S0-ADM-487

SMALL AND MEDIUM ENTERPRISES IN MALAYSIA

Small and Medium Enterprises in Malaysia

Policy issues and challenges

MOHA ASRI ABDULLAH
Deputy Director
Centre for Policy Research
University Science Malaysia

Ashgate

Aldershot • Brookfield USA • Singapore • Sydney

© M. A. Abdullah 1999

All rights reserved. No part of this publication may be reproduced, stored in a retrieval system, or transmitted in any form or by any means, electronic, mechanical, photocopying, recording or otherwise without the prior permission of the publisher.

Published by
Ashgate Publishing Ltd
Gower House
Croft Road
Aldershot
Hants GU11 3HR
England

Ashgate Publishing Company
Old Post Road
Brookfield
Vermont 05036
USA

British Library Cataloguing in Publication Data
Abdullah, Moha Asri
  Small and medium enterprises in Malaysia : policy issues and
  challenges
  1. Small business - Malaysia 2. Small business - Government
  policy - Malaysia
  I. Title
  338.6'42'09595

Library of Congress Catalog Card Number: 98-73758

ISBN 1 84014 884 5

Printed and bound by Athenaeum Press, Ltd.,
Gateshead, Tyne & Wear.

Contents

CHAPTER SIX: LOCATION AND INFRASTRUCTURE FACILITIES

CHAPTER SEVEN: FISCAL POLICY AND INCENTIVES FOR SMEs

List of Figures

List of Maps

List of Tables

Preface

The significant contributions that Small and Medium Enterprises (SMEs) make in national development is widely recognised in many countries, developed and developing countries alike. Concomitant to this, SMEs occupy a prominent position in the development agenda and essentially become part of the overall national development strategy in most countries. Literature shows that contributions of SMEs can be observed in a number of aspects including labour absorption, income generation and distribution, poverty alleviation, training ground for the development and upgrading entrepreneurship skills, and important vehicles for promoting forward and backward linkages in geographically and economically diverse sectors of the economy in many countries. The policy support programmes, therefore has become a major concern of development policy in their respective countries. Malaysia in this relation, is no exceptional to this when the government gives a high priority to the development of SMEs in her national economic development strategy.

It has been increasingly realised that the high priority is given to the promotion of SMEs is not just because of the above mentioned contributions, but more significantly due to Malaysia's industrial structure. Since the last two decade, the industrial structure of the country become increasingly export-oriented resulting in potentially vulnerable. This is because of her narrow concentration in electronics and textiles and a heavy reliance on large-scale enterprises, Free Trade Zones-based enterprises which are dominated by foreign investment, engaged in enclave-type, capital and import-intensive activities that contribute little to the deepening and widening of Malaysia's domestic industrial structure. Linkages with the rest of the economy remain relatively weak. In order to achieve a counter-balancing force of this increasingly global-linked economic development, the promotion and support programmes for SMEs are an upmost importance particularly in view of reducing an imbalanced industrial structure of the country, widening pattern of manufacturing activity and inducing indigenously-based and a more balanced industrial development. Therefore, the SMEs' development strategy involves provision of a range of support services through numerous public and private agencies. Presently, there are as many as 13 ministries and nearly 30 government agencies engaged in various types of SME's support programmes, while some others have been initiated by private agencies.

Despite the fact that small and medium enterprises (SMEs) are very important for the national economic development in Malaysia, very few studies have been available. Observation shows that all the studies on SMEs in Malaysia are either quite outdated or restricted in terms of its focuses. This always prevents the reader to arrive at any definite conclusion on the general nature and characteristics of SMEs, the current type, form and the focus of support programmes for SMEs in the country. In this relation, the objective of this study is to present a comprehensive and a more up-to-date scenario of SMEs in Malaysia by compiling together selected materials from previous studies other than the study's experience of the author in some current case studies of SMEs in Malaysia in order to enable readers to have a clearer picture of the important role of SMEs, problems and prospects in the general development of the Malaysian economy. In addition, policy support programmes for the development of SMEs and its ourtreach, accessibility and effectiveness, its strength and weaknesses will also give a much clearer picture of the general phenomenon of SMEs in the country as a whole.

This book therefore covers numerous aspects relating to SMEs and support programmes for the development of SMEs including: i) the existing policies and support programmes; ii) some empirical evidence on the accessibility of policy support programmes on SMEs in Malaysia; iii) major problems, issues and needs of SMEs in general; iv) institutional structure and overall measures needed to enhance the competitive position of SMEs in the country; and v) recommendations and measures to more effectively promote the development of SMEs in general. Towards the end, the book is divided into nine chapters. Chapter One provides an overview of the current economic development in Malaysia, including a discussion on a major structural transformation and its problems in the industrial structure over the past two decades. In addition, definition of SMEs, characteristics and roles of SMEs in Malaysia are also presented. Chapter Two examines some conceptual perspectives underlying the development of SMEs, and the rationale in promoting SMEs in developing countries is also revealed. This is followed by a review of policy SMEs in selected developing countries. This is done before highlighting the main types of the existing policy supports for the development of SMEs in Malaysia. Chapter Three touches specifically on financial and credit assistance for SMEs in

Malaysia along with major agencies and institutions involved in the provision of such assistance. Chapter Four discusses entrepreneurial development and management training programmes for SMEs in the country. The role of some major agencies which provide this particular assistance such as National Productivity (NPC), Malaysian Entrepreneurial Development Centre (MEDEC), Small and Medium Industries Development Corporation (SMIDEC), Small Business Development Centre of University Putra Malaysia, Federation of Malaysian Manufacturers (FMM) and others. Chapter Five provides a review of human resources development, technical and vocational training programmes for SMEs in the country with the main agencies and institutions which provide such programmes. Infrastructural supports and fiscal incentives respectively for the development of SMEs are discussed in Chapter Six and Seven respectively. Chapter Eight provides some empirical evidence on the accessibility of the government and non-government support programmes for SMEs in Malaysia based upon two specific-case studies. Finally Chapter Nine critically analyse issues, needs and challenges aimed at upgrading the efficiency, productivity and modernising SMEs toward a more export-orientated as well as enhancing the overall economic contribution of SMEs in Malaysia and achieving a more balanced-industrial structure.

The study recognised that data on small and medium enterprises (SMEs) in Malaysia are not easily available and quite inadequate. Official data and record are scanty and still fragmented and not consistant since no institution or individual in the government and outside government have the resources to collect a comprehensive data on SMEs. Although, effort towards this has recently been initiated by Small and Medium Industries Corporation (SMIDEC), it is still too early to gather information and data in a systematic and comprehensive manner as well as up-to-date which will be adequate for estalishing a data-based on national scale. It is for this reason that this book has been initiated.

Finally, this book would not have been successfully completed without the generous assistance and kind support of many individual and organisations. First and foremost, I wish to express my sincere appreciation and profound gratitude to Caren Levy for her wise counseling throughout the preparation of the thesis which forms the significant part of the book. To all owners/managers of the sampled forms, I owe a special debt of gratitude for permitting me to obtain the relevant data, particularly for their time given to me, and their "open" attitudes and views towards the questionnaire, although it directly touched on the firms' core financial attributes. Thanks also goes to several officers and staff at several agencies and institutions from which materials and information were collected. My sincere appreciation is also extended to Himmat Ratnoo for reading through some chapters of the book and Arif Butt for having kindly read the entire first draft. To all my colleagues at the Centre for Policy Research, I am indebted for comments and suggestions raised during the process of writing up. Many thanks also goes to Mr. Mohammad Idris Ahmad and Mrs. Noor Ain Ismail who play the key role in typing the manuscript with patience and skill particularly Idris for preparing a camera-ready-copy version. Last but not least, I also wish to express the debt I owe to my wife for her understanding and cooperation in looking after our children thoughout the writing and preparation of the drafts of the manuscript and who was a constant source of inspiration. For my parents, I will always remain indebted for the sacrifices they made throughout my education.

Dr. Moha Asri Abdullah
Deputy Director
Centre for Policy Research
University Science Malaysia
11800 Penang, MALAYSIA

List of Abbreviations

ADB	Asian Development Bank
AJDF	ASEAN-Japan Development Fund
ASEAN	Association of South East Asian Nations
BIMB	Bank Industri Malaysia Berhad
BNM	Bank Negara Malaysia
BPMB	Bank Pembangunan Malaysia Berhad
BPM	Bank Pertanian Malaysia
CCDSI	Coordination Council for Development of Small Industry
CGC	Credit Guarantee Corporation
CIAST	Centre for Instructor and Advance Skills Training
DEB	Dasar Ekonomi Baru
FRIM	Forestry Research Institute of Malaysia
FMM	Federation of Malaysian Manufacturer
FTZ	Free Trade Zone
IBA	Industry Building Allowance
ICA	Industrial Coordination Act
IDRC	International Development Research Centre
IKS	Industri Kecil dan Sederhana
IMP	Industrial Master Plan
ITI	Industrial Training Institute
KDNK	Keluaran Dalam Negara Kasar
LMW	Licensed Manufacturing Warehouse
MARA	Majlis Amanah Rakyat
MARDI	Malaysian Agricultural Research and Development Institute
MATRADE	Malaysian External Trade Development Corporation
MEDEC	Malaysian Entrepreneurial Development Centre
MESEAM	Medium and Small Enterprises Association of Malaysia
MIDA	Malaysian Industrial Development Authority
MIDF	Malaysian Industrial Development Fund
MIEL	Malaysian Industrial Estate Limited
MIMOS	Malaysian Institute of Microelectronic System

MITI	Ministry of International Trade and Industry
MPSM	Majlis Pembangunan Sumber Manusia
MTDC	Malaysian Technology Development Corporation
NIF	New Investment Fund
NPC	National Productivity Centre
RA	Reinvestment Allowance
SCX	Subcontract Exchange Scheme
SEDC	State Economic Development Corporation
SIRIM	Standard and Industrial Research Institute of Malaysia
SMIDEC	Small and Medium Industries Development Malaysia
TPM	Technology Park Malaysia
TPSM	Tabung Pembangunan Sumber Manusia
TUB	Tabung Usahawan Baru
UPM	Universiti Putra Malaysia
UDA	Urban Development Authority
UNDP	United Nations Industrial Development Organisation
UNIDO	United Nations Industrial Development Organisation
VDP	Vendor Development Programme

1 Introduction

Introduction

After the World War II, many developing countries gained independence from their respective colonial powers. Numerous policies and strategies have been planned, introduced and implemented, with different forms, levels and focuses through many ways and ideologies such as socialism, communism, capitalism, lasex faire or adaptation of these are aimed at harnessing the resources of the country that would ensure rapid economic development for the benefit of the people in their respective countries. This process of the so called industrialisation may symbolise the acquisition of new technologies, comfortable life styles, reduce poverty, better education and greater opportunities in many aspect of life. One of the most significant symbols, nonetheless, is the structural transformation of economic activities from a predominantly traditional sector i.e. agricultural-based to a more modern sector i.e. industrial-based in the composition of the value of Gross Domestic Product (GDP). In this context, some countries in Asia, especially the East Asia, are rather fortunate with numerous improvements have been achieved. These are especially so as compared to countries like Sri Lanka, Bangladesh, Somalia, Afghanistan and many other countries in the African continent (see Table 1.1).

The phenomenal economic development has been fundamental for some countries in Asia with the growth rate as high as 10 percent per year in the late 1980s and 1990s (see Table 1.2). The high rate of overall economic growth has continued to be associated with rapid structural transformation. The role of the agricultural sector has declined considerably in some Asian countries. For instance, in Indonesia it declined from 56 percent in 1965 to only 17 percent in 1994; Philippines from 26 percent to 22 percent during the same period; Thailand from 32 percent to 10 percent; China from 44 percent to 21 percent.

1

Table 1.1 Basic Indicators of Selected Developing Countries in the Asian and African Regions, 1994

Country	Population (million)	GNP Per capita (USA)	Life Expectancy	Adult Illiteracy
ASIA				
Bangladesh	117.9	220	57	62
India	913.6	320	62	48
Pakistan	126.3	430	60	62
Sri Lanka	17.9	640	72	10
Indonesia	190.4	880	63	16
Philippines	67.0	950	65	5
Thailand	58.0	2,410	69	6
Malaysia	19.7	3,480	71	17
AFRICA				
Mozambique	15.5	90	46	60
Ethiopia	54.9	100	49	65
Kenya	26.0	250	59	22
Nigeria	108.0	280	52	43
Zimbabwe	10.8	500	58	15
Algeria	27.4	1,650	69	38
Botswana	1.4	2,800	68	30

Source: World Bank 1996, *World Development Report*, Washington D.C. (p. 188-189).

The rapid economic transformation, in the reverse, has raised the share of industrial sector during the same period. For instance, in Indonesia it raised from 13 to 41 percent; Philippines from 28 to 39 percent; Thailand from 23 to 33 percent. The figures also revealed that manufacturing recorded the fastest growing sector in these countries. Malaysia as one of the country in the region is not exceptional. The rapid economic development in the country has indeed resulted in the change in the structure of economy, a full employment, a full employment level, increase demand for labour, brought about a chronic shortage of labour and more essentially raised many issues and implications on human resources development. This chapter attempts to examine the current the economic development with focusing on the development of manufacturing sector and its consequences on changing economic structure, inflation rate, unemployment rate as well as the demand for human resource in the country. The fourth part of the chapter will also discussed the definition of SMEs in Malaysia while characteristic and contributions of SMEs are reviewed in the fifth and sixth parts respectively.

Table 1.2 The Changes in Structural Composition of the Value of GDP by the Industrial Origin for Some Asian Countries between 1965 - 1994

Country	Agriculture			Industrial			Services			Manufacturing		
	1965	1980	1994	1965	1980	1994	1965	1980	1994	1965	1980	1995
China	44	30	21	39	49	47	17	21	32	31	41	37
Indonesia	56	24	17	13	42	41	31	34	42	8	13	24
Philippines	26	25	22	28	39	33	46	36	45	20	26	23
Thailand	32	23	10	23	29	39	45	48	50	14	20	29
Malaysia	28	22	14	25	38	43	47	40	42	9	21	32
Singapore	3	1	0	24	38	36	74	61	64	15	29	27

Note: - Agriculture covers forestry, livestock and fishing.
- Industry comprises value added in mining, manufacturing, construction, electricity, water and gas.
- Services include whole sale, retail and trade, transportation, government and other services.
- Manufacturing was already included in the industry but is purposely shown separately in table since it is the most dynamic part of industrial sector.

Source: (i) World Bank 1990, *World Development Report 1990*, Washington D.C. (p.182-183).
(ii) World Bank 1996, *World Development Report 1996*, Washington D.C. (p. 210-211).

Current Economic Development in Malaysia

For the last three decades, Malaysia is rather fortunate having experienced a phenomenal economic growth. It is noted that between 1971 and 1990, the Malaysian economy has been growing at a rapid rate of an average of 6.7 percent per annum. Eventhough, this average rate of percentage is slightly below the original target of 8.0 percent anticipated and set by the First Outline Perspective Plan (1971-1990), this economic performance of Malaysia, by any international standard has been very impressive. During the period of 1971-1990, moreover, real Gross Domestic Product (GDP) has recorded an increase of almost four-fold that is between RM21.5 billion and RM79.1 billion (in 1978 prices). Since late 1980s, the rate of economic growth of the country even higher and strongly advocated by many international agencies such as World Bank and United Nations as one of the most rapidly growing economies in the world. During the period of 1991-1995 the Malaysian economy has been growing at an average rate of 8.4 percent per annum (see MALAYSIA 1996). This rate is indeed well above the target of an average 7.0 percent per annum anticipated in the Second Outline Perspective Plan (1990-2010) and surpassing the Sixth Malaysian Plan target of 12.2 percent (1991-2000). It is strongly believed that impressive economic performance country makes it possible for the country to join the ranks of newly industrialised countries.

One of the most prominent features of the high growth rate of the overall Malaysian economy is that, it is closely associated with the rapid growth of the manufacturing sector. This growth can be seen through the high increase in the output of manufacturing sector i.e. 13.4 percent in 1987, 17.6 percent in 1988, 15.7 percent in 1990 and at average of more than 12 percent between 1991 and 1995. It is recorded that this sector contributed almost 45 percent to overall economic growth of the country during 1991-1995 period (MALAYSIA 1996). Continuing increase in the manufacturing sector since 1970s up to the late 1997 has consequently transformed the structure of the Malaysia economy. This transformation can be observed from the declining role of agricultural sector (including forestry and fisheries sub-sectors) in Malaysia Gross Domestic Product (GDP) i.e. from 30.8 percent in 1970 to about 14.9 percent in 1994 and increase a little bit to 16.4 percent in 1995 (see Table 1.3). In the reverse, the share of the manufacturing sector to GDP has raised substantially from 13.4 percent in 1970 to 31.4 percent in 1994 and 39.8 percent in 1995. It is further expected that the sector's share will reach 66.2 percent by the year 2000 (MALAYSIA 1996).

The export demand as well as buoyant domestic demand largely led the high growth of the manufacturing sector. The electronic and electrical products and machinery provided the main impetus for the rapid export-oriented demand. The manufacturing sector has also the substantial share of employment of 24.6 percent while manufactured product represent 79.5 percent of the Malaysia's total export. By the year 2000, it is expected that the manufactured output to exceed 81 percent of the total Malaysian export. As many other Asian countries, electronic and electrical products increased significantly from 48 percent in 1980 to 63 percent of the total manufactured product exported in 1994 and 68 percent in 1995. It is also pertinent to note that structural changes in the Malaysian economy has been very rapid in terms of output as compared to the similar change in terms of the structure of employment. It is estimated that about 53.2 percent of the total employment was in agricultural sector (including livestock, forestry and fishery sub-sectors) in 1970 and reduced to 31.3 percent in 1985 and 18.0 percent in 1995. Although the share declined sharply, it has changed at a much slower pace than that of the share of agriculture in GDP. The high growth rates have also been followed by low inflationary rate. After coming out of short but severe economic recession in 1985-1986, the Malaysian economy maintains to have experienced price stability, despite the fact that its annual economic growth rate has been generally high. It is recorded that the Consumer Price Index has been below 5 percent during the last ten years of 1986-1995.

Meanwhile, the share of manufactured exports to total exports which recorded a sharp increase are largely due to the electrical and electronic products industry with a share of almost 66 percent of the manufactured export in 1995. The strong growth performance of the electrical and electronic products industry, with a growth rate of 19 percent per annum, was mainly attributed to the large increase in production and demand for refrigerating and air-conditioning using machinery as well as radios and television sets. Despite the significance of electrical and electronic products in total exports, analysis of export trends showed that diversification and expansion of the export base has constantly taken place. Although the newly emerging export-oriented industries such as transport equipment chemical and its related-products, furniture and relatively small in proportion, but they recorded high rates of growth.

Among the domestic market-oriented industries, the fabricated metal products, basic iron and steel, and non-metallic products industries, registered double-digit growth rates in output of 36 percent, 15.7 percent and 12.8 percent per annum respectively. Indeed, the growths of these industries were limited to the rapid progress of the industrialisation process in the country and expansion of related-activities such as the construction, services and implementation of infrastructure-related projects.

Table 1.3 Malaysian GDP Composition by Economic Sector 1970-2000

ECONOMIC SECTOR	1970	1980	1990	1995	2000
Agriculture, livestock, forestry & fishing	30.8	23.4	18.7	13.6	10.5
Mining & quarrying	6.5	5.0	9.8	7.4	5.7
Manufacturing	13.4	20.5	26.9	33.1	37.5
Construction	3.9	4.5	3.6	4.4	4.8
Electricity, gas & water	1.9	2.2	1.9	2.3	2.7
Transport, storage & communication	4.7	6.3	6.9	7.3	8.3
Whole sale & retail	13.3	12.4	11.1	12.1	12.7
Finance, insurance, real estate & business services	8.4	7.8	9.8	10.7	11.9
Government services	11.1	12.5	10.6	9.7	8.1
Other services	2.5	2.6	2.1	2.0	2.1
TOTAL	100.0	100.0	100.0	100.0	100.0

Source: MALAYSIA 1981, 1991, 1993 and 1996.

The location of foreign investors in Malaysia has in a way influenced the growth in the economic activity and the manufacturing sector, especially in the more developed region such as Selangor, Penang and Johor. The increase in investment and production activities among the manufacturing firms and Multinational Corporations (MNC) in the Free Trade Zone (FTZ) in the above mentioned states have contributed to the rapid economic growth and the Gross National Domestic Product (GDNP), which are higher compare to the other states. In the period of 1990-1995, Selangor recorded an average growth of 12.9 percent, Penang with 12.4 percent and Johor with 11.8 percent which are higher than the national rate of economic growth and GDNP (see Malaysia, 1996). Penang, as one of the region in Malaysia that has strong linkage with the process of globalisation has managed to attract around 750 foreign firm n its Free Trade Zone area, with investment worth around 5.21 billion. Table 1.4, shows that the ratio of foreign investment in Malaysia throughout 1980 - 1995 has increased steadily i.e. from 34.7 percent to 49.4 percent. It is well known fact that the process of globalisation, the transfer of foreign investment and the involvement of firms and MNCs have actually played an important role in the economic growth, structural transformation of economy and the process of spatial industrial development in Malaysia. This has been clearly reflected in the Malaysian economic growth, especially since 1970s. The main factor contributing to this phenomenon is the increased in investment and production of manufacturing sector of more than 10 percent throughout 1995. It is expected that with the identification of 4 zones or development corridors namely East-Coast, Western, North-South and East-West, which spatially span across the nation (East-West and North-south configurations) will further enhance the process of industrialisation in Malaysia, especially, the high technology.

Table 1.4 Percentage of Ratio of Investment (foreign and local) in the Manufacturing Sector 1980-1995

Year	Local Investment	Foreign Investment
1980	65.3	34.7
1985	83.1	16.9
1990	37.4	62.6
1993	54.3	45.7
1994	51.4	48.6
1995	50.6	49.4

Source: Ministry of Finance, Annual Economic Report (various issues), Kuala Lumpur.

9

The Demand for Work Force

Among the factors that have influenced and brought about high demand for manpower at various level of skills and economic sectors are globalisation, economic growth, structural transformation of economy and rapid growth of industrial sector. The rapid growth of the manufacturing sector, construction and services has therefore created employment opportunities. Modernisations of the agricultural sector and estate have also created new job opportunities. The requirement of a workforce resulting from rapid growth of manufacturing sector can be seen from various reports and previous studies. The Ministry of labour has estimated that around 600,000 are professional and semi-professional labour are required by the year 2000 in an effort to facilitate the nation industrial development endeavour. Malaysian should be able to create about 100,000 skilled workforce in the technical field yearly up to the year 2000 (see Moha Asri 1995b). Studies by the Ministry of Human Resource on 1461 giant international companies from Malaysia Industrial Development Authority's (MIDA) list of approved industries showed that between 1990-1998, these companies required 314,955 additional workforce especially the semi-skilled worker (162,480) and unskilled workers (92,485). The detailed requirement for skilled labour by these companies can be gleaned from Table 1.5. The future demand for labour force of this nature reflects the magnitude of problem faced by the manufacturing sector in getting the human workforce.

The Demand for Labour: A Case of Penang

Nesadurai (1991) and Salih and Young (1986) have provided a quite comprehensive account of the industrial growth and development of Penang since the sixties. They have also discussed the labour implication of such economic growth. A current study (see Nooriah, Morshidi and Abibullah 1995) has provided a more recent account of the labour supply problems in the state as a result of the increasing integration of Penang with the international production system and Penang economic development. Table 1.6 summarises the dynamics of industrial growth in Penang since 1970. Between 1970 and 1980, 276 manufacturing firms were established in various production complexes and this has increased to 695 in 1994, 723 in 1995 and 736 firms in 1996. The total of investment (paid up capital) has also increased drastically, i.e. from RM29.4 million in 1970 to RM3.9 billion in 1993, RM4.46 billion in 1994, RM4.99 billion in 1995 and RM5.31 billion in 1996. The increased number of manufacturing firms and

10

amount of investment has also resulted in the increase of the total workforce i.e. from only 2,784 to 162,703 between 1970 and 1993, and 177,250 workers in 1994, 195,264 workers and 196,774 workers in 1995 and 1996 respectively (see Table 1.6).

In 1970 manufacturing industries was basically import-substitution in nature with low capital and based on simple production technology. Beginning in the late 1970s however, the manufacturing industries became labour-intensive and export-orientated. Production process was also partly automated but the demand for labour is very high. Typical among this group of manufacturing industries is the electronic and electrical products, rubber footwear, textiles, chemicals and food processing sub-sectors. Majorities of these operations are limited to the multinational corporations. From 1990 onwards there is a great trend among manufacturing plants in Penang Industries Complexes to automate and become high-tech industries. This trend is concomitant with strategy of the state's industrialisation which put greater emphasis on high-tech industry and higher value-added, among other, to overcome the existing problems of labour supply and to remain competitive.

Table 1.5 The Need for Labour by Category of Worker, 1990-1998

Category of worker	1990	1991	1992	1993	1994	1995	1996	1997	1998	Total
Engineering graduates	1,313	2,222	1,973	1,626	1,196	635	249	60	0	9,274
Science graduates	99	146	205	101	89	70	21	6	0	737
Other graduates*	1,131	1,713	1,521	981	769	332	154	33	0	6,634
Technicians	1,688	3,132	2,894	2,409	1,732	915	435	107	0	13,312
Craft-skills workers	3,190	4,763	4,422	3,629	2,801	1,394	592	258	28	21,077
CAD-CAM operators	2,080	1,721	1,509	1,437	1,443	413	272	121	0	8,966
Semi-skilled workers	27,785	44,073	33,942	22,735	17,003	10,621	5,195	926	200	162,480
Unskilled workers	18,124	25,623	18,364	2,284	10,314	4,326	2,782	472	196	92,485
TOTAL	55,410	83,393	64,830	45,202	35,347	18,706	9,700	1,983	424	314,995

Note: *Includes lawyer, accountant, system analyst, computer programmer and management group forms the largest (i.e. 3,889 from 6,634 workers needed).

Source: Ministry of Human Resource 1993, Department of Research and Planning, Ministry of Human Resource, 1993, Kuala Lumpur.

12

**Table 1.6 Growth of Manufacturing Firms, Workforce and Capital
in the Penang Industrial Complexes between 1970 - 1996**

Year	Number of Plant	Number of Workers	Paid up Capital
1970	31	2,784	0.29
1985	276	59,625	1.16
1990	430	100,953	1.23
1993	637	162,703	3.99
1994	695	177,250	4.46
1995	723	195,264	4.99
1996	736	196,774	5.31

Source: Penang Development Corporation: Annual Reports (various Issues), PDC: Penang

A study on 60 manufacturing firms in FTZ of Penang and Seberang Prai was conducted, for example to asses the demand for labour in the state. The findings reveal that the demand for labour in these production complexes is so heavy that more and more manufacturing firms are experiencing problems between 1992 and 1994 (see Table 1.7).   The findings of the study also shows that some initiative has and will be taken by the firms in overcoming the problem of labour shortage which among other include: (i) the usage of automation and changes in the technique of production which is more inclined to higher technology, (ii) increase the basic wages with to the attractive incentive and also a more conducive working environment, (iii) resort to foreign workers, iv) sub-contracting of production components, (v) upgrading of workers skill through training, and (vi) relocation of firms. Recent development in Penang has shown the increased in the number of foreign workers employed by firms in FTZ.

Table 1.7 Manpower Problems by Types of Manufacturing Plans in Penang, 1994

INDUSTRY	No. of plants surveyed	No. of plans with problem	Percent
Electronics/Electrical	26	22	84.6
Rubber based	7	6	85.7
Textiles/Garments	7	7	100.0
Plastic & Plastic products	5	5	100.0
Paper, paper products & printing work	6	4	66.7
Professional and scientific Measuring & controlling Equipment & optical goods	1	1	100.0
Basic metal industries	5	2	40.0
Non-metallic & mineral products	3	2	66.7
TOTAL	60	49	81.7

Source: Nooriah, Morshidi and Abibullah 1995.

According to report by Immigration Department, between June 1992 to June 1995, a total of 19,772 foreign workers have been officially employed. In the FTZ area, foreign workers account for about 5.4 percent or 10,3609 of the total workforce. In the FTZ area, foreign workers accounts for about 5.4 percent of the total workforce. However, it was also widely believed that in Penang, the number of foreign workers being employed whether legally or illegally has increased. A different study on 60 firms in the FTZ shows that 28 percent of the firm having foreign workers are in the textile and apparel sub-industry which account for about 28 percent of the total workforce (Moha Asri, et al, 1996). It is therefore clear that the need for workforce has increased. This is because the average number of labour entering the market yearly throughout 1991-95, is around 2.9 percent compare to 3.4 percent yearly in term of the average number of job opportunity available (see Malaysia 1996).

Manpower Participation

Although there had been an increased in the labour force participation and high growth of the working-age population as well as large inflows of foreign labour, the labour force increased at an average annual rate of 2.9 percent during the period of 1991-1995. This rate is clearly much lower as compared to employment expansion i.e. at the rate 3.4 percent per annum (MALAYSIA 1996). It is indicated that the increase in the overall labour force participation from 65.9 percent in 1990 to 66.9 percent in 1995 involves both male and female. The male labour force participation rate increased from 86.3 percent to 86.8 percent, while the rate for females increased from 45.8 percent to 47.1 percent. This means that were slightly over one million additional entrants (220,000 persons per year) into the labour market during the same period. Labour force participation also indicates that there was a gradual decline in the proportion of the labour force in the age group 15-24 i.e. from 78.4 percent in 1985 to 71.3 percent in 1994. However, registrants from the Manpower Department show that labour force in the age groups 25-29 and 30-39 increased from 12.2 percent and 77.7 percent in 1985 to 15.1 percent and 9.9 percent in 1994 respectively. Thus, the data obviously explain three main reasons. Firstly, there was a decline in fertility rate among Malaysian. Secondly, there was an increase in the length of the schooling period, and thirdly, people were also generally entering the labour market at older ages.

Manpower by Sectors

An Impressive expansion in the demand for labour was indeed a direct result of rapid industrialisation process and buoyant economic conditions especially since the late 1980s. During the period of 1991-1995, for example, a total of about 1.6 million new jobs was created, exceeding the 1.1 million jobs forecast (see Table 1.8). Therefore this clearly shows that, although labour force growth remained high, the relatively stronger growth of employment resulted in labour shortage in most sectors of the economy. The manufacturing sector, which produces the most rapidly output growth, accounted for about one quarter of total employment. More importantly, this sector generated almost 60 percent of net employment creation during the period of 1991-1995. The strong demand for labour in the sector growing at 9.0 percent per annum during the same period, coupled with industrial restructuring towards higher value-added products and activities, resulted in labour shortages not only at the production level but also at the skilled and semi-skilled levels. Although there has been increasing utilisation of modern technology such as computer-numerically-controlled machines, computer-aided design and manufacturing and robotics, the transition to greater capitalisation was low. This is because of high capital costs, shortage of skilled manpower, especially in new technology areas.

The *services* sector accounted for about one half of the total employment and 47 percent of total job creation during 1991-1995. Among the main contributors to employment creation in this sector include finance, the whole sale and retail trade, hotels and restaurants. A total of 443,500 jobs were created in those sub-sectors during the same period. Meanwhile employment in the *construction* sector grew at an average rate of 9.2 percent per annum and accounted for about 19 percent of total job creation. It well noted that a creditable growth of jobs creation in this sector arose from the massive investments in a number of infrastructure projects. In addition, there was substantial development of residential and commercial property. With the strong growth of employment in this sector, its share to total employment increased from 6.3 percent in 1990 to 8.3 percent in 1995. However, employment in the agriculture sector declined by 3.6 percent per annum as a result of a slower growth of output and increasing mechanisation in the sector.

It is expected that during the period of 1991-1995 along, a reduction of about 309, 300 jobs in obsolete terms. The share of agricultural employment fell from 26.0 percent in 1990 to 18.0 percent in 1995. One the labour supply side, nonetheless, the sector continued to face labour shortages as local labour moved into other economic sectors because of better prospects and wages.

It is clear that the stronger growth of employment resulted in labour shortages and with the expected continuing rapid industrialisation and manufacturing expansion in the near future, the heavy demand for labour will continue to be a major challenge for the country. This phenomenon has indeed made Malaysia the most attractive destinations for foreign workers. Followed by the decision of the government in 1991 to liberalise the policy on the employment of foreign labour, an estimated number of more than 1.3 million recent legal and illegal immigrant labour in Malaysia. It is recorded that by the end of 1995, a total of 649, 680 work permits was issued to migrant workers with 76 percent were issued in Federal Territory, Johor, Sabah and Selangor. The number of illegal immigrant workers is said to reach more than 800, 000. From the sectoral level, about two-thirds of the temporary work permits were issued for work in the plantation and construction sectors, domestic helpers accounted for 23 percent and 11 percent for work in the manufacturing sector.

Manpower by Occupation, Wages and Productivity

Concomitant to the high employment growth in the manufacturing and services sectors during the past two decades, the demand for workers in the professional and technical as well as administrative and managerial categories expanded rapidly. Between 1991 and 1995, the average annual rates of growth of jobs in these categories reached 6.8 percent and 5.5 percent respectively. This reflects a strong demand for human resource with higher levels of education especially tertiary, technical and professional training. These two categories accounted for almost one quarter of the total number of jobs created during the same period. As a result of rapid process of industrialisation, there was also a strong demand for production workers especially in manufacturing firms. With regard to engineering assistants along, the demand was higher than the supply of 26, 600 from local tertiary institutions.

Table 1.8 Employment by Sector 1990 - 2000 ('000)

Industry	1990	%	1995	%	2000	%	Average Annual Growth Rate		Net Job Creation			
							6MP	7MP	6MP	%	7MP	%
Agriculture, Forestry, Livestock & Fishing	1,738.0	26.0	1,428.7	18.0	1,187.7	13.1	-3.8	-3.6	-309.3	-25.2	241.0	-20.9
Mining & Quarrying	37.0	0.6	40.7	0.5	44.5	0.5	1.9	1.8	3.7	0.3	3.8	0.3
Manufacturing	1,333.0	19.9	2,051.6	25.9	2,616.3	28.9	9.0	5.0	718.6	58.5	564.7	49.1
Construction	424.0	6.3	659.4	8.3	845.4	9.3	9.2	5.1	235.4	19.1	186.0	16.2
Electricity, Gas & Water	47.0	0.7	69.1	0.9	84.0	0.9	8.0	4.0	22.1	1.8	14.9	1.3
Transport, Storage & Communications	302.0	4.5	395.2	5.0	506.9	5.6	5.5	5.1	93.2	7.6	111.7	9.7
Wholesale & Retail Trade, Hotels & Restaurants	1,218.0	18.2	1,327.8	16.8	1,469.6	16.2	1.7	2.1	109.8	8.9	141.8	12.3
Finance, Insurance, Real Estate & Business Services	258.0	3.9	378.5	4.8	479.0	5.3	8.0	4.8	120.5	9.8	100.5	8.7
Government Services	850.0	12.7	872.2	11.0	894.2	9.9	0.5	0.5	22.2	1.8	22.0	1.9
Other Services	479.0	7.2	692.2	8.7	938.6	10.4	7.6	6.3	213.2	17.3	246.4	21.4
Total	6,686.0	100.0	7,915.4	100.0	9,066.2	100.0	3.4	2.8	1,229.4	100.0	1,150.8	100.0
Labour Force	7,042.0		8,140.0		9,327.1		2.9	2.8				
Local	6,752.0		7,490.0		8,546.1		2.1	2.8				
Foreign	290.0		650.0		781.0		17.5	2.7				
Unemployment	356.0		224.6		260.9			3.7				
Unemployment Rate	5.1		2.8		2.8							

Source: Seventh Malaysia Plan (1996-2000), National Printers, Kuala Lumpur

During the period 1991-1995, the professional and technical category accounted for 18.6 percent of the total employment created (or 228, 900 jobs). A demand for engineers and engineering assistants reached about 36, 350 and 48, 800 respectively, generated especially by upgrading production technology towards more sophisticated and automated processes (see Table 1.9). There was also a high demand for health professional such as physicians and surgeons, and allied health professionals such as nurses, medical assistants, laboratory technologists and dental paramedics. The net increase in the employment of medical and health professionals was about 5, 200 jobs and allied health professionals reached 12, 500. Shortages were also reported in all fields of specialisation such as psychiatry, forensic, medicine, haematology, paediatrics, and obstetrics and gynaecology. Shortage of school teachers particularly those teaching mathematics, Islamic education, living skills and technical subjects was also obvious.

The demand for administrative and managerial manpower grew at an average rate of 5.5 percent, accounting for 4.1 percent of total job creation. In the service sector category, occupation grew at 4.8 percent and accounted for 16.6 percent or 203, 900 jobs created during the period of 1991-1995. The rapid expansion of hotels and increasing tourist arrivals led to the increased demand for tourism-related workers to about 40 percent. The largest number of jobs created was in the production workers category, totalling 702,800 jobs or 57.2 percent of the total jobs created during the period. Demand for production workers in manufacturing sector both skilled and unskilled reached about 6.7 percent per annum.

Labour productivity for the economy as a whole as measured by Gross Domestic Product (GDP) per workers (in constant 1978 prices) has also been increased since 1986. The overall growth rate of annual labour productivity during the period of 1991-1995 recorded at 5.1 percent, much higher as compared to 3.3 percent during the period of 1991-1995. Output per worker in the manufacturing sector reached at RM19, 410 in 1995, higher than that of the economy as a whole, i.e. 3.9 percent per annum. Meanwhile, labour productivity growth in the agriculture and services sectors were 6.1 percent and 5.9 percent, respectively. In the services sector in particular, the growth of GDP per worker at 5.9 percent per annum as compared to 1.8 percent during the 1986-1990 reflects higher efficiency in the use of labour resources and greater use of information technology.

The short labour supply resulted in upward pressure on wages during the past decade. Data from the Department of Statistics indicated that the average nominal manufacturing wages increased by about 27 percent between 1990 and 1994 or about 6.2 percent per annum. The growth of real product wage or normal wage deflated by producer prices during this period was 13.8 percent, while real sales value per worker, which is used as an indicator of productivity, experienced an increase of 7.3 percent. With productivity growth lagging behind wage growth in the sector, there was pressure on unit labour costs. This phenomenon was particularly marked in 1990-1992, where high wage growth unaccompanied by corresponding productivity growth resulted in rising unit labour costs. Although productivity growth in manufacturing sector began to experience an upward trend (with growth at 4.6 percent and 6.8 percent in 1993 and 1994 respectively) indicating some effects of labour market adjustments, unit labour costs in the manufacturing sector started to increase again in the last two or three years.

Table 1.9 Employment by Major Occupation Group, 1990 - 2000 ('000)

Occupational Group	1990	%	1995	%	2000	%	Average Annual Growth Rate (%)		Net Job Creation			
							6MP	7MP	6MP	%	7MP	%
Professional, Technical & Related Workers	586.4	8.8	815.3	10.3	1,097.0	12.1	6.8	6.1	228.9	18.6	281.7	24.5
Administrative & Managerial Workers	163.8	2.4	213.7	2.7	290.1	3.2	5.5	6.3	49.9	4.1	76.4	6.6
Clerical & Related Workers	652.6	9.8	799.5	10.1	933.8	10.3	4.1	3.2	146.9	11.9	134.4	11.7
Sales Workers	768.9	11.5	894.4	11.3	1,042.6	11.5	3.1	3.1	125.5	10.2	149.2	12.9
Service Workers	777.6	11.6	981.5	12.4	1,169.5	12.9	4.8	3.6	203.9	16.6	188.0	16.3
Production & Related Workers, Transport Equipment Operators & Labourers	1,846.0	27.6	2,548.8	32.2	3,046.2	33.6	6.7	3.6	702.8	57.2	497.5	43.2
Agricultural, Animal Husbandry & Forestry Workers, Fishermen & Hunters	1,890.7	28.3	1,662.2	21.0	1,486.9	16.4	-2.5	2.2	-228.5	-18.6	175.4	-15.2
TOTAL	6,686.0	100.0	7,915.4	100.0	9,066.2	100.0	3.4	2.8	1,229.4	100.0	1,150.8	100.0

Source: Seventh Malaysian Plan (1996 - 2000), National Printer, Kuala Lumpur.

Definition of Small and Medium Enterprises (SMEs)

There was never been a consensus on what criteria should be applied to define a small and medium enterprises in developing countries despite the fact that there is a proliferation of definitions. One study by the Georgia Institute of Technology for instance, identified over 55 different definitions in 75 countries (Manuh and Brown 1987). It is noted that most definitions appear to have been governed by the interest of the perceiver, the propose to be served and the staged of development of the particular country and economic environment in which the definition is to be employed (ILO 1986). A general tendency among empirical researchers is, however, to define SMEs by certain size of enterprises which are normally measured by either the number of person employed or the value of paid up capital (and/or fixed assets) or a combination of both. Others use less common methods such as share holders' fund, value and/or volume of output, sales, turn over, legal status, capital/labour intensity etc.

Having acknowledged this, it is illustrative at this juncture to explore some existing definitions formulated by different government agencies and researchers in Malaysia before establishing our operational definition. Indeed, like other countries, a similar difficulty is felt in considering the definition of SMEs in the country. So far, there has not been a formal, legal or clear-cut categorisation of what 'constitutes' the small and medium enterprises in Malaysia. Various government agencies and or institute have adopted different definitions. A review of such situation is further extended in this sub-topic.

The first example to state is the practice of the Ministry of International Trade and Industry (MITI) which is responsible for licensing the manufacturing establishment of the country, has been to define the small and medium enterprises (SMEs) differently over time. For instance, under its Industrial Co-ordination Act (ICA) which was introduced in 1975, all new and existing industrial establishments with more than 25 workers and paid up capital of more than M$250,000 were, required to apply for a new manufacturing license. In 1985, ICA amended its existing provision to cover establishments with paid up capital of up to RMl million and a full-time workforce of less than 50 employees. A year later, another amendment was adopted extending its regulation to establishments with paid up capital of RM2.5 million and engaging 75 full-time employees. The purpose of these amendments is understood to allow more small- and medium-sized enterprises to operate without having to register with the ICA, and hence giving them more responsibility for their own survival and market conditions (see MIDA 1990:2).

Meanwhile, the Co-ordination Council for Development of Small Industry defined a small firm as one that has fixed assets of less than RM250,000. Recently, this Council was transferred to the Ministry of International Trade and Industry and was renamed the Small-Scale Enterprises Division (SSED) which is responsible for co-ordinating government policies and programmes for promoting the development of small and medium-sized enterprises. It has now classified a small enterprises as having paid up capital not exceeding RM500,000 and medium-sized enterprises as having paid up capital not exceeding RM2.5 million (Ministry of International Trade and Industry, 1990). Meanwhile, under the Credit Guarantee Corporations (CGC), a small and medium enterprises is defined as one with having paid up capital that does not exceed RM100, 000 for "non-Bumiputera" enterprises and RM200,000 for a "Bumiputera" enterprise. The National Trust of People (MARA) has also used its own definition, classifying all enterprises with paid up capital less than RM200,000 as being a small and medium enterprises.

It is indeed widely acknowledged that the different definitions of small and medium enterprises serve specific purposes for the respective establishments. In three studies conducted in Malaysia by three international agencies, i.e. World Bank (1984:4), United Nations Development Organisation (1986:15-16) and Asian Development Bank (1990:9), they adopted the following definition:

i. small-scale enterprises - establishments employing less than 50 workers;
ii. medium-scale enterprises - those having between 50 and 199 workers; and
iii. large-scale enterprises - enterprises having more than 200 employees.

Besides, a few other independent researchers have used several other measures to define the small and medium enterprises in the country. Chee 1985:2-3), in his study of small industry in the manufacturing sector, has defined small and medium enterprises as those employing less than 50 and below 200 full-time workers respectively. In a study of a specific small and medium Bumiputera entrepreneur in Johor Bharu, Aziz also proposed a small and medium enterprises as having less 200 employees. On the other hand, Clapham (1982:2-5) classifies small and medium enterprises in Malaysia as those having a workforce between 10 and 100 full-time

23

employees. Similar to the definitions adopted by Lim and Aziz, Salleh has categorised small and medium enterprises as enterprises having less than 50 employees and 200 employees respectively (1990:1 and 1991:2-3).

Having observed some definitions of small and medium enterprises in Malaysia into consideration, the term 'small and medium enterprises' in this study refers to a firm that has full time employees of less than 200 and has fixed assets of less than RM2.5 million. These two criteria of the number of employees and fixed assets applied in the study are thought to be important relevant in view that small and medium enterprises may adopt a high-technology and capital intensive mode of production that would result in less capacity for generating employment and vice-versa.

A General Review of Small and Medium Enterprises in Malaysia

The significance and characteristics of small and medium enterprises many developed in general are well documented. It is also widely recognised that small and medium enterprises could and should become an essential component of Malaysia's industrialisation process. The overall situation of the development of small and medium enterprises has been acknowledged in several previous studies. Stewpanek's article on the development of small and medium-scale enterprises in the Federation of Malaya (1960) was probably the first initiative ever conducted. This study constrained by very limited statistical data since there was no field study carried out. Wong and Schiper's (1970) are also among the earlier independent studies. However, the research is restricted to the desirability of the consultative approach rather than on the development of small and medium enterprises. Chee (1978, 1982, 1984 and 1985) has written several encouraging articles on the characteristics and general development of the country's small industry. However, his study covered a sample population of only 377 firms across economic sectors throughout the country and may be regarded as under-representative. The detailed situation of small enterprises has not yet received special attention.

In addition, the World Bank (1982) and Asian Development Bank (1990) have also been involved in the study of SMEs businesses in Malaysia. Both studies generally concentrated on technological development and the major obstacles facing SMEs in manufacturing and repairing firms, suggesting the need for changes and the adoption of new policy instruments and institutions. In addition to the above studies, there are also a few other individual studies focusing on SMEs but with a limited scope. For instance, Poponoe (1970) and Mahmud (1981), focused on Malay Entrepreneurship, while Othman and Aziz's (1981) study is restricted to small and medium 'Bumiputera' enterprises in Kuala Lumpur and Johor Bharu.

Having considered these previous studies coupled with information from the Manufacturing Sector Surveys and Census of Industries made available from Department of Statistics, some general characteristics on the development of Malaysian small and medium enterprises will be presented. Table 1.10 shows the relative percentage share of the number of establishments by size of enterprises (measured by the number of employees) and the number of employees by size of enterprises from 1978 to 1988. Table 1.11 illustrates the total value of output and the total value of fixed assets by size of firms over the period of 1978 to 1994.

In 1994, small and medium enterprises accounted for 79.6 percent of the total manufacturing establishments and 41.5 percent of the total employment. SMEs, while consisting of about 44.3 percent of the total value of output, contributed 30.2 percent of the total value of fixed assets. This data implies that although over two-thirds of the total number of manufacturing firms are small and medium enterprises, their percentage share in employment, output and fixed assets are relatively smaller, i.e. below than 50 percent of the total. Indeed, there exists an inverse relationship between firm's size and the shares of employment, output and fixed assets. The figures also indicate a general decline in the relative significance of small and medium enterprises during the period 1978-1988, in terms of percentage share of establishments, contribution to employment, total value of output and fixed assets. For instance, from 91.3 percent of the number of manufacturing establishments in 1978 to 79.6 percent in 1988. In the share of the number of employees, the importance of small and medium enterprises' contribution had declined to about 2.8 percent over the same period, from 44.3 percent to 41.5 percent in 1994. In absolute terms, however, the number of small and medium enterprises has increased dramatically, from 2,219 in 1978 to 7,381 enterprises in 1994. A similar trend is also observed in terms of the numbers in employed increasing from 79,128 to 92,416 over the same period.

Table 1.10 Percentage Share of the Total Value of Establishments and Total Share of Labour Force by Employment Size of Firms in Malaysian Manufacturing Sector from 1978-1994

Number of Employee	1978 Est	1978 Emp	1983 Est	1983 Emp	1985 Est	1985 Emp	1994 Est	1994 Emp
0 to 49	66.3	16.5	64.2	16.3	64.0	16.5	58.8	11.7
50 to 99	16.3	13.4	16.6	13.9	17.0	14.6	17.2	11.8
100 to 199	8.7	14.4	11.4	18.5	11.1	18.3	13.6	18.0
200 to 499	6.0	21.2	5.2	19.4	5.4	20.1	6.9	20.1
500 or more	2.7	34.5	2.5	31.9	2.5	30.5	3.5	38.5
TOTAL	100	100	100	100	100	100	100	100

Notes: Est= Establishment of output, Empt = Employment .
Sources: Department of Statistics, Manufacturing Sector Surveys and Censuses of Industries, various issues, Government Printer, Kuala Lumpur.

Table 1.11 Percentage Share of the Total Value of Output and Value of Fixed Assets by Employment Size of Firms in Malaysian Manufacturing Sector 1978-1994

Number of Employee	1978		1983		1985		1994	
	Pro	Ast	Pro	Ast	Pro	Ast	Pro	Ast
0 to 49	12.6	10.4	9.5	8.5	9.1	7.8	9.8	6.3
50 to 99	13.7	12.4	13.1	9.8	13.4	8.8	11.8	9.0
100 to 199	18.5	16.3	23.7	18.0	24.2	14.8	22.7	14.9
200 to 499	29.2	27.2	21.9	19.7	23.2	28.5	23.0	29.3
500 or more	26.0	33.7	31.8	44.0	30.1	40.0	32.7	40.5
TOTAL	100	100	100	100	100	100	100	100

Notes: Pro= percentage of output, Ast= percentage affixed assets.
Sources: Department of Statistics, Manufacturing Sector Surveys and Censuses of Industries, various issues, Government Printer: Kuala Lumpur.

The large enterprises have been expending most rapidly, not only in terms of the number of establishment and employment, but also in terms of value of output and fixed assets. It is not known whether the decline in the significance of small and medium enterprises in the manufacturing sector is due to the relatively higher rate of bankruptcy during the period, or to an increase in their numbers employed which has pushed them into cohorts representing larger firms, or merely to the technical coverage of the surveys conducted by the Department of Statistics.

What is quite obvious from Table 1.12 above is that the value added per worker has risen in all firm sizes. Over the period 1983 to 1994 for instance, value added per worker in the small establishments had increased from RM48,800 to RM60,800, while the capital/output ratio has increased from RM339,300 to RM591,000 in the same period. Likewise, it is also reported that fixed capital per unit of output and fixed capital per worker had also increased irrespective of firm sizes (except in 1983) (see Industrial Surveys, Department of Statistics 1984 and 1994). These figures also show that the larger the firms, the higher the value added per worker and capital-output ratio relatively.

Table 1.12 Labour Productivity (in RM'000) and Capital/Output Ratio (in RM) by Employment Size in the Manufacturing Sector between 1983 - 1994

Number of Workers	1983		1985		1994	
	Lab	Cap	Lab	Cap	Lab	Cap
0-49	0.0488	0.3393	0.0529	0.5910	0.0608	0.5910
50-99	0.0794	0.2871	0.0877	0.3079	0.0971	0.4841
100-199	0.1078	0.2885	0.1264	0.2875	0.1249	0.4092
200-499	0.0952	0.3421	0.1104	0.5778	0.1185	0.7012
500 & more	0.0622	0.2708	0.1041	0.6239	0.1210	0.8838
Average	**0.0600**	**0.5333**	**0.0975**	**0.4691**	**0.1022**	**0.5989**

Notes :   Lab= Labour productivity, Cap= Capital/Output ratio
Source: Department of Statistics, Manufacturing Sector Surveys and Censuses or industries, various issues, Government Printer, Kuala Lumpur.

Prior studies to date show that the characteristics of small-scale and to some extent, medium-sized enterprises in Malaysia as in many other developing countries their organisation, marketing orientation and location are universal in nature. It has been documented that small and medium enterprises in Malaysia are typically family or significantly sole proprietorship businesses, utilising relatively low levels of capital. In view of this phenomenon, they tend to be more labour intensive, involving simple management and specialisation of labour, being run largely as one-person or family tied-operations and with a very simple division of labour. These small and medium enterprises have restricted access to capital, modern technology, and marketing information. These characteristics result in limited expansion and many of them remain sole proprietorship business (see for example, Chee 1988:7-29, Salleh 1991:3-6). Although these general characteristic have gradually changed over recent years due to government effort to modernise local SMEs to be more efficient and competitive in global market, only less significant proportion is sensitive towards this change (see Moha Asri 1997b, ADB 1990, FMM 1996).

The location of these businesses is spread across the country, in the countryside as well as urban areas. In the case of urban areas, the activities are generally situated only in the commercial and industrial centres but also in backyard operations and residential areas. A few small and medium enterprises were said to have located their operations in dedicated industrial sites. Nonetheless, there is a tendency for SMEs particularly those in the manufacturing sector to locate their operations in a specific area of so-called "small-medium enterprises" zones. A study on 185 SMEs in Penang recently indicates that 34.1 percent of them have located their operations in industrial zones for SMEs as opposed to only 16.8 percent in residential areas (see Table 1.13). The rests are situated in business areas (11.9 percent), shop houses and shop buildings (33.5 percent) and industrial zones (2.2 percent). Small and medium enterprises are also reported to produce goods significantly for lower and medium income households, concentrating on domestic products, which are locally orientated and are in many cases not suitable for export. A very limited number of them are reported to have been exported (Fong, 1986). Small and medium manufacturing firms have also been reported as basically owned by Malaysians, especially Chinese who account for almost 80 percent of the total establishments, illustrating the traditional Chinese dominance in trade, commerce and manufacturing activities (Asian Development Bank 1990:13). Nevertheless, the number of small and medium enterprises owned by "Bumiputera" are increasing, notably in the 1980s in several types of eco-

30

nomic activities such as handicraft, batik, food processing and furniture production (Aziz 1981 and Othman 1982).

Table 1.13 Operation of Small and Medium Enterprises by Location.

Location of Enterprises	Number	Percent
Industrial Zone	4	2.2
SMEs Industrial Zone	63	34.1
Shophouses/ Shopbuildings	62	33.5
Business Area	22	11.9
Residental Area	31	16.8
Illegal Area	1	0.5
Others	2	1.1
Total	185	100.0

Source: Moha Asri (1997c)

The Important Role of Small and Medium Enterprises in Malaysia

Prior independence up to now, Malaysian economic development has been closely related to development of global environment and international economy. From 1970s onwards, these had been the rise in the importance of non resource-based industries, particularly electronic and electrical sub-industries, replacing predominant by agricultural-based industries. In other words, these had been a shift from domestic-oriented import substitution to export-oriented industrialisation. In the 1980s, the country had witnessed with an export-oriented economic development. However, the focus was largely on development and growth of electronic and electrical sub-industries and textile and clothing sub-industries. Those were seen as potentially vulnerable to adverse external and global economic environment. For instance, global recession in the early 1980s and severe worsening Malaysian external terms of trade led to decline in the growth of trade performance. As consequences, it led to unbalance growth, high fiscal and external deficits, a rise in external debt as well as requiring structural adjustment to restore balance and stability. Since 1983, government introduced several adjustment measures which involved sharp reduction in public investment, restrain on external borrowing reforming financial system and encouraging private investment. In the 1980s, electronics and electrical goods, and textile and clothing products were generating nearly two-thirds of the total manufacturing value added and employing about 40 percent of all full time employees in manufacturing sector. Hence, the share of manufacturing exports in total gross national export reached 26 percent in 1991 and increased to almost 80 percent in 1995 (Malaysia 1996). In view of this global development, Malaysian industrial structure has become increasingly export-orientation.

This trend of development with narrow concentration on electronic and electrical, and textile and clothing industries but more significantly its heavy reliance on large-scale and Free Industrial Zone (FIZ) is seen to be potentially vulnerable. These firms largely dominated by foreign investment engage in enclave-type of activity, capital and import intensive modes of production. This nature of production indeed contributes little to deepening and widening of Malaysian domestic industrial structure. Linkages with the down and up stream economy remain scarce. In this connection, the government policy support programmes for SMEs are potentially viewed as highly important with respect to achieve a counter-balancing force which could reduce an existing imbalance industrial base and hence leading to widening the pattern of domestic manufacturing activity. It is therefore, highly thought that in order to achieve a more balanced-industrial structure, the promotion of SMEs can also be effectively integrated into the mainstream of industrial development. In particular, SMEs are largely local owned-business. In this relation, supporting SMEs would have the potential in reducing the dependency on large foreign-based investments which predominantly control many industrial sub-sectors in the country.

In addition, SMEs which are mostly endogenously-based enterprises, their linkages with large-multinational corporations in Malaysia can be seen as a mean or the same goal indirectly by encouraging large firms to foster the growth and expansion of SMEs. It has indeed to be realised that, as Malaysian economy move into a more complex phase of industrialisation and much more global, involving backward and forward integration of an efficient network of suppliers industries is extremely essential for export-orientated activities. Furthermore, many assembler firms of SMEs in Malaysia are either joint venture with foreign companies or at least licensees of foreign firms. In this view, technological transfer and other spin off to domestic supplier firms are both relevant with respect to the issues of inter firm linkages. Most of all, as feeder industries to larger firms, SMEs could provide ready business networks and distribution channels from which further industrial deepening and diversifying could be enhanced.

Moreover, SMEs represent the most platforms through which our indigenous entrepreneurs can progressively upgrade their investment and management skills. Moreover, SMEs have played many vital roles in providing avenues for local investors to diversify into manufacturing outputs. This sector has provided affordable investments opportunities that can be comparable to domestic investor availability and managerial capability. In this relation, it is highly important to note that the role of SMEs should be even greater, not just as a feeder industry, but more significantly as a backbone economic transition of the country especially in the wake of achieving industrialised nation by the year 2020.

To conclude, the strategic significance of SMEs in the overall economic growth and development of the country is attributable to among others things: SMEs account for nearly 80 percent of the total number of establishments, their ability to employ more worker per unit of capital, contributing to more equal income distribution, their role as a major vehicle for transferring or developing technical know-how, providing impetus for inter-firm linkages to the domestic economy, reducing import requirement and foreign exchange savings, and inducing endogenous and balanced industrial development. Furthermore, there was a concurrence that in most cases the importance of SMEs did not diminish as an economy went through different stages of economic development and industrial expansion. Based upon this realisation that numerous support programmes and strategies have been adopted and implemented in many countries to promote the development of SMEs. As one of the most rapidly growing economies, Malaysia in this relation is no exception. These support programmes for SMEs will be discussing further in the coming two chapters ahead.

Conclusion

Rapid industrial development and process of industrialisation in Malaysia has given considerable impact on the demand for labour, acute shortage of local labour and consequently on human resource development in general. In other words, the on-going industrialisation process of the country has led to the basic transformation of its economic structure which requires large supply of manpower also come from various categories of jobs such as professional and technical; administrative and managerial; and semi-skilled, production workers and unskilled.

In the light of the anticipated strong economic growth and industrial development in the next five years or so, the demand for manpower is expected to be the main challenge. With the unemployment rate is expected to stabilise at around 2.8 percent by the year 2000, and employment creation is expected to reach at more than 3.4 percent, the shortage of manpower will remained high in most sectors of the economy. In this regard, the transformation of Malaysian economic structure has led to substantial inflow of foreign labour into various employment sectors of the economy and Malaysia has become the most attractive destination country. It is roughly estimated that foreign labour comprises about eight percent of the total Malaysia population. However, depending excessively on foreign labour would affect long term development objectives of the country and also the socio-political problems resulting from the influx of foreign workers. As such, there is a need to re-examine closely the present human resource development strategy to cope with future challenge. It is therefore clear that the transformation of economic structure and rapid growth of manufacturing activity over the years has raised serious consequences on the issues of human resource development in this country. It is also clear that the transformation of economic structure needs fuller contributions of SMEs realising that rapid industrial growth become increasingly export-oriented and remains potentially vulnerable because of its narrow concentration on electronics and textiles sub-industries and heavy reliance on large scale, Free Trade Zone (FTZ)-based firms. These firms are exceptionally dominated by foreign investment, are engaged in enclave-type, capital and import-intensive activities which contribute little to the deepening and widening of Malaysia's domestic industrial structure. Linkages between SMEs and the rest of the economy remain weak. In this respect, SMEs have been officially recognised as important parcels that have to be effectively integrated into the mainstream of Malaysia's export-oriented industrialisation.

2 Policy Supports for Small and Medium Enterprises in Developing Countries: Rationale and Practice

Introduction

The recognition of the significant contribution of small and medium enterprises to national economic development has gradually led to a prominent position of these enterprises in the policy agendas of many developing countries (World Bank 1984, ILO 1986, UNIDO 1986 1991, ADB 1990). Nonetheless, systematic studies and evaluation, issues and challenges, on the particular characteristics of policy supports which have reached individual small and medium enterprises and their effects on the development of targeted firms have been lacking in the available literature (World Bank 1978, Sharma 1978, Gibb 1981, Neck 1983, Harper 1984, Richardson 1984, Hill 1985).

This section will, therefore, briefly review the nature of different conceptual approaches in relation to policy promotion of SMEs. Secondly, the rationale for promoting the development of SMEs will be summarised alongside the main policy supports proposed in the available literature. Lastly, a review of the main types of policy programmes in different developing countries is presented before a general outline of the existing policy support programmes in Malaysia is highlighted.

The Conceptual Approaches Underlying Policy Supports for Small and Medium Enterprises

In the development studies literature, there are, among others, three distinct analytical approaches which are concerned explicitly with the position of small and medium enterprises in developing economies. The theoretical arguments underlying these approaches are marked by differing conceptual frameworks and discussed differently in terms of development prospects of these enterprises in promoting the development of small and medium enterprises in developing countries. There are other than some concern which has been expressed about the purpose and implication of policy supports programmes for small and medium enterprises.

This sub-topic provides a review of these three approaches, namely dualist, petty commodity production (PCP) and flexible specialisation (FS), all of which are espoused to serve as the theoretical background to the study in this book.

The Dualist Approach

The term "dualist" has been used by Moser (1984a and 1984b) to describe the conceptual approach which divides, economic activity especially urban areas of developing countries into two separate sectors which in turn have two critical characteristics, i.e. the small and medium sector is seen as evolutionary and independent of their large-scale counterparts, and the inter-linkages between small-medium and large enterprises as being benign and beneficial. The term "dualist" is exclusively used in this book refer to this body of arguments.

The study of economic activities in developing countries within the general framework of the dualist approach which began three decades ago, has generated different coupling-terms regarding the dualist units of production. Among these, to mention a few, are: bazaar-type and a centred firms economy (Geertz 1963), the modern and traditional sector (Todaro 1969), informal-formal sector (ILO 1972), family and non-family enterprises (Friedman and Sullivan 1974), unprotected and protected enterprises (Mazumdar 1976), unorganised and organised activities (Joshi 1976) etc. These various terms broadly refer to small-medium enterprises on the one hand, and large-scale enterprises on the other (Schmitz 1982, Moser 1984b). Nonetheless, among those numerous terms employed, the informal-formal sector is the most widely used in the literature of small enterprises as Banerjee, for instance, points out:

> The co-existence of standard western-type employment along with other amorphous kinds of work has been labelled as the formal/informal sector dichotomy and has since been adopted as a general characteristic of the economies of less developed countries. (1981:36)

Although the originator of the term is Hart (1973:61-89), who used the term "informal sector" to describe urban workers outside the wage sector, its broad acceptance as a tool in urban analysis is due to the efforts of the ILO (International Labour Organisation) and WEP (World Employment Programme). The term 'informal sector' was developed as a pivotal concept with the various policy-oriented, studies set up within the framework of ILO-WEP studies, beginning with the Reports of the Kenya Mission (ILO, 1972). In the years following, the ILO produced a series of reports from intensive studies on a number of countries and cities with special focus on the potential role of small-medium economic enterprises in relation to employment problems. From the beginning, therefore, the term informal sector as an avenue to explain the characteristics of the working population in developing countries in accordance with the general aim of solving the problems of the unemployed and under employed segments of the labour force. In recognising the significance of small-medium enterprises in the development process in Ghana, Hart distinguishes employment in two forms, i.e. the 'informal activity' described as an unorganised sector of self-employment which differs from the 'formal' sector an activity of waged workers, recruited on a permanent and regular basis

Soon afterwards the ILO Kenya Mission extended the scope of the concept covering the characteristics of activities rather than forms of employment. The study related explicitly to small-medium based on several criteria, included the following: 'ease of entry' reliance on indigenous resources, family ownership of enterprises, small-medium operation, labour intensive and adopted technology, skills acquired outside the formal school system, and unregulated and competitive markets' (ILO, 1972:5-6). On the other hand, characteristics of the formal sector were simply stated as the opposite of those identified above (ILO, 1972:6). The absence of a relationship between small-medium and large enterprises was noted in the ILO report which later recommended recognising or establishing such links for the promotion of small and medium enterprises due to their potentially complementary role.

The report was the most prominent argument depicting the importance of small and medium enterprises inspiring a number of independent studies which have taken place in many parts of the three continents (Africa, Asia and Latin America). Despite the ILO emphasising, the concept of dualism in terms of the characteristics of small-medium and large enterprises, there have been attempts to apply the term to individuals, households, certain geographical areas, occupational groups (Peattie 1974:102 and Amin 1982:11-13) and certain types of technologies (Schumacher 1973, Dicksom 1974, Gilbert 1982, Widiono 1989, Kaplinksy 1990). Nonetheless, limited links between small-medium and large enterprises has been one of the main attributes of the dualist approach.

In addition, although the ILO's (1972) definition of small and medium enterprises is the most significant, there has been no consensus on how to classify small and medium enterprises in precise terms. It appears that researchers usually adopt their own definition either priori or interpreting, empirical data to determine the dividing points between dichotomous activities of the economy (Moser 1982, Richardson 1984). This has resulted in employing numerous criteria which appeared to have equal weight, as for example, Joshi (1980:641) notes as:

> Dichotomisation of urban economic activities into the dual formal-informal framework is strictly speaking justified only when the several dividing lines between large-scale and small-scale, high-productivity and low-productivity, foreign and indigenous, high-wage and low-wage, more or less coincide and also when they mark some discontinuity which does not have to be arbitrarily drawn across a continuum.

This is one of the most significant points on which the early critiques of the dualist approach focused, that is, to define economic activities as being small-medium and large enterprises. Faced with the difficulties of developing a sound basis for the dichotomisation of productive activities, some researchers proposed triple or even plural divisions (Steel 1976, Bienefeld and Godrey, 1975, Standing 1977, Jalloul 1988). Indeed, the definition of small and medium enterprises from this approach appeared to be problematic and it is difficult to justify a straight-forward conclusion. The division between various activities within small-medium enterprises, particularly between trading activities and productive activities was not sufficiently clarified. Moreover, this approach does not explain the, complexity of linkages between various forms of production in economic activity and also does not describe the significance of the socio-economic environment and political forces in a given society in determining the growth or decline of individual small and medium enterprises.

Having noted these difficulties in dividing the economies of developing countries, the several findings regarding the basic concept of this approach may generally be summed up as follows: the first is that the dualist approach depicts economic activities in urban areas being divided into two separate entities and conceptualises small-medium enterprises as *having evolutionary growth and being independent* from large firms. This conceptualisation is linked to an ideological framework of the "modernisation school". The second is that although *they rarely recognise the existence of relationship*[1] between small-medium and large enterprises, they assume both parties will benefit from this relationship. This assumption finds its best express on in the policy recommendations supporting the small-medium enterprises which be fostered, among other, via subcontracting with large enterprises.

In general, the classification of economic activities into two largely homogeneous entities causes severe problems to the conceptual usefulness of the dualist approach and weakens its explanatory and analytical power. In addition, its refusal to recognise the existence of various inter-firm linkages between different sizes and forms of organisation of production and that these linkages may not always be positive, and to underline the importance of the socio-economic environment and political forces in determining growth/decline or transition from one form to another, show the ideological nature of the dualist approach.

Petty Commodity Production (PCP) Approach

After the mid-1970s, the dualist approach received vigorous criticism which resulted in utilising an alternative perspective that evolved within the Marxian-based concept of "petty commodity production" (PCP) and its inter-linkages with the capitalist mode of production. The PCP approach distinguished itself from the previous one by its recognition of a multisectoral system of production in the economy. It highlights the existence of petty-commodity producers as one form of production within a "continuum mode", bridging from petty-commodity production to a full capitalist mode of production. While there is the notion of "bridging" or progress within the (PCP) approach (not dissimilar from a Rostowian conceptualisation), what distinguishes it is the concept of articulation of modes of production within a given economic activity.

In conceptualising small and medium enterprises as a form of production, Marx's treatment of petty commodity production as a transitional form that emerged in 19th century Europe in a transitional

---

[1] This may be seen in ILO (1972), Hart (1873), Chana and Morrison (1975), Sethuraman (1977 and 1981) etc. with the exception of Webb (1975:48) who seems to disagree with the non-existence of links between small and large enterprises.

period from feudalism to capitalism received considerable modification in view of the present-day situation in developing countries. It is proliferation rather than dissolution of petty production activities that has been the general pattern (Moser 1982, 1984b). Thus, the "vast majority of small and medium enterprises of the type described in the informal sector fit into the category of petty commodity production" (Moser 1978:1057).

Although both "form" and/or "mode" of production are used in explaining economic activities, it has been increasingly accepted that PCP should be regarded as a "form" of production (see Davies 1979:203 and Scott 1986:31 and also in Gerry 1979, Smith 1986, Basok 1989). This is due to the fact that petty-commodity production exists "at the margin of capitalist mode of production but is nevertheless integrated into it and subordinate to it" (Le Brun and Gerry 1975:20), and that it has never performed as a dominant mode of production as compared to the large-capitalist mode of production.

The earlier explanation of the persistence of non-capitalist forms of production (small and medium enterprises) in the economies, lies in the basic functions of these firms for the dominant capitalist mode of production. It is claimed that *unequal linkages* appear to prevail and that capitalist enterprises benefit from the continuing existence of other forms of production. The most common mechanism is that small and medium enterprises are useful in lowering the costs of the reproduction of labour power and/or transferring surplus through various multitudes of linkage, including sub-contracting works (Le Brun and Gerry 1975, Gerry 1979, Gerry and Bickbeck 1981). Therefore, the conservation/dissolution effect of the capitalist mode of production on other forms of production (small and medium enterprises) are for the purpose of reproduction of capitalism. Due to small and medium enterprises dependent position, there are constraints and limitations on their level of capital accumulation and development and in many respects a loss of autonomy (Gerry 1979). Based upon subordination and their dependent position, it is argued that Policy Proposals for small and medium enterprises will only end up with the total transfer of benefits to large capitalist enterprises (Leys 1975:117 Breman 1976:86-87).

Within this approach, not all analysts agree with the above-mentioned position (see Schmitz 1982, Basok 1989, Scott 1986a[2] and Bernstein 1988). These authors generally recognise that the analysis of small and medium enterprises needs to be expanded with greater emphasis being placed on the level of production as against merely a total system of production and inter-linkages among various enterprises. As Blincow (1986:114) contends, for instance, an analysis of "petty commodity producers" must concentrate on the specifics of the domain of production as the essential locus within which the process of transformation occurs. Freedman relates this issue to what she calls the "problem of totality" (1986:119) in which she stresses the mistake of previous writers in assuming that everything is capitalist in the "capitalist world system" (1986:120).

Besides primarily concentrating on external linkages between multiple levels of producers, the internal dynamics of small and medium enterprises, *their management practices and organisation of production* are also important by these analysts. The internal dynamics are said to have given small and medium enterprises opportunities to develop and respond to the linkages with large firms under the constraints of capitalist system, allowing small and medium enterprises the possibility of favourable development (Basok 1989:63-64). Besides this shift, deriving from the petty commodity production approach, its terminology and theoretical framework has also been drawn upon to explain issues such as class relations, kinship, gender and ethnicity in the analysis of small and medium enterprises (see also in Scott 1986b, Isik 1992). In other words, the internal characteristics of small and medium enterprises (including personal characteristics and management practices of the owner/managers, and the labour process of individual small and medium enterprises) which inevitably play their role (in various degrees), have also to be considered as parts of the overall-discussion in respect to the position, progress and development of small and medium enterprises in a given context or specific socio-economic environment.

---

[2] This reference entails a change from the argument made by Scott (1979), previously. See A.M. Scott 1986a 'Introduction: Why rethink Petty Commodity-Production' in Scott A. (ed.) "Rethink *Commodity* Production", in Social Analysis Special Issue Series, 20 (December) (pp. 3-10).

Flexible Specialisation (FS) Approach

From the late 1980s, there has been discussion on the applicability of a new approach known as "flexible specialisation" (FS) in an attempt to describe the existing position of small and medium enterprises in developing country. The flexible specialisation approach is thought to have emerged from a wider discussion over the past decades on the changes in industrial organisation and production technology in the international economy, and investment activities of multi-national corporations (MNCs) that have brought about considerable changes in the policies of economic management and production processes at the national and regional levels of many countries, developed and developing countries alike (see for instance Hirst and Zeitlin 1992:70). According to Drakakis-Smith (1987:26-28), these changes result from several circumstances including: rising cost of production in Western Europe and U.S.A. not only for wages but also rents and raw material imports too; the availability of cheaper labour resources in the cities of developing countries; the liberalisation of economic activities in some developing countries as a result of the role of international agencies (like the World Bank, UNIDO and ILO) and national governments, to bring employment to inhabitants of these cities and promote their industrial development. From the theoretical perspective, there is a great deal of confusion about how to characterise these changes, especially in the process of industrial production and manufacturing organisation. These have resulted in a number of approaches, among which are; "regulation theory", "post-Fordism" and "flexible specialisation" (detailed discussion of these approaches can be seen in Hirst and Zeitlin 1992:70-115).

The flexible specialisation approach was originally pinpointed by Piore and Sabel (1984) who used this concept to indicate new ways of organising industrial production in specific advanced countries notably, in northeastern Italy (and to some extent Japan), where they allegedly differed from the decline of general Fordist pattern (mass production system) in many other advanced economies. The approach emphasises the change from a dominant mass production system, where stable markets, economies of scale, factor-cost reductions, strict division of labour, the homogeneous market and stability etc. exists, to more diversified and ever-changing markets, products and production processes. The main characteristics of flexible specialisation which differ to that of mass production are summarised in Table 2.1.

Table 2.1 Characteristics of Flexible Specialisation and Mass Production

Main Feature	Flexible Specialisation	Mass Production
i) Size of Firm	Scope for small-medium and large	Large only
ii) Technology	General purpose machinery	Specialised dedicated machinery
iii) Labour	Broadly trained, multi-skilled and varied tasks	Narrowly trained, fragmented and routinised tasks
iv) Attitude to labour management	Seen as a resource, flat hierarchy, informal	Seen as a cost, hierarchical and formal
v) Product strategies	Variety, customised, rapid response and innovation	Standardisation, high volume and limited range
vi) Inter-firm	Close, co-operation and long-term	Arms-length, short-term and adversarial
vii) Competitive behaviour	Fast adaptation to change	Strategy to control market
viii) Institutional framework	Decentralised and local institutions which fuse co-operation and competition	Centralised national and multinational Keynesianism

Source: Schimtz (1989:11) and Kaplinsky (1991:7).

According to Schmitz (1989:12), the existence of the (FS) approach does not stand up as the new "mega theory of capitalist industrial development but the approach stands at a more modest level in advancing the understanding of past and current industrialisation".[3] Besides, this approach attempts to reconstruct a "historical trajectory of industrial development by identifying empirical forms of 'craft production' throughout the modern period in a given society" and therefore, it "rejects the notion of linear development and gradual progressive stages, and

---

[3] This article illustrates a new approach from H. Schmitz who was earlier considered as a petty commodity analyst.

classical theory of technical choice" (Lyberaki 1989:28). The application of the FS approach[4] to the study of small and medium enterprises developing countries recently been adopted by a number of scholars (see for instance Schmitz 1989 and 1990, Lyberaki 1989, Kaplinsky 1991, Lowder and Morris 1992, Ramussen, Schmitz and Dijk 1992, Dawson 1992, Hansohm 1992, Sverrisson 1992 and Aeroe 1992).

This approach distinguishes itself from the previous two approaches by its wider recognition of flexibility and innovation of production systems (including times of crisis "just in time") in a given economic and socio-cultural environment of developing countries. It recognises historically the fact that small and medium enterprises have not occupied the same inferior position in all countries. Rather, their strength has been affected by the degree of large firm domination, state policies, and differences in the socio-cultural environment (Rasmussen 1992:21). The approach also regards existing small and medium enterprises as being more flexible and more efficient for a more intensive use of labour instead of scarce capital, as compared to large firms (Schmitz 1989:24). Therefore essential element in their survival are exploitation of internal economies of scale and their capacity to adapt to rapidly changing markets (Schmitz 1989:24, Rasmussen, Schimitz and Dijk 1992:4).[5] In this relation, the growth potential of small and medium enterprises and their resilience during crises depends critically on their efficiency and flexibility to adjust faster to change circumstances in a specific economic, political and socio-cultural context (Sabel 1986 and Kaplinsky 1991).

The concern with flexibility (including innovation) and efficiency of small and medium enterprises has extended the conceptual discussion of small and medium enterprises on a number of crucial and inter-related issues. The most important is that of inter-firm linkages which are regarded as part of the flexibility and efficiency of small and medium enterprises. The analysis of linkages covers intra- and inter-firm levels implying that enterprises' interaction occurs in clusters among equal partners (among small and medium enterprises in an industrial locality/district) and more

---

[4] This is despite the fact that the concept of FS has been used in various ways, purpose and has often been confusing (see Lovering 1990:159, Rainnie 1991:353, Harrison and Kelly 1993:213 etc.). This may be because of its newness in the theoretical debate of SMEs.

[5] For a detail analysis of the changes in scale of economies at the product, plant and firm level which show how SMEs respond to the changing circumstance, see Kaplinsky (1990 and 1991).

frequently with input/output suppliers and/or vertical sub-contracting arrangements with large firm counterparts. The most common practice is vertical disintegration which segregates the production functions economically and geographically via the development of a diffused sub-contractors net (Sverrisson 1992:32). However, the extent of intra- and inter-firm linkages and the benefits of such links on the development of individual small depend upon consumer markets, demand and the specific environments in which small and medium enterprises operate.

The FS approach conceptualises the internal characteristics of small and medium enterprises in terms of management adjustments in response to changing markets and customer demanding a specific time and locality. The internal adjustments are said to include the ability of the owner/managers of small and medium enterprises, to make more effective use of employees[6] or "human resources" in their pursuit of efficiency and flexibility (Hill 1991:39 Overall, three adjustments with respect to the flexibility of owner/managers in SMEs are given priority (Harrison and Kelly 1993:213-235). These are: i) functional flexibility, i.e. efforts of owner/managers to redefine, work tasks, redeploy resources and reconfigure relationships with suppliers and distributors; ii) wage flexibility, which refers to various efforts by owner/managers to reintroduce greater competition among individual workers; and iii) numerical flexibility, i.e. redesign of jobs to substantiate or substitute part-time, piece-rate, home workers etc. where necessary. Nonetheless, the features and level of flexibility of internal adjustments very much correlate with "socio-cultural dimensions such as the existence of ethnic, religious, and groups which have a major influence on how business relations develop" (Rasmbssen, Schmitz and Dijk 1992:4), and that eventually effects the development of individual SMEs.

The approach also recommends policy support for SMEs. In its recognition, the emphasis is given to the existence and effective operation of flexible institutions which could provide a supportive environment for specific types of industry in a particular locality (Morris and Lowder 1992:196). Moreover, according to Hirst and Zeitlin (1992:111-112), the institutional route to "flexible specialisation" is the existence of political,

---

6 Opportunities for SMEs (the owner/manager to utilies the existing "surplus labour" (in many developing countries including unregistered, part-time, piece-rate and unpaid workers) to obtain high labour turnover as compared to wages paid were clearly described by Schmitz (1989:30-34) under labour market conditions in many of these countries.

normative and organisational means of creating relationships to foster co-operation and co-ordination. Two broad ways are foreseen. There are: i) building up strategy, i.e. linking up firms with collaborative institutions to form industrial districts, and seeking to generalise and link such districts so as to form the dynamic core of a national economy, and ii) the strategy of building down, i.e. through reorganisation of major multinational firms into constellations of semi-autonomous sub-units that may cooperage one with another or with other firms in an industrial district. The question of "how and to what extent flexible specialisation can be fostered through policies of government or other institution" is indeed dependent upon the locality where SMEs -operate (Schmitz 1989: 8), and therefore would be analysed in the specific context of sub-industry and country (Rasmussen 1992:21).

As the flexible specialisation approach to the study of SMEs in developing countries is being recently developed, some criticisms have been raised. The most important one being argued concerns "overly flexible and insufficiently specified specialisation" (Sayer 1986:666). Therefore, the concept has been used for different purposes resulting in inconsistencies between different versions (Lovering 1990:159 and Harrisson and Kelley 1993:213). In addition, critics also argue that general dichotomies between a mass production system and flexible specialisation are not clear, the changes over-stated, and that they fail to grasp continuities of industrial development in many parts of the world where the mass production system is still expanding (Morris and Lowder 1992:190,200). In some respect, their reality is that the ideal types of FS are united with other forms of industrial organisation in varying degrees (Hirst and Zeitlin 1991). The FS is also claimed to be an advocative idea rather than an empirical generalisation and hence, largely hypothetical and difficult to test empirically.

Besides these criticisms, some issues relating to its conceptual underpinnings are indeed relevant to be summarised, especially in its explanation of flexibility and efficiency of industrial organisation. The approach's recognition of both intra- and inter-linkages between firms has extended the conceptual discussion a step ahead of the previous two approaches presented earlier. The management adjustments on various levels of operation including flexibility towards readily available "labour surplus" in many parts of developing countries are among the recent advancing theoretical spectrums. The importance of specificity of policy support for SMEs with respect to the economic sub-industry and socio-cultural environment is a distinctive feature. However, as this approach is relatively new, many issues raised on these aspects are largely untested.

The Rationale for Policy Promotions

The arguments in favour of promoting the development of small and medium enterprises in developing countries are closely related to their *potential and actual role* as well as their importance in economic development, for which there now exists considerable and mounting evidence. These two correlated-issues will be highlighted simultaneously under three element viz. *economic, social* and *political* aspects.

In terms of the economic impact of SMEs, employment and income generations are the main reasons advanced. World Bank reports (1978) and ILO studies (1982) in many different countries statistically show a significant share of employment, which in turn provides income. It is noted that small and medium enterprises account for between 60 and 92 percent of total employment in the manufacturing sectors of developing countries during the period 1967-1975 (Andersson 1982). This percentage even larger in other sectors of the economy. Recently, Little, Mazumdar and Page (1987:300) observed that more than half of all manufacturing employment in India, Indonesia and many African countries came from small and medium enterprises. The rational promoting SMEs is also relevant to enhance international competitiveness and enabling the quickening of the process of economic structural change and to take advantage of the shifting economic comparative advantage. In addition, assistance to SMEs would enable a number of them to move gradually through a process of transformation to emerge as producer of high-tech products or to act as suppliers of components or parts to larger firms through sub-contracting or to become producers of import substitution products. SMEs promotion is also seen one of the channels that would help increasing number of new entrepreneurs which would be of vital importance in any economy.

The significant contribution of SMEs to total manufacturing output has also been put forward to argue in favour of policy supports. It was found that in 1980 small and medium enterprises in Brazil contribute more than 30 percent of the value of production in the manufacturing. In Indonesia and Sierra Leone, the corresponding figures were 38 and 58 percent in 1974/75 (ILO 1986:8). There are other economic reasons. According to Soon (1983) in some newly industrialised countries like Singapore, Taiwan and Korea, an import role of SMEs is to support the large local and multinational companies. It has also been noted that SMEs will become even more important and will be accorded even greater priority as the country develops (see Lim 1985, ADB 1990 etc.). There is a tendency to associate large enterprises with highly developed countries such as the U.S.A., Japan, Germany, and Canada. Nonetheless, SMEs remains a highly vital component in the manufacturing sectors and its importance has increased rather than diminished in all these countries recognise the growing importance of SMEs and have continued to extend various forms of assistance to their SMEs. A few examples is illustrative to point out here. First, examples from the limited states show that in 1976, the U.S.A. Congress (by public law) created the Office of Advocacy within the Small Business within the Federal Government. This is created to ensure that small and medium enterprises would be the "cornerstone" of the U.S.A. free enterprises system.

The significance role of SMEs in the Japanese economy is well known. This can also be observed through numerous government assistance legislation's and several government agencies involve in the development of SMEs in Japan. The most well-known agency is the Small and Medium Enterprises Agency. In Canada, there is a Minister of State for Small-Medium Business which provides unequivocal support to SMEs.

Under social considerations, income re-distribution, greater use of local products for local needs, rectification of regional imbalance, greater job satisfaction for workers and provision of a source of livelihood for particular groups such as youth and refugees are among the reasons put forward (see for instance, in Harper 1984). All these may lead to a reduction of poverty, unemployment and inequity in the society. With respect to political consideration, basic principles of democracy and social justice are well explained by Bromley (1985:250) who points out that policy supports are the government obligation as part of its "power base". Detail elaboration may be also observed in Diawana and Kinga (1977).[7]

Specific Assistance Activities for Small and Medium Enterprises in Developing Countries

The policy recommendations of many policy makers and academics of related disciplines (see in Neck 1977, World Bank 1978, 1982, Sharma 1979, Gibb 1982, Harper 1984, UNIDO 1986, 1991, Levy 1991) may be summarised in the following four broad areas: i) financial or credit assistance; ii)management training and technical assistance; iii) extension and advisory services; and iv) infrastructure supports. A brief reference to

---

[7] In P. Nect (1977).

the support programmes in some developing countries is made under these headings.

Financial or Credit Assistance

Lack of finance or access to the resources of organised credit facilities is recognised as a major obstacle to the development of SMEs. A common feature of most financial support activities observed in practice and in the literature is credit assistance, which may take the form of low interest rate loans, and/or direct subsidies, and occasionally tax and customs relief. Frequently, a much lower interest rate merely covering bank costs might be adopted or imposed for investment loans; or SMEs might be made exempt from paying specific income and other taxes during their first few years of operation.

Another policy typically adopted is to oblige banks to allocate a set minimum proportion of lending to small and medium enterprises or otherwise face penalties. This policy follows reluctance on the part of the banks to provide loans to SMEs on the grounds of risk and overall profitability. Consequently, in Korea for example, commercial banks operating on a nation-wide scale must reserve at least 35 percent of their loanable funds for SMEs while other local banks are obliged to allocate 50 percent (UNIDO, 1986:39).

In the light of the reluctance of banks to lend to SMEs, credit guaranteed by government agencies has also been adopted in some countries, for examples the policy of setting up special institutions to provide financial assistance to SMEs. In Thailand, the Industrial Finance Corporation of Thailand (IFCT) was established in 1973, to finance SMEs purchasing raw materials, new technology or imported technology to process local raw materials into new products. The Small Industry Finance Office (SIFO) in Thailand provides the financial supports at a relatively low interest rate, i.e. 14.5 percent per annum with a repayment period of 5 to 6 years for small and medium enterprises in manufacturing services and handicrafts. It was recorded that up to 1988, a total of 1,203 loans were approved with a total value of 397.5 million bath (Khanthachai 1990: 17-34). The Industrial Bank of Korea (IBK) is believed to be the main source of credits for small and medium-sized enterprises in Korea. This is apart from the Korea Credit Guarantee Fund (KCGF) which was established in 1971 extending credit guarantees to commercial banks that provide loans to SMEs.

Besides the Bank of Malawi and Grameen Bank which are the main credit sources for Malawian small and medium enterprises under the special loans up to K2,500.00 and 11 percent interest rate, Malawian Saving and Credit Organisation (MUSCO) is also active (Beza 1989:80). In Philippines much financial aid to SMEs is directed through the Cottage Industrial Guarantee and Loan Fund (CIGLF). It is a joint programme of public and private financial institutions, the Ministry of Trade and Industry as well as the National Cottage Industrial Development Authority (NACIDA) with a credit maximum of P100,000. Collateral is required for 50 percent of a loan, the rest being covered by CIGLF guarantee (Conti 1990:81-95). In Sri Lanka, the Credit Guarantee Scheme is issued by the Central Bank that covers 60 percent of the total loans (UNIDO 1986). Indonesian Credit Insurance in Indonesia provides the guarantee and bears the risk resulting from non-repayment of the bank credits supplied to small and medium-sized SMEs, while the Institute of Co-operative Credit Guarantees (ICCG) guarantees the credits granted by Bank Rakyat Indonesia to co-operatives and SMEs (ADB 1989).

Credit guarantee apart, special institutions have been set up to provide credit to SMEs. These can be found in virtually all the countries referred to above and many others. A typical example is the Gujarat Industrial Investment Corporation (GIIC) in India. A public limited company, its objectives are to promote new entrepreneurs in SMEs, to develop non-traditional new-industries, and to undertake those functions which existing institutions do not give a chance, Patel (1982) gives details of Technical, Scheme whereby Gujarat Industrial Investment Corporation provides 100 percent finance of project costs of SMEs and requires no collateral or third party guarantees. Additionally, the loan attracts the following terms: i) no repayment for the first three years, followed by annual instalments spread several years; and ii) a 50 percent subsidy applies on interest for the first three years. A significant development with respect to institutions is the increasing interest in and support by the World Bank and its affiliated organisations in Development Finance Companies (DFCs) through which assistance is channelled to SMEs (UNIDO 1986, 1991). DFCs may either lend directly or, as is more often the case, provide funds for participating commercial banks for on-lending to SMEs. DFCs feature prominently in, SMEs promotion policy in several countries such as Singapore, Korea, and Thailand.

Financial assistance is also provided by the public banks of several countries specifically to develop and upgrade the technological improvements or R&D in SMEs' operation. For instance, the Industrial Development Bank of India decided to impose five percent levy on all technology import payments to create a venture fund. With the involvement of several other main agencies in the country such as Venture Capital Schemes, the Unit Trust of India (UTI), the Industrial Credit and Investment Corporation of India, several objectives are formulated along this line, inter alia: i) assessment of innovative technology, products, processes, markets and services; and ii) upgrading of technology through in house R&D and commercialisation of new domestic technology (ADB 1989). Several banks/agencies in Indonesia with the help of the Asian Development Bank are also involved in a similar form of arrangement. These agencies include Bank Pembangunan Indonesia (BAPINDO), Regional Development Banks (RDBS) and Indonesian Small and Medium-sized Enterprises Institute (ISMEI) (see ADB, 1989).

A few more programmes could be cited, perhaps the most notable being venture capital. The foregoing typify financing policy and programmes in several countries. For instance, in India the above mentioned institutions also provide venture capital where equity participation is restricted to 49 percent of the invested enterprises paid up capital. SMEs are given assistance in the forms of: i) conventional loans, i.e. loans granted under certain predetermined conditions (e.g. interest rate and grace period etc.); ii) developmental loans, i.e. allow profit and risk sharing with the project proponents; and iii) equity investment, i.e. the financial assistance takes the from of a direct subscription to the shares of enterprises undertaking the project (see ADB 1989:199-205). In the Philippines, the Venture Capital Co-operative plays a leading role as the business partner with the small-medium entrepreneur rather than a lender (Yonzon 1990:132-139).

Entrepreneurial Training and Technical Assistance

There are two main support activities, which may generally be identified, in technical and training assistance. The first is entrepreneurial development training for potential entrepreneurs who desire to establish new and small and medium scaled businesses. This support activity usually focuses on the development of a business plan, accessing financial sources, viability of business proportions, company formations and basic management skills. This can be seen in many of the above mentioned countries. With assistance from United Nations Industrial Development Organisation (UNIDO) and ILO, for instance, the Industrial Services Division was established in Thailand in 1972 to provide management training for potential small and medium business. Meanwhile, the Thailand

51

Management Development and Productivity Centre (TMDPC) is set up to promote small and medium industries by providing continuous technical assistance and conducting seminars to manufacturers on management techniques, inventory control, production planning and control (Khanthachai 1990: 17-29).

The Institute of Small Scale Industry (ISSI) was established in 1966 in the Philippines to provide technical and training assistance to entrepreneurs, namely on managerial production and marketing aspects of small and medium businesses. Meanwhile the Small Business Advisory Centres (SBAC) provides the technical know how for young entrepreneurs. In Myanmar (Burma), "Small Scale Industrial Development in the Co-operatives Sector" was established in 1972 under the initiative of UNDP (United Nation Development Programme) and ILO to disseminate of their own training facilities and technology upgrading (UNIDO 1986:18).

Other examples of similar institutions include: the Malawian Entrepreneurs Development Institute (MEDI) and Small Enterprise Development Organisation of Malawi (SEDOM) in Malawi; the National Science and Development Board and the Design Centre of the Philippines; the Small and Medium Industry Promotion Corporation (SMIPC) in Korea; the Medium and Small Business Administration, Industrial Technology; and Research Institute of Taiwan and China Textile Research Centre in Taiwan.

The second support activity under the technical and training assistance is technical skill oriented-training technology for engineers and workers. It is provided mainly to improve various aspects of technical production broadly including processing techniques, equipment/tool selections, handling processes and overall technology-manufacturing techniques. A course of this type of assistance varies from one country to another. For example, the National Institute for Development of Skilled Labour (LIDHL) in Thailand provides training for skill improvement of industrial workers ranging from six months to three years. The same technical advice to engineers and workers in small and medium enterprises are also given by the-Textile Industry Development Centre (Khanthachai 1990:17-29). A similar example can also be found in India where the Birla Institute of Technology appears to have developed very successful integrated programmes (Patel 1982).

Extension and advisory services are normally the follow up assistance provided to entrepreneurs who are already involved in business. While technical training assistance is given to potential entrepreneurs, engineers and workers, extension and advisory services are apparently provided for only the owner/manager of small and medium-sized activities. Three main types of extension and advisory services may generally be noted under extension and advisory services. The first is management consultancy services. This is given either in seminars or short-courses about professional management in business. The organisation of these activities as found in the literature and in practice differs from one country to another. In Indonesia, the Management of Indonesian Enterprises (P.T. BAHANA), for example, is the only major national institution giving assistance in the field of management, amongst other things, to SMEs. This institution is apparently involved in all fields of business activity of the private sector and in management consultancy services of enterprises in which it has an interest.

Small Enterprise Development Organisation (SEDOM) which was established in 1982 plays a crucial role in providing extension and advisory services to potential and existing entrepreneurs in Malawi (Beza 1989:80). In the Philippines, the Institute of Small Scale Industries (ISSI) is again the major government institution whose primary function is to conduct managerial and entrepreneurial consultancy development SMEs. The Institute provides training courses and entrepreneurial development programmes in pursuit of various objectives. Another extension and advisory services is the Small Business Advisory Centre (SBAC) launched in 1975 to provide "post-loan assistance" in the form of techno-managerial consultancy services to SMEs' clients funded by World Bank (UNIDO 1986:17).

The second type of extension and advisory service is courses related to marketing and market research. These courses include knowledge of market opportunities, products' innovation and development, attractive packaging etc. The objectives of these courses are generally to identify target markets and customers, to assess their buying habits, price promotion and distribution strategies. Some countries focus their scope of assistance largely on marketing and market-orientation programmes that encourage small and medium enterprises to manufacture export-oriented products, such as in Korea and Thailand. They also provide useful information on the various potentials domestic as well as overseas markets. Moreover, the promotion of greater linkages, especially vertical integration with the large firms, can be observed. In Thailand, for instance, the marketing outlets are provided by collecting products from producers throughout the country and displaying them at the Naraiphon Store in Bangkok for local buyers and foreign importers. This centre too promoted sub-contracting and vertical linkages among enterprises in the country especially between SMEs and large firms.

In India, the promotion of linkages is well known as "ancillarisation" or development of feeder industries. This activity involves in an abiding relationship between SMEs and large industries where the SMEs provides a substantial portion of its production of parts, components, sub-assemblies or services to large firms, which use these in the production process or final product. Several state-owned companies in particular have taken the lead by issuing comprehensive guidelines to SMEs units registered as ancillary to such companies. In 1982, a total of 7,068 SMEs registered with total value of supplies of RM2,330 million and provided employment to 26,702 workers in several sub-industries including textile (UNIDO 1986:7).

The last type of extension and advisory service is courses related to product quality, quality and design improvement. There are normally several agencies in the above-mentioned countries, which provide consultancy services to SMEs to upgrade the quality, design of their product and quality control system. In some countries, there is one main institution to carry out a broad range of functions relating to standard testing, registration for quality control, Research and Development (R&D) and consulting.[8] In the Philippines, for instance, ISSI is also involved in managerial consultancy so as to enable enterprises to upgrade their financial planning, to control procedure, to introduce systematic accounting techniques and to upgrade quality and design of products (Yonzon 1990: 132-140). The Naraiphon Store in Thailand also provides assistance in other areas such as product design, available raw material, production technique and other necessary assistance.

---

[8] It can also be a government agency established to provide for the testing of commodities, processes, practices and encourage establishment of quality services providing for the registration for Certificate Making of Quality Control and regulate its use (see ADB 1991).

It has long been recognised that the scattered location of SMEs poses a major challenge in efforts to assist them. The extra cost of travel make the appraisal and supervision of small loans less economic, and individual advisers may spend more time travelling than working with clients. The problem in question may also frustrate attempts to provide assistance with raw materials, marketing outlets and specialised technical services. The setting up of industrial sites is usually combined with special incentives and supportive measures (i.e. provision of industrial premises, common production facilities, guaranteed supply of raw materials and services, sub-contract arrangement etc.) to locate and develop small and medium enterprises.

Such recognition has led to the consideration of a cluster of SMEs on sites which are not only more convenient for the promotion agency, but also enables tenants to benefit from an integrated package of services which would be uneconomic otherwise (UNIDO 1986). The case for industrial estates appear strong both for relocating existing business and for encouraging new businesses to start in clusters. Not surprising the literature abounds with evidence of policy supports for SMEs in this area such as The Industrial Estate Authority of Thailand and the Jurong Town Corporation (JTC) in Singapore. Two specific industrial estates for SMEs were built at Liwonde and Lilonwe by the Ministry of Trade, Industry and Tourist of Malawi in order to promote greater incentive for small-medium producers especially in the manufacturing sector (Beza 1989:80). In the Philippines, the Omnibus Investment Code is the major agency for providing industrial estates nowadays and includes incentives to encourage the location of industries in non-urban centres thereby, proposing to improve regional industrial development.

Finally, a review of literature on the types of support and assistance specifically designed to promote SMEs indicates the fact that the notion is widely accepted in the majority of developing countries, though the scope and extent commitment vary greatly one country to another. Some countries have embarked upon comprehensive programmes designed to promote the development of SMEs an integral part of national plans. This is particularly true in the case of some countries in Asia. While others have periodically implemented a of plans patchily designed under social/political pressures, to alleviate economic conditions of the poor. This is particularly true in the case of many African countries were economic resources are relatively scarce (Manuh 1989 and Levy 1991).

The Existing Policy Support Programmes for Small and Medium Enterprises in Malaysia

During the early period of Independence, there was no precise government policy programmes design specifically for the development of small and medium enterprises. The development of the traditional rubber and tin industries led to the growth of various workshops and foundries to cater for these industries. These became the forerunners of SMEs' development in country. The palm oil industry provided further impetus to the small and medium enterprises especially in the area of processing and machinery fabrication and repairs. The development of SMEs was hence, regarded as incidental to this.

When Malaysia embarked on an industrialisation drive in the 1960s, the government policy support programmes for the small and medium-sized enterprises were originally outlined in the First Malaysian Plan (1966-1970). The government emphasis was however, still on bigger industries and attraction of foreign investment as, for instance, shown by the introduction of the Investment Incentives Act 1968. Nonetheless, the significance of promoting the development of small and medium enterprises in general and small and medium manufacturing establishments in particular was restated under the New Economic Policy (NEP) in 1971 and reaffirmed in subsequent five-year National Development Plans. The main attention of the Government's small-medium industrial policy promotion and programmes has been focused on the development of indigenous, i.e. Bumiputera entrepreneurs. Various public agencies involved in promoting SMEs' development and entrepreneurial know-how with the central focus on the Bumiputera community.

The Mid-Term Review of the Fourth Malaysian Plan (1981-1983:1983) provides the most comprehensive listing of the government's guidelines for small-medium enterprises development. These guidelines, among other things, emphasise the following: i) small and medium enterprises should not duplicate activities already under taken by the bigger-scale enterprises, and that preference be given to small and medium enterprises which complement the activities of bigger-scale businesses; ii) the selection of industries must satisfy the need to achieve the New Economic Policy, particularly in encouraging Bumiputera participation in businesses and other commercial activities; and iii) the promotion of SMEs should be considered as an integral part of the overall manufacturing sector development (see Mid-Term Review of the Fourth Malaysian Plan, 1983).

The government policy supports for the development of small and medium enterprises were under further review, in late 1988. Since this time new policy initiatives have been progressively introduced, such as through the 1989 and 1990 National Budgets. These together with any other major new initiatives such as the First and Second Industrial Master Plans associated with the policy review, were consolidated and reflected in the Sixth Malaysia Plan which covers the period 1991 to 1995 and Seventh Malaysia Plan which covers the period 1996 to 2000.

Overall, it is observable that before 1980, government policy support programmes were essentially "inward-looking", i.e. domestic market-oriented. This was not reviewed until the recession-related downturn in the economy in the early 1980s. As outlined in the Fourth Malaysian Plan (1981-1985:1980), the increasing concentration of local products-orientated is now being replaced by the need for a more outward-looking, i.e. export-oriented development of SMEs. This strategy includes the policy support programmes for small and medium industrial expansion and modernisation through provision of financial assistance, improvement of the incentive system, promotion of R&D activities and the strengthening of the institutions responsible for small and medium enterprises.

Under the institutional framework, the first to be noted is the Small and Medium-Scale Enterprise Division (SSED at MITI). It has primary responsibility for co-ordinating the Government's small and medium industrial development programmes. The main functions of this division can be summarised as follow: i) to study and evaluate the existing and forthcoming policies for the development of SMEs; ii) to identify opportunities in industries for involvement of SMEs; iii) to provide advice and guidance to entrepreneurs on policies and programmes implemented by government agencies through conferences, dialogues, talks and workshops; iv) to collect and distribute publications on projects, studies and pamphlets on SMEs; and iv) to create and implement specific programmes for the development of small firms (MITI 1989: 4-14). Presently, SSED was upgraded to bigger role when the Small and Medium Industries Development Corporation (SMEDEC) was established in May 1996. The establishment of SMEDEC is in line with the recognition of the need for a specialised agency to further promote the development of SMEs to be an integral part of the national industrialisation programme and become global and world class enterprises. The main task of this corporation is among others: i) to co-ordinate the overall development of SMEs in the country, ii) to promote the development of   modern and sophisticated indigenous SMEs in tandem with the strategic direction of the industrial development, and iii) to develop the SMEs into an efficient and competitive sector, capable of producing high value added and quality products, components and related services for the global market.

Presently, there are as many as 13 ministries and 30 government agencies with varying responsibilities and offering a wide variety of programmes to promote small and medium enterprises development. To avoid repetitiveness in reviewing the existing assistance activities, the responsibilities and functions of those existing government agencies will be reviewed with respect to the six main chapters of policy support identified in earlier: financial and credit assistance; entrepreneurial development and business management; human resource development, technical and vocational programmes, locational and infrastructural facilities; and fiscal incentives (see for instance Lim 1986, MIDA 1985 and 1990, MITI 1990, ADB 1990 Bank Negara 1989 and 1991, Moha Asri 1997a and 1977b etc.). All these will be presenting exclusively in the respective few chapters ahead.

3 Financial and Credit Assistance

Introduction

The financial system in Malaysia is relatively well developed. Under the Bank Negara (the Central Bank) which is the main controller of the country's financial policy, there were 38 commercial banks operating a total of 911 branches by the end of 1980s. Moreover, financial companies which total 47 with 486 branches, comprise the second largest group of deposit-taking financial institutions in Malaysia, in addition to several development finance institution (Bank Negara, 1989). In order to make credit more readily and cheaply available to SMEs, commercial banks, finance companies and government related financial institutions had certain criteria imposed on them by the Central Bank. The most important one is the Priority Lending Guidelines which imposes qualitative lending targets introduced in 1974.

This guideline requires commercial banks and other financial agencies to allocate a prescribed proportion of their loans outstanding to SMEs. The guidelines are reviewed each year, specifying required levels of lending to the four priority group of: the Bumiputera community, small-medium enterprises, farmers and enterprises engaged in agricultural food production; loans to buyers of low cost owner-occupied homes, at interest rates below the market rate. Failure to do so means a penalty would be imposed. Since commercial banks, finance companies and government financial-related institutions are the major sources of credit assistance for SMEs, a review of the amount of loans, basic interest rate charged and number of recipient enterprises are briefly presented under these headings respectively.

Commercial Banks

Commercial banks are the major of credit for SMEs consisting of about 20 percent of total new bank credit each year. Under the priority lending guidelines, the maximum interest rate which can be charged by commercial

59

banks is fixed at 1.75 percentage points above the average of the Base Lending Rate (BLR) of the two main commercial banks in Malaysia (i.e. Malayan Banking Berhad and Bank Bumiputera Malaysia Berhad) or 9 percent per annum, whichever is lower. In line with the reduction in the BLR of these two banks, the maximum interest rate for priority sector loans in 1988, for instance, was 8.5 percent. It has been recorded that Commercial Banks loans to the manufacturing sector rose steadily, from RM7.4 in 1983 to RM13.2 million 1989. The number of SMEs, which had received loans through commercial banks also, increased over the same period from 39,581 to 57,751 businesses (Bank Negara 1990).

The Finance Companies

As in the case of commercial banks, finance companies had similar lending guideline imposed on them by the Central Bank to direct funds to priority sectors. Among these guidelines, a total of 15 percent of their total loans had to be given to SMEs and 20 percent of this had to be to the 'Bumiputera community'. By 1989, a total of RM2,807 million credit was granted to small and medium businesses. The minimum credit for SMEs is RM10,000 and the maximum is RM50,000. However, only between 4 and 6 percent went to the small and medium-manufacturing enterprises.

The Merchant Banks

There were only 12 Merchant Banks in Malaysia in 1988 but the number is believed too have increased significantly in 1990s. They play a significant role in providing finance to small and medium-sized enterprises especially in the manufacturing sector. For instance, in 1989, it is recorded that these banks provided a total of 7.9 percent of the total loans to the manufacturing sector. These banks also act as special financial intermediaries in the financial market and are engaged in professional, investment advice, financial advisory services and management services. They are also involved in operations such as accepting deposits and making loans, discounting, leasing and bridging finance as well as equity financing.

The Development Finance Institutions (DFIs)

There are four specialised Development Finance Institutions in Malaysia catering for loans on concessional terms to support and promote industrial and agricultural development. Besides providing medium and long term capital to businesses, they also provide finance, managerial and limited technical advice to enterprises involved in the development of new business projects. Basically, DFIs provide the loans to clients who would normally not be able to secure credit from the commercial banks and finance companies. The following role is played by the four individual Development Finance Institutions.

Malaysian Industrial Development Finance Berhad (MIDF)

This financial institution was launched in 1960 to accelerate development and modernisation in the manufacturing sector in Malaysia. Since its foundation, it has granted more than 3,800 loans and leases of over RM1.8 billion to manufacturing enterprises. It also provides finance in the form of loans or lease for plant, equipment and machinery. By 1988, it was recorded that its approved a total of RM120.4 million to 152 applicants. The average size of loans was RM792,000. Loans or leases for Bumiputera accounted for 18.4 percent of the total number and 9.1 percent of the total value. At present, MIDF has widely diversified its sector coverage to include infrastructure and utilities sectors, tourism and services sectors. Under this diversification, MIDF provides a wide range of facilities through two major schemes, i.e. fixed rate loan scheme and special loan scheme.

Fixed rate loan scheme There are four types of loan facilities provided under this scheme i.e. project loan, machinery loan, factory mortgage loan and lease financing. *Project Loan* provides up to 70 percent financing of the fixed assets (including land factory building, plant and machinery of the project based on actual cost). Under this *project loan*, the borrower puts up equity capital of not less than the loan amount to pay for the balance of the fixed assets cost and to meet pre-operating/preliminary expenses and part of the working capital. Therefore, the balance of the working capital could be sourced from commercial banks and other financial institutions. Interest rate varies according to the period of loan as the following: up to 5 years the rate is between 8.5 percent and 9.5 percent per annum; for 5 years to 10 years (9.0 percent to 10.0 percent per annum) and above 10 years (9.5

61

percent to 10.5 percent per annum).

Machinery Loan provides facilities up to 75 percent of cost of plant and machinery. This is dependent on the shareholders funds of the project and other existing borrowings. Interest rate and period of repayment are the same as the project loan above. Meanwhile, *Factory Mortgage Loan* provides facilities up to 70 percent of the land and factory building together with basic installations such as electrical installations, fire fighting equipment and air conditioning. Interest rate and period of repayment are similar to that of the project loan. Different than other facilities mentioned earlier, *Lease Financing* provides up to 100 percent of lease financing to assist in acquiring plant and machinery. This facility is believed to be an alternative to the machinery loan, designed to help SMEs operators who require higher percentage financing than is possible with machinery loan. This facility also focuses on providing credit/loan to on-going ventures with acceptable track record. Interest rate and period of repayment depend on the amount of facility that is granted, but normally not more than 7 percent per annum.

Special loan schemes There are three main facilities provided under the special loan schemes including Industrial Adjustment Fund; Bumiputera Industrial Fund; and Modernisation and Automation Schemes for Small and Medium enterprises. *Industrial Adjustment Fund* was launched in January 1991 with the amount of about RM500 million fund. This fund specifically established by the government to give assistance and financial requirement in the restructuring and adjustment programmes of three major industrial sub-sectors namely the wood-based, machinery and engineering; and textile and garment industries. This fund offers facilities to any firm with at least 51 percent Malaysian ownership with the loan amount ranges between RM1000, 000,00 and RM10 million. Interest rate is 7.75 percent per annum and subject to a maximum repayment period of 8 years.

Modernisation and Automation Schemes for Small and Medium Enterprises is aimed at enhancing the modernisation and automation of SMEs through the utilisation of a new technology. This scheme was launched in 1993 with RM50 million funds approved under the sixth Malaysian Plan. This scheme offers to manufacture enterprises with shareholders not more than RM2.5 million and comprise at least 70 percent Malaysian equity ownership. Loan amount is up to a maximum of RM1 million and offers to Bumiputera SMEs (70 percent equity) and is granted together with fixed assets loans under the scheme. Interest rate is considerably low, i.e. 4.0 percent per annum, with repayment period between five and ten years including grace period.

Bumiputera Industrial Fund was launched in 1993 to provide Bumiputera individuals or corporations with shareholders funds not exceeding RM2.5 million and least 70 percent of the total is Bumiputera shareholding and management control. An initial allocation of this fund is RM100 million. Maximum amount of loan is up to RM2.5 million. Interest rate for this facility is 5.0 percent per annum with repayment period of 8 years maximum including the grace period.

Bank Pembangunan Malaysia Berhad (BPMB)

This institution was established in 1973 to develop and accelerate Bumiputera participation in the industrial and commercial sectors of the economy. It has played a key role in financing the start-up and growth of new small and medium enterprises and has focused its lending mainly on manufacturing, tourism and the mining (excluding tin-mining) sectors. It provides term loans, plant hire and leasing facilities and conducts entrepreneurial development and advisory programmes for Bumiputera enterprises. The entrepreneurial development programmes were introduced in 1981 with the objective of developing Bumiputera entrepreneurs in the industrial sector. Entrepreneurship development courses are conducted with the co-operation of MARA, the National Productivity Centre (NPC) and Malaysian Entrepreneurial Development Centre (MEDEC). Currently there are a number of loan schemes provided by BPMP. These include special Loan Scheme for small and medium-sized industries, Special Loan Schemes for Bumiputera only, special scheme for furniture and food industries, seed capital scheme and few other facilities.

Special loan schemes for small and medium-sized enterprise This scheme was initiated in 1984 under the collaboration of the World Bank with the aim at assisting SMEs in commercial and industrial sectors to obtain credit and technical assistance. In line with these schemes four specific funds are provided. First is *Industrial Adjustment Fund (IAF)* with amount of loan available is between RM100, 000 and RM10 million. This fund is available for registered enterprises in Malaysia with at least 51 percent equity owned by Malaysian citizens. Interest rate is at 7.75 percent per annum with maximum period of repayment is eight years. Second is *Special Fund for Tourism* (SFT). This fund is provided for enterprises which are registered in Malaysia with at least 51 percent owned by Malaysian citizens.

This fund is provided for the tourism sector and is given to enterprises

63

registered in Malaysia with at least 51 percent equity owned by Malaysian citizens. Minimum loan amount is RM100,000 and maximum is RM2.25 million. Interest rate is lower than the former fund which is 6.5 percent per annum with maximum loan period of ten years. The third one is the *New Enterprises Fund* provided facilities to Bumiputera owned enterprises or Bumiputera partnership enterprises particularly in manufacturing, tourism and export-oriented projects. Loan ranges amount from RM30,000 to RM2 million. Cumulative maximum loan given for each borrower is not more than RM2.0 million. Purposes of the loan is to finance a few provisions such as fixed asset; working capital (fixed and revolving) and lease financing of machinery or equipment. Interest rate for this fund is considerably low at 5 percent per annum with a maximum loan period of eight years. The last one is *Bumiputera Industrial Fund* which provides facilities to at least 70 percent Bumiputera owned enterprises which paid-up capital not more than RM2.5 million and registered as vendors with either Kumpulan Guthrie Bhd, National Automotive or Besta Distributors Sdn. Bhd only. This fund focuses on manufacturing and export-oriented projects with the amount of loan varies from RM100,000 to a maximum of RM2.5 million or 85 percent of the additional project cost. The purpose of the fund is to finance Bumiputera enterprises in a number of areas such as fixed asset, working capital and machinery or equipment.

Seed Capital Scheme This scheme provides loan facilities to Bumiputera registered enterprises with at least 70 percent equity owned by Bumiputera and paid up capital must not be less than RM100,000 but not exceeding RM5 million. The purpose of the loan is to finance fixed asset through syariah financing system, working capital and share financing. Seed Capital Scheme concentrates on a number of industrial sub-sectors such as tourism, services and manufacturing especially vendors and franchisers. The amount of loan available is RM5 million or 75 percent of cost of assets to be purchased. The rate of interest varies depending upon types of loan. For loan and share-financing loan, maximum interest rate is 4.5 percent per annum while others types are negotiable. Maximum period of loan under the scheme is ten years.

Normal Loan Scheme for Bumiputera Under this scheme, there are three main forms of credit facilities provided for Bumiputera entrepreneurs. The first one is *Project Loan,* which provides credit facility to Bumiputera individual, and Bumiputera designated companies/co-operatives with at least 51 percent of equity owned by Bumiputera. Sectors that are eligible for this facility are manufacturing, utilities and transportation. The purpose of loan is to finance fixed assets, working capital and syndicated loans. Minimum loan given is RM100,000 and maximum is RM2.5 million. Interest rate is 2 percent above the Base Lending Rate per annum. Maximum period of repayment is 12 years for fixed assets loan and from 2 to 4 years for working capital loan. The second is *Leasing Loan* provided facility to Bumiputera individual and Bumiputera designated enterprises with at least 51 percent of equity owned by Bumiputera. The purpose of this loan is to enable them to finance the purchase of machinery or equipment with maximum lease amount is RM100,000 while minimum interest rate is 5 percent.

The last is *Share Financing* facility. Under this facility individuals can take up equity in companies which are listed in Kuala Lumpur Stock Exchange (KLSE), companies which have obtained the Security Commissions approval to be listed at KLSE and companies which have fulfilled the listing conditions for one year and can be listed within three years. Therefore, Bumiputera individuals, Bumiputera professionals partnership enterprises or Bumiputera designated companies with at least 51 percent equity owned by Bumiputera are eligible to apply. Loan amount ranges from RM100,000 to RM5 million with rate of interest is 4 percent per annum above the market rate. Maximum period of repayment is five years.

Other facilities and services offered by Bank Pembangunan There are three other facilities and services provided by BPMB i.e. Syndicate Loan, Financing for External Trade and Nursery Factory Scheme. Syndicate Loan is introduced to co-finance large projects with other institutions where a substantial loan amount is involved. The maximum loan period is up to 15 years. Financing for External Trade is provided for firms which need credit facility to import raw materials or semi-finished goods for manufacturing. While Nursery Factory Scheme a credit facility given to small factories at attractively low rentals. It is available for selected Bumiputera who wish a commerce operation on a small-scale. Along side with credit facility, advisory services are also offered by BPMB. Currently, a number of facilities provided by this bank. These include Small and Medium Scale Industry Promotion Programme (SMIPP), Financing for the Manufacturing Sector, Export Credit Scheme-Capital Goods and Trade Financing Facilities.

Bank Industri Malaysia Berhad (BIMB)

This bank was established in 1979 to stimulate development of export-orientated and high technology industries. Its primary aims are to: provide long-term and other financial assistance to capital-intensive industries, especially export-oriented industries and other manufacturing sub-sectors designated as high priority by the Government; to encourage and promote exports through the financing of domestic and international trade; and to finance and assist expansion and modernisation of manufacturing enterprises. In its lending policy, Industrial Bank has adopted a target market approach, selecting specific segments of industry. Other than the shipping industry, recently in focused on the engineering segment of the manufacturing sector including metal-based manufacturing, electronics, electricity, foundry, tool and die forging, machining and manufacture of component parts. Currently, a number of facilities provided by this bank. These include Small and medium-Scale Industry Promotion Programme (SMIPP), Financing for the Manufacturing Sector, Export Credit Scheme, Capital Goods and Trade Financing Facilities. All these are presented in the following sub-sections below.

Small and Medium Scale Industry Promotion Programme (SMIPP) This programme was introduced with the main purpose is to provide financial assistance to SMEs to enable them becoming dynamic and productive enterprises in the country. This is includes services procured in order to upgrade technology and/or transfer technical and management know how in the country. The focus of the programme is on a few sub-sectors such as engineering (including electrical and electronic industry) plastics and pharmaceutical industries, shipping or shipyard and marine related industries. The facilities are offered to Malaysian enterprises established in Malaysia whose paid-up capital do not exceed RM5 million at the time of application for the loan. The facility gives priority to enterprises which need credit to acquire equipment and machinery and construction of plant and factory. Other aspects of facility include working capital requirement acquisition of share and purchase of land are also given priority. Credit provided normally is up to 75 percent of the total cost project with maximum amount not exceed RM5 million. Interest rate facility given is seven percent per annum with maximum period of repayment is 15 years including five years grace period.

Financing for the manufacturing sector This specific financial assistance is introduced to further promote and enhance the government's drive towards industrialisation programme. In this relation, a comprehensive manufacturing sector facility is provided covering major and also ancillary and auxiliary sub-industries. Among these include providing support to start-up and on-going projects seeking expansion or upgrading. Industrial sub-sectors that are eligible for the facility include; component manufacturing, die-casting and machining, electrical and electronic, electroplating, fabrication, forging, foundry, machinery and equipment manufacturing machining, material technology, metal stamping, mould and die, plastic technology and pharmaceuticals. The credit facility provided normally to enable companies to equip machinery and equipment factory building. The credit facility covers up to 85 percent of the total project cost without maximum amount of loan. Rate of interest is very low, i.e. from 65 percent to 8.5 percent per annum with maximum repayment period of the loan is 15 years.

Export Credit Scheme-Capital Goods Bank Industri Malaysia Berhad also provides export credit facilities to Malaysian enterprises in term of capital goods with a minimum of 30 percent local content and 20 percent online-added. Enterprises which export non-capital goods are also eligible, however, they have to have a minimum of 50 percent local content and 30 percent value added. This credit offers to both parties, i.e. Supplier's Credit and Buyer's. Credit offered to the later consists three categories i.e. pre-shipment, post-shipment and buyer's credit. Facilities offered to *Pre-Shipment* category is available to local exporters for production of manufactured goods meant for export. The purpose is to assist the exporters to finance part of their working capital especially during the production stage. The total amount of credit given is up to a maximum of 85 percent of the export order value. The interest rate differs from time to time as approved by the Central Bank. In the previous five years, the rate was 9 percent per annum. The maximum loan period provided is 120 days. Credit is also extended to *Post Shipment* category which is available to local exporters to enable them to provide attractive credit terms to foreign buyers for the export of their manufactured goods. The main objective of this facility is to extent funds to the exporters for their export sales on credit. Maximum amount of credit is 95 percent of the total export invoice value for financing transacted under letter of credit while a maximum of 85 percent of export invoice value for transacted without letter of credit. The interest rate for this facility is about the same as the pre-shipment category. The current maximum period of loan under the Central Bank is 180 days. However under the BIBM facility, tenure greater than 180 days is possible. Buyers' Credit is provided by BIMB in order to facilitate and encourage the purchase of Malaysian manufactured goods by foreign importers. In this relation, the attractive terms of this facility will provide local exporters the competitive edge when bidding for jobs overseas. The amount of financing provided is up to maximum of 85 percent of the total contract value. Minimum interest rate is 9 percent per annum with maximum loan period of 10 years inclusive of graced period. Respective buyers are also required to have an international bank guarantee.

Trade Financing Facilities There are two main type of facility under the scheme i.e. short and long terms of financing scheme. The former scheme, i.e. Short Term Financing Facility is offered by BIMB on behalf of the Islamic Development Bank (IDB) based in Jeddah, Saudi Arabia. The primary purpose is to assist Malaysian importers in purchase of needed development inputs from member as well as non-member of IDB. Bank Industri Malaysia Berhad, in this respect, plays as an executing agent and provides a guarantee facility to the Malaysian importer. This scheme focuses on a number of import trades' goods such as raw materials for industry, industrial intermediate goods and construction materials. Loan repayment period is between 9 and 24 months. This scheme does not have any interest conforming to the Syariah Law. Instead, a mark up of 6 percent per annum of the total purchase price will be charge if procurement of raw materials are from member countries. Otherwise, it is 6.5 percent per annum. In addition to that, BIMB will charge a guarantee fee of 1.5 percent per annum of the total outstanding amount guaranteed. Nevertheless, this scheme offers additional advantage when a rebate of 15 percent of the mark up is granted if the repayment if effected on or before the due dates. While the Long Term Trade Refinancing Scheme is designed to promote trade among OIC member countries. The financing is extended to the importer and the transaction is based on Murabaha concept under which the IDB undertakes to purchase the goods directly from the exporter and re-sells the goods to the importer at a mark up of presently 6.5 percent per annum. The repayment under the facility could range from 6 months to 60 months depending on the good purchase. The importer is required to provide an international bank guarantee acceptable to the IDB.

Credit Guarantee Corporation Malaysia Berhad (CGC)

The Credit Guarantee Corporation Malaysia Berhad was established in 1973. The main purpose is to provide small and medium-sized enterprises to gain greater access to credit facilities at reasonable interest rate. The corporation's task is to provide guarantee cover to commercial banks for loans extended to SMEs. This task is implemented by formulating and implementing various guarantee scheme aimed at assisting small and medium-sized entrepreneurs to have access to credit facilities. Under this corporation, there are three main credit facilities provided, inter alia; New Principal Guarantee Scheme (New PGS), New Entrepreneurs Fund Guarantee Scheme (NEF), and Integrated Lending Scheme (ILS).

New Principal Guarantee Scheme This scheme provides credit facilities to Malaysian SMEs with a good credit record and it covers a number of facilities such as loans overdrafts, letter of credits trust receipts, export credit refinancing, bill purchased, bankers acceptances, shipping/performance/bank guarantees, hire purchase and leasing. Amount of loan facility provided under the scheme ranges according to sectors. Those who in the manufacturing sector are eligible up to a maximum of RM7.5 million, other priority sectors are RM5 million. Rate of interest under this scheme is two percent above than the Base Lending Rate of the two leading banks.

New Entrepreneurs Fund Guarantee Scheme (NEF) This loan scheme is given to a new entrepreneurs who is starting up businesses or newly started up businesses. This scheme is provided specifically for Bumiputera registered SMEs with next assets or shareholders' funds up to RM1.5 million. Among business areas given priority are manufacturing, export oriented industries, tourism and agriculture. The amount of loan from this scheme is RM2.0 million to cover mainly fund-based facilities such as overdrafts and term loans. Rate of interest for the scheme is very low i.e. 5.0 percent per annum with the maximum of guarantee's coverage is 80 percent of the principal loan and period of guarantee is not more than eight years. There are ten commercial banks that are participating in this scheme, inter alia; Perwira Affin Bank, Maybank, Bank Utama, DCB Bank, Public Bank, Sabah Bank and Bank of Commerce.

Integrated Lending Scheme (ILS) This is also another scheme offered to registered SMEs with net assets or shareholders' funds of up to RM2.5 million. Entrepreneurs must be Malaysian or Malaysian majority shareholders with a good credit record. Industrial sub-sectors that are eligible to apply include metal-based, plastic, electric and electronics, chemical and pharmaceutical manufacturing as well as other sub-sectors identified from time to time by the CGC and participating banks. A total of up to RM7.5 million of loan is eligible for the said entrepreneurs. Credit facilities covered under this scheme include term loans, overdrafts, letters of credit/trust receipt, export credit refinancing, bills purchased, bankers acceptances and bank guarantees. While other facilities is determined by the corporation from time to time. Maximum rate of interest charged under this scheme is two percent above the Base Lending Rate (BLR) of the two lending commercial banks. Amount of guarantee covered by the CGC is RM2.5 million. Among participating commercial bank joined this scheme include, Maybank Berhad, Bank Bumiputera Malaysia Berhad, OCBC Bank Malaysia Berhad, Hong Kong Bank Malaysia Berhad, Hock Hua Bank Berhad and Bank Industri Malaysia Berhad.

Majlis Amanah Rakyat (MARA)

MARA was set up in 1960 to provide assistance to the Bumiputera's entrepreneurs in the country. This agency focuses on almost all types of assistance and credit facility is one of them. However, its concentration is largely on small-sized enterprises especially in commercial and industrial sectors. Maximum net assets or shareholder fund for business to be eligible for the facility is up to RM500, 000. Most of credit facility given is for working capital and the purchase of fixed assets. Specifically, industrial and commercial and other sub-sectors that are eligible for credit facility include manufacturing companies, commerce (such as retailers, wholesalers, agents) services (technical professional), contracts (construction, suppliers and services) and transport. Rate of interest is only 5.5 percent for loan below RM5, 000.00 and 7 percent for loan above RM5, 000.00. Period of repayment varies according to the amount of loan. Loan which is below than RM20, 000, the period of repayment is between one and three years, amount of loan from RM20, 000 to RM50, 000 between, one and five years, while amount of loan above RM50, 000, the maximum period of repayment is RM50, 000.

Special Loan Scheme There are a number of other credit schemes being offered to SMEs in the country. These include ASEAN-Japan Development Fund (AJDF), Industrial Adjustment Fund (IAF), The New Investment Fund (NIF), The Enterprises Rehabilitation Fund (ERF), Bumiputera Industrial Fund (BIF), Export Credit Refinancing Scheme (ECRS) and Modernisation and Automation Scheme for Small and Medium-Scale Industries. One of the credit facilities is the *ASEAN-Japan Development Fund*. This fund provides loan to SMEs with the main objective of promoting the development of Malaysia-controlled (shareholding of 51 percent or more) SMEs in the manufacturing, agriculture and tourism sectors in Malaysia. The SMEs or borrowers that eligible for the fund are those having paid up capital not exceeding RM5 million and loan amount should not exceed RM5 million. Rate of interest is relatively low i.e. 6.5 percent per annum with loan repayment period varies from 3 to 6 years.

The New Investment Fund (NIF) and The Enterprises Rehabilitation Fund (ERF) In 1985, the New Investment Fund was launched with RM1 billion fund to encourage investment in new productive capacity in the manufacturing, agriculture, tourism and mining sectors which are considered as a part of the government efforts to foster exports and ensure that funds at reasonable cost were readily available to investors in stated sectors. Two years later the fund was increased to RM1.7 billion. The NIF funds, were made available to the manufacturing sector in areas such as the construction of new factories, purchase of new plant and equipment, improvement of existing factories and plant expansion and the manufacture of new products. The minimum amount of fund is RM50,000 and the maximum is RM250,000 per project. By the end of 1989, 75 percent of allocated fund was used with more than RM762 million going to the manufacturing sector. *Enterprises Rehabilitation Fund* (ERF) was established in 1988 to help the small and medium-sized enterprises that need soft loans or seed capital to assist them sort out their difficulties. The Malaysian Industrial Development Finance (MIDF) acts as the secretariat, of ERF for assessing and approving the projects. In 1989, a total of 823 applications were submitted to the MIDF. *The Export Credit Refinancing Scheme (ECRS)* This scheme was introduced in 1977 to assist exporters to obtain pre-shipment and post-shipment funds in the manufacturing sector including small and medium enterprises. The assistance is given by the Central Bank through commercial banks. Later in 1986, the full package of reforms was made to provide greater access to credit for exporters, including the suppliers of inputs used in manufacture of export products. In 1988, the interest rate reduced to as low as 4 percent per annum.

4 Entrepreneurial Development and Business Management Training

Introduction

Rapid economic growth needs efficient, productive and effective entrepreneurs, managers administrators and business leaders. The increase in the high level of competitiveness at domestic and global markets gives a greater need for highly qualified and well equipped entrepreneurs managers and business leaders. This need becomes not only more significant in making sure some successful and development of SMEs, but more importantly to promote SMEs to be capable enterprises which that can provide products, goods, components and services to heavy and large sized enterprises. This need is even been felt with respect to the national's vision to become a fully industrialised and dynamic nation by the year 2020. Therefore, entrepreneurial development and programme is not merely important in terms of general knowledge but also essential equipping them with specific skills and training in conjunction with the trend in production technique which tend to be mechanised, automated and high-tech industries.

To deal with those challenges, entrepreneurial and management development and business programmes have been introduced and provided to equip training and experience to SMEs entrepreneurs in every aspects relating to management system and business management training. Entrepreneurs development and business management training programme is normally conducted through a number of short courses or workshops. Among others things that are given attention include; entrepreneurial motivation, basic exposure of entrepreneurial, production aspects, marketing, accounting and financial management. In terms of duration of each programme varies from three days to eight weeks depending upon type of programmes and agency or institution involved. There are also workshops on entrepreneurial development and business management training along side with other facilities such as financial and credit assistance, technical training and others. A number of government agencies and institutions are involved in providing these programmes. These among others, include: National Productivity Corporation (NPC); Malaysian Entrepreneurial Development Centre (MEDEC); The Council of Trust for Indigenous People (MARA); Federation of Malaysian Manufacturers (FMM); Centre of Small Enterprises Development of the University Putra Malaysia, Small and Medium Industrial Development Corporation (SMIDEC); and several others.

National Productivity Corporation (NPC)

National Productivity Corporation was established in 1962 as a statutory body under the Ministry of International Trade and Industry known as National Productivity Centre. However, the name was changed to the National Productivity Corporation effective from 1991 when it was corporatised by the government to enhance its management. The NPC is a premier provider of short courses entrepreneurial development and management with the main mission is to contribute significantly towards the productivity and quality enhancement of the nation for economic growth. The corporation has a complement of more than 150 staffs including more than 50 full-time professional trainees with skills in applied research and management consultancy. The NPC has also received considerable technical and staff development assistance to strengthen its capacity to provide high quality training programmes as well as consultancy and advisory services. The NPC is located in the commercial centre of Petaling Jaya and walking distance of banks , hotels, post office, eating outlet and shopping centres, public transport is easily available other than its regional branches throughout the country. This corporation also has an outstanding training facilities such as 23 lecture rooms, five syndicate or meeting rooms, library, multi-purpose hall, language laboratory, computer facility, audio-visual aids, studio rooms and demonstration kitchens.

The overall objectives of the NPC, inter alia, are: to provide inputs for policy formulation and planning in the area of productivity and quality; to enhance the development of human resources and enterprise towards excellence and to upgrade local expertise in the area of productivity and quality. In this respect, the core service provided by the corporation is Productivity and Quality Enhancement. There are four main activities which NPC attempts to promote i.e. Research Training and Accreditation Joint Ventures, Advisory and Consultancy, and Information

73

Management. Other than those, NPC also offers in-plant courses on request and accrediates training programmes conducted by private institutions.

There is also a division known as the Bumiputera Services Division (BSD) in the NPC which responsible for providing entrepreneurial training. It is also responsible for implementing short course training for SMEs entrepreneurs. These training programmes cover a broad spectrum of areas including sales, marketing, export and import procedures, management development, industrial relations, quality control, industrial engineering, automation and hotel and tourism management. These courses are conducted at the NPC at Petaling Jaya headquarters and its regional centres in Kuantan, Kuching, Johor, Kota Kinabalu and Penang. In addition, the NPC undertakes the following other related functions:

i. research and analysis of productivity issues and productivity measurement, organisational climate and development training needs analysis;
ii. marketing management and productivity, and quality improvement methods;
iii. dissemination of knowledge and data on productivity issues; and
iv. provision of a forum for discussion on organisational management and supervisory issues.

In 1995 for instance, the NPC offers 19 short courses relating to entrepreneurial trainings according to several main sub-topics such as entrepreneurial motivation, motivation and job satisfaction, production management in SMEs, implementation of ISO 9000 in SMEs, the practice of 5S (short, set, shine, standard and self-discipline), improvement of productivity and quality in furniture production, improvement in competitiveness, quality control for group leaders, quality process and method, productivity management in SMEs, total quality management in SMEs, quality control for SMEs, practice in quality improvements and usage of seven QCC equipments. These courses are offered to individuals who have the interest in starting up business, planning to start up business, those who wish to change their careers to be entrepreneurs, entrepreneurs, owners, proprietors, executives managers and supervisors, accountant and development officers in government and private agencies or institutions. Methods of instruction used by the NPC are various. These include teaching, questions and answers as well as discussions are emphasised. Informal instruction and interaction in the form of lectures, syndicate discussions and case studies creates a more conductive atmosphere to adult training. The instructors also carry out follow up visits to give further guidance and assistance, particularly in the case of in-plant practical projects being carried out by the course participants. The course are normally supplemented with relevant management picture and film, simulation exercises, video recordings, computers and study visits. Admission opens to all Malaysian who have had at least attended secondary level of education. Application for admission should be made on the Course Registration Form. Applicants should have some interest or experience in the particular subject relevant to particular course applied. Course Registration should be made with or sent to the headquarters or the following regional officers at the addresses given below:

1.   National Productivity Corporation (NPC),
   P O Box 64,
   Jalan Sultan
   46904 Petaling Jaya.

2.   Director,
   National Productivity Corporation (NPC),
   East Coast Region,
   18th Floor Teruntum Complex,
   Jalan Mahkota,
   25000 Kuantan.

3.   Director,
   National Productivity Corporation (NPC),
   Southern Region,
   3rd Floor Pertronas Building,
   4 ½ Miles, Jalan Skudai,
   P O Box 105,
   88718 Johor Bharu.

4.   Director,
   National Productivity Corporation (NPC),
   Northern Region,
   Locked Bag 206, Jalan Bertam
   13200 Kepala Batas,
   Pulau Pinang.

5. Director,
   National Productivity Corporation (NPC),
   Sarawak Region,
   5th Floor, Bank Negara Building,
   Jalan Satok, P.O Box 2679,
   93752 Kuching, Sarawak.

6. Director,
   National Productivity Corporation (NPC),
   Sabah Region,
   No. 8, Tingkat 7, Blok E,
   Kompleks KUWASA,
   88000 Kota Kinabalu.

Malaysian Entrepreneurial Development Centre (MEDEC)

The centre was established in 1975 at the MARA Institute of Technology in Shah Alam, Selangor. The establishment of MEDEC is to provide training for Bumiputera to assist them start up new business. The main focus of the centre is on providing management courses to potential, new and young entrepreneurs to run their business operation on SMEs. Therefore, the centre has two main entrepreneurial training programmes, i.e. entrepreneurial training for the public and entrepreneurial training for students of the MARA Institute of Technology.

Entrepreneurial Training for the Public

Entrepreneurial training for the public is the main training programme conducted by MEDEC. It normally offers the training on a full time basis over a number period of week i.e. from one to six weeks. The course provided usually covers four main parts, inter alia these include: the first one is *entrepreneurial motivation*. This particular lesson mainly attempt to prepare participants morally and psychologically for the task of establishing new business. Second part is *project selection and identification*. The main objective of this lesson is to provide participants with tools for doing feasibility analysis of their proposed business ventures. Among the major sub-topics being discussed under this part is to recognise market opportunities, market surveys and the preparation of a working paper on the proposed business ventures. The third part touches on *management.* Management component consists of a number of sub-topics including small and medium business managements, production management, book keeping, financial management, costing, credit control, distribution and retailing, price setting, marketing strategy, salesmanship, taxation, cash control and management, and business communications. The last part of the course concentrates on the *formation of companies.* The major aim of this part is to provide information on the fundamentals of actualising a business. In this part, discussion on legal forms of business and registration of business are also included. There are two other specific entrepreneurial programmes conducted by MEDEC as part of its efforts to assist Bumiputera's entrepreneurs include the following:

i.   Graduate Enterprises Programme. This specific programme began in 1987 designed to assist graduates who wish to establish their own business enterprises. The content of the course is very much similar to the earlier entrepreneurial development programme. Its involves the period of eight weeks course work. For part timers, the course conducted in evening classes each weekdays and over weekends.

ii.   Entrepreneurial Development Programme for Government Staff. This was introduced in 1983 and designed for government employees to assist them to start their own business after they leave the public service. This programmes is also more extensive than any other programme conducted by MEDEC because its requires attachment period to related factories or enterprises for practical experience. The whole programme covers five months on a full-time basis i.e four month course and one month attachment. The main entrepreneurial training programmes for the public, graduate enterprises programmes, graduate enterprises programmes and for government staff are advertised in the local newspapers two or three months prior to the course. Candidates are also expected to have a business proposal. Those who interested should send and submit their application form to the MEDEC office at the Institute of MARA Technology (ITM) in Shah Alam, Selangor.

Entrepreneurial Training for ITM Students

Since July 1988, all students doing their Diploma at the ITM should take a basic entrepreneurial course as a compulsory subject. This course is taught over a period of 15 weeks or one semester course focusing mainly on the basic principles of entrepreneurship and is only offered to final year students. Before this course is offered, students at the ITM also have the opportunity to undertake the Student Entrepreneur Co-curriculum Programme (REMUSA) which was introduced in 1980 with the aim at exposing student to entrepreneurial skills. This programme is guided with practical activities including planning and running a weekly night market, direct selling and managing a retail store in the campus. All enquires and application forms should be directed to the address below:

Director,
Malaysian Entrepreneurial Development Centre (MEDEC),
Institute Technology of MARA,
40450 Shah Alam,
Selangor, Malaysia.

The Majlis Amanah Rakyat (MARA)

This Majlis Amanah Rakyat (the Council of Trust for Indigenous People) plays a major role in training Bumiputera entrepreneurs and responsible in creating and adding the number of Bumiputera entrepreneurs as well as upgrading their level of participation in the small and medium commercial and industrial enterprises. The principal objective of MARA is to motivate, guide, train and assist Bumiputera generally and rural areas specifically to enable them to become actively involve in industrial and commercial activities in the country. Since the establishment of MARA in 1960 it has conducted more than 7,000 entrepreneur development courses involving more than 200,000 participants as the end of 1997. MARA has also provided credit extension facilities amounting to more than 1 billion to more than 150,000 beneficiaries, constructed business premises to the value of more than RM300 million and recorded to have spent more than RM25 million on entrepreneurial training. MARA is one of the largest organisation in the country with a staff of more than 4,800 persons at its headquarters in Kuala Lumpur, other than that its regional network of 54 district officers and 14 state officers who supervise the work of the district officers. In its programmes MARA has adopted a more integrated approach to entrepreneurial training, counselling and advisory services and the provision of business premises for rental at subsidised rates to Bumiputera entrepreneurs. In order to encourage, guide, train and assist Bumiputera entrepreneurs, three basic types of entrepreneurial development training courses are provided. These include the following:

i.   Precreation Programmes. These are generally two weeks courses and conducted on a full-time basis. The programme is designed in such a way to provide potential entrepreneurs with an understanding of the challenges, activities, responsibilities and risks involved in starting up a new business.

ii. Creation Programmes. These are designed to motivate and assist potential entrepreneurs to develop a business proposal and evaluate the potential of the project. These courses are also conducted over a two-week period on a full-time basis.

iii. Entrepreneur Advancement Programme. These courses are provided to help existing entrepreneurs upgrade their business skills and knowledge. Courses under this programme are conducted over a three or four-day period and focus on a specific area.

Under the above three types of entrepreneurial development training course, there are many sub-topics being offered, inter alia, include; book keeping, financial management, business management, costing, marketing, distribution, salesmanship, import/export, contract management, factory management, automobile workshop management, retail management, food catering management, tourism and construction. It is pertinent to note that most of the entrepreneurs assisted by MARA establish tiny family businesses as petty trades, small retail outlets, mini markets, sundry shops, small handicraft, manufacturing, food processing and other small rural town businesses involving low technical skills and little capital.

Experience shows that large portion of participants have been from school dropouts persons and those who have not proceed beyond secondary level of education. Observation also notices that the short duration of the entrepreneur creation programme greatly limits to scope and depth of training provided. For instance, coverage of key subjects such as basic management, book keeping and marketing remain weak. Figures indicate that only about 10 to 15 percent of participants who complete the entrepreneurial creation courses are actually going on to establish new businesses. Nonetheless, MARA has updated many of its existing courses to match with the current business trend and to encounter some most obvious weaknesses through their almost 39 years experience. For those who interested to participate in the entrepreneurial development training courses should approach MARA's headquarters in Kuala Lumpur or its regional or district officers across the country, as stated below:

Entrepreneurs Development Division,
Majlis Amanah Rakyat (MARA),
Tingkat 17, Medan MARA,
Jalan Raja Laut,
50609 Kuala Lumpur.

Selangor's MARA Office,
Tingkat 2, Kompleks PKNS,
40607 Shah Alam.

Johor's MARA office,
Tingkat 5, Bangunan MARA,
Jalan Segget,
80700 Johor Bahru.

Kedah's MARA Office,
Tingkat 4 & 5,
Bangunan Perniagaan Pekan Rabu,
05000 Alor Setar.

Melaka's MARA Office,
Tingkat 4, Kompleks MARA,
Jalan Hang Tuah, Peti Surat 226,
75750 Melaka.

Negeri Sembilan's MARA Office,
Tingkat 6, Bangunan Yayasan Negeri Sembilan,
Jalan Yam Tuan,
70990 Seremban.

Perak's MARA Office,
Bangunan Sri Kinta,
Jalan Sultan Idris Shah,
30770 Ipoh.

Penang's MARA Office,
Tingkat 8, Bangunan MARA,
5, Lebuh Birmingham,
10607 Pulau Pinang.

Pahang's MARA Office,
Tingkat 3, Kompleks MARA,
Jalan Gambut, Peti Surat 310
25750 Kuantan.

Kelantan's MARA Office,
Tingkat 6&7, Komplek MARA,
Jalan Dato' Pati,
15000 Kota Bharu.

Terengganu's MARA Office,
2, Bangunan MARA, Jalan Masjid,
20100 Kuala Terengganu.

Sabah's MARA Office,
Tingkat 1&2, Bangunan Bank Rakyat,
Peti Surat 1040,
88718 Kota Kinabalu.

Sarawak's MARA Office,
129, Jalan Satok,
Peti Surat 1352,
93728 Kuching.

Small Business Development Centre (SBDC), Universiti Putra Malaysia (UPM)

Universiti Putra Malaysia (UPM) previously known as Agricultural University of Malaysia established Small Business Development Centre

(SBDC) in 1981 to provide training and extension services to small businesses and potential entrepreneurs. This centre also gives strong emphasis on applied research on small and medium enterprises business. Although the centre has a small complement of full-time staff, its also depend on the professional expertise of the large Faculty of Management in UPM. To achieve its objectives, two main course training programmes for SMEs is provided by the centre. These include: a) an entrepreneurial training programme for unemployed graduates which extends over a three-month period. This programme covers intensive full-time training on business management. And b) entrepreneurial development for school leavers who are involved in the development of a business plan. Other than courses offered above, the centre also has some collaboration with the Malaysian Institute of Management to provide business management training programme to the public. This programme is designed to offer a Certificate in Business Management conducts the course at the SBDC during the weekends.

The other role played by the SBDC in providing entrepreneurial development programme is Junior Achievement Project. This project provided for secondary school students involving staff from the SBDC visit the school each week to conduct workshop on small business management. The students in this programme form small companies, produce handicrafts for sale and operate small stalls to sell foods and other suitable items. They receive practical training in the formation of companies, development of business plan, account-keeping in the other aspects of business management. The SBDC also conducts a number of studies on especially on the inter-firm comparison. This particular project involves research, provision of extension services as well as some individualism and group training of small business entrepreneurs registered with the project. A comprehensive set of financial ratios and standard against which they are able to evaluate their own performance. Individual counselling is provided to participating enterprises on problems encountered. The SBDC is also involved in actively promoting entrepreneurship to undergraduate student of UPM through a series of elective course in Small Business Management and Entrepreneurship. Further information regarding entrepreneurial development programme at the Small Business Development Centre is available from the address below:

Small Business Development Centre
Faculty of Management
Universiti Putra Malaysia
43400 Serdang, Selangor
Malaysia.

Federation of Malaysian Manufacturers (FMM)

Federation of Malaysian Manufacturers (FMM)plays a very active role in its efforts to provide an adequate and efficient supply of work force in the country. For this particular reason, Entrepreneur and Skill Development Centre (ESDC) was established in 1991 to focus fully on the creation and upgrading skills in industrial development and management capabilities of the work force. This concentration is translated from the main objectives of the establishment of the centre, among others include to equip employees of member enterprises with skills and knowledge needed to carry out their assigned jobs effectively; to upgrade existing technical skills and knowledge of the manufacturing industry so as to enable them to keep abreast with and to anticipate constant technological changes; to provide a vehicle for constant exchange of experience and ideas in the improvement of work ethics; and to stimulate enterprise and creativity in the Malaysian business community through upgrading of human recourses and skills development.

Since the establishment of ESDC, its has conducted a wide range of training programme particularly pertaining to SMEs in manufacturing sector. These training programmes aimed at upgrading the existing skills of industrial workers through the acquisition of knowledge, methods and attitudes towards managing people, system and technology. The training programmes which have been given great emphasis include the following subject areas:

i.   Quality and Productivity Related Training. Training programmes under this category are aimed at improving quality of systems and products within any manufacturing organisation. Examples of such programmes are Work Procedure and Manual Writing, Practical Quality Auditing, Statistical Process Control, Total Quality Management and 5S Towards a Quality Environment.

ii. Production and Operation Management. Under this category, concentration of the programmes is mainly on **manufacturing**, resources training, materials planning and control, store and warehouse operation, inventory system and distribution system. The aimed of this programme is to assist manufacturing firms improving their work flow and efficiency.

iii. Industrial Automation. This programme is designed to enable enterprises to upgrade their operations and enhance their value-added operations. The programme focuses on a range of low-cost automation. This includes introduction to pneumatics, electro-pneumatic and hydraulics as well as programmable logic controllers.

iv. Plant Maintenance. The programme under this particular category is design to assist member to avoid hazards and waste. Predictive maintenance and maintenance management are examples of programmes.

v. Management Skills. The programme under this category is designed to offer the most needy areas of manufacturing enterprises especially in SMEs i.e. to constantly develop their human resources. Course offered, therefore include team-building for managers, supervisory management, staff training and development, report writing, problem-solving techniques, management and supervisors skills and leadership for line leaders.

vi. Entrepreneurial Development. This specific programme is designed to cater the need for joint ventures between the various Malaysian communities and domestic investment in numerous manufacturing projects. This programme therefore, covers topics such as business planning, financial management, human resources management, production, manufacturing resources planning, as well as marketing.

Training programmes in the areas of industrial automation, plant maintenance and manufacturing technology have been granted the Approved Training Status by the Ministry of Human Resources in the country. Therefore, enterprises which send their participants to attend these programmes at ESDC will be eligible for the Double Deduction Incentive for training. The ESDC is a registered training provider with the Human Resources Development Council (HRDC). A majority of its programmes has been granted the Approval Training Programme (ATP) status which automatically allows employers to claim from HRDF through its Approval Training Scheme (PROLUS). Further information and procedures on a wide range of training programmes provided by the ESDC, FMM, can be

obtained from its headquarters in Kuala Lumpur or any FMM regional
offices across the country, at the following addresses:

Federation of Malaysian Manufacturers (FMM)
Tingkat 8 and 17, Wisma Sime Darby,
Jalan Raja Laut,
50350 Kuala Lumpur.

Federation of Malaysian Manufacturers (FMM),
Northern Branch,
23, Tingkat Kekek 7,
Taman Inderawasih,
13600 Perai,
Pulau Pinang.

Federation of Malaysian Manufacturers (FMM),
Perak's Branch,
130, Jalan Kampar,
P.O. Box 290
30730 Ipoh, Perak.

Federation of Malaysian Manufacturers (FMM),
Selangor's Branch,
Tingkat 3, Bangunan Electrulux,
Lot 2c, Jalan Keluli, Seksyen 15,
40200 Shah Alam, Selangor.

Federation of Malaysian Manufacturers (FMM),
Melaka's Branch,
164/3, Tingkat 3,
Kompleks Munshi Abdullah,
75100 Melaka.

Federation of Malaysian Manufacturers (FMM),
Johor's Branch,
Rumah FMM,
19-A, Jalan Bukit Chagar,
80300 Johor Bahru, Johor.

Federation of Malaysian Manufacturers(FMM) ,
Eastern Branch,
Suite 8, Tingkat 11,
Kompleks Teruntum,
Jalan Mahkota,
25000 Kuantan, Pahang.

Malaysian Agricultural Research and Development Institute (MARDI)

The Malaysian Agricultural Research and Development Institute (MARDI) is established by the Government to encourage potential entrepreneurs in SMEs to participate in manufacturing of food industry in the country. The Institute is also responsible for providing exposure to entrepreneurs concerning new technology in food processing and quality control. Participants who follow the course will normally receive practical training in handling food processing machine under the supervision of the Institute's staffs. Under this Food Technology Industrial Division, a number of courses being conducted by the Institute which mainly emphasises on the exposure and advancement of food processing industry using modern and more updated technology. Since its establishment in 1982, this Division has identified more than 700 small-scale food producers who have the potential to develop, mechanise and increase volume of production and quality for both local and overseas markets. Three major types of course provided by this division, as the following:

i.   Adaptation programme. This programme covers a period of up to three years which offer range of topics from advancement of the use of technology in production process, quality and packaging of food industry. Under this programme, some collaboration is also initiated with MARDI to assist entrepreneurs to obtain credit facilities for new location, tools and machines.

ii. Basic Food Technology Processing Course. This course offers a range of basic knowledge in food processing industry such as food introduction to food industry, types of food industry, major needs in the industry, basic technology and technique used in food processing, market, opportunities and challenges. Priority for this course is extended to new and existing entrepreneurs and those are interested in the food processing industry. Other than this, relevant officers and staff from other government agencies who are interested in the food industry are also encouraged to participate in the course.

iii. Advanced Food Technology Processing Course. This is an advanced course which is provided for those who are actively in the business and need further exposure and advance in knowledge and skills in Food processing technology. This course is offered according to selected and particular types of food industry which is relevant to food processing technology and quality control.

Interested entrepreneurs should be 18 years old and at least completed low level of secondary school. A minimum fee is also needed for every course which will be used for every course materials, practical works, stationary and tea. All these courses are offered in its headquarters in Serdang, Selangor and all its regional offices throughout the country. Further information and application forms are available from the addresses shown below:

Director,
Food Technology Industrial Division,
Malaysian Agricultural Research and Development Institute (MARDI),
Peti Surat 12301, Pejabat Pos Besar,
50774 Kuala Lumpur.

Director,
Malaysian Agricultural Research and Development Institute (MARDI),
Lot PTB, 17514 Larkin By-Pass,
KM 7, Jalan Tun Abdul Razak,
80200 Johor Bharu, Johor.

Director,
Malaysian Agricultural Research and Development Institute (MARDI),
Jalan Balik Bukit,
20300 Kuala Terengganu, Terengganu.

Director,
Malaysian Agricultural Research and Development Institute
(MARDI),
Padang Pak Amat,
16900 Pasir Putih, Kelantan.

Director,
Malaysian Agricultural Research and Development Institute
(MARDI),
Peti Surat 1,
06707 Pendang, Kedah.

Director,
Malaysian Agricultural Research and Development Institute
(MARDI),
Lot 411, Block 14,
Santubong Road, Petra Jaya,
93055 Kuching, Sarawak.

Small and Medium Industries Development Corporation (SMIDEC)

The Small and Medium Industrial Development Corporation (SMIDEC)
was established in May 1996. It was previously a small division under the
Ministry of International Trade and Industry (MITI) known as Small Scale
Enterprises Division (SSED) which co-ordinated government policies and
programmes for promoting the development of SMEs. Therefore, the
establishment of SMIDEC was in line with the recognition of the need for a
specialised agency to future promote the development of small and medium
enterprises (SMEs) in the country. The Corporation current efforts are to
create resilient and efficient SMEs in the country and able to complete in a
more liberalised future market in the global world. The SMIDEC is also
responsible for promoting SMEs to be an integral part of the
industrialisation programme, a national focus point on the overall
development programmes for SMEs in the country and to become global
and world class manufacturers. Toward this vision, the main objectives of
its establishment are among others: to co-ordinate the overall development
of SMEs in the country; to promote the development of a modern and
sophisticated indigenous SMEs in tandem with the strategic direction of the
industrial development; to develop the SMEs into an efficient and

competitive sector, capable of producing high value added and quality products, components and related services for the global market.

In order to promote the development of SMEs in the country, a wide range of support programme is provided by the Corporation. These among others include, the following: providing technical support and advisory services for the enhancement of the growth of SMEs; seeking opportunities for industrial linkages within the various industrial clusters; promoting human resources development in the SMEs; undertaking promotional activities for the growth of SMEs including participation in specific technology exhibition, seminar domestically and abroad; promoting mutual co-operation among SMEs through amalgamation of business, technical co-operation, establishment of mutual fund or co-operative enterprise and the procurement of common equipment; acting as a referral and dissemination centre of information related to SMEs; and co-ordinating with other agencies on programmes pertaining to the development of SMEs.

Currently, the Corporation offers a number of programmes and schemes towards achieving its objectives, including:

i.   *Modernisation and Automation Scheme for SMEs*. This scheme is aimed at promoting the modernisation and automation of SMEs through utilisation and application of modern technology. The scheme is in the form of soft loan to assist acquisition of new machinery and equipment capable of automating manufacturing operations. Potential SMEs are encourage to apply especially those engaged in manufacturing activities, firms with shareholders fund of below RM2.5 million and 70 percent of the shareholders are Malaysians. Items eligible for financing are machinery and equipment with loan exceeding 75 percent of the total cost. This scheme offers a very low interest rate, i.e. 4 percent with a loan period of between 5 and 10 years.

ii. *Scheme for Quality Enhancement of SMEs*. The purpose of the scheme is to provide flexible support services for Bumiputera SMEs involved in the manufacturing sector. This scheme is introduced to promote the modernisation and automation of SMEs through the utilisation and application of modern technology. Assistance is provided for the acquisition of new machinery and equipment which reflects modern features and more capable automating manufacturing operations. The maximum loan amount is RM100 million at an interest rate of 4 percent per annum and the loan period is from 5 to 10 years.

iii. *Technology Development and Acquisition Programme.* It is highly realised that innovation and technology will be the competitive edge in the global market. A dynamic, efficient and resilient SMEs with appropriate and state of the art technological and R&D capabilities is critical in the country vast phase of industrialisation programme, in order to sustain competitiveness globally. The Technology Development and Acquisition Programme is formulated to achieve the following objectives; to develop and strengthen the capacity and capability of potential SMEs to adopt best manufacturing and management practices; to inculcate total quality management and R&D culture among SMEs; to identify weakness within the SMEs manufacturing processes and management with the view to overcoming them; to enhance the competitiveness of SMEs; and to obtain acquisition of appropriate technology which will help developing technology of SMEs especially in product development engineering, designing and processes. SMEs engaged in manufacturing and related services, shareholder's fund of below RM2.5 million with least 70 percent of the shareholders are Malaysians are eligible for the scheme. A fund of RM100 million has been allocated under The Seventh Malaysian Plan (1996-2000) to support the scheme whereby the assistance will be given in the form of matching grant for SMEs. To implement the scheme, the Corporation will identify and appoint technical and research institutions as panel consultants for SMEs. Under the scheme, SMEs will be encouraged to develop their competitiveness through conformation to international standards (i.e. ISO 9000 series). This will then facility SMEs to penetrate the international market. Among the programmes available under the scheme are; Factory Audit for Industrial Linkages; New Product Development Scheme; Financing of R&D for SMEs, upgrading Technology for SMEs and Technology Database.

iv. *Industrial Linkages Programme (ILP).* This programme is a cluster-based industrial development programme in tandem with the Second Industrial Master Plan (1996-2005). Through ILP, local SMEs will be further promoted and matured into becoming reliable manufacturers and suppliers of critical component and services to the larger enterprises or MNCs within the a particular industry cluster as well as across other clusters. The programme serves two important objectives: a) deepening and diversifying

90

the country's industrial base towards high value added activities; and b) reducing the country's dependence on imports of intermediate products and inputs, thus improving its balance of payment position.

v.   *Export Development Programme.* This programme is being formulated to develop and nurture export-oriented SMEs to become world class manufacturers. The programme is conducted with the assistance of Malaysian External Trade Development Corporation (MATRADE). Its opens to all registered SMEs engaged in manufacturing activities with shareholder's fund of below RM2.5 million and at least 70 percent of the shareholders are Malaysians. Among the main activities organised under this programme include; establishment of small and medium Enterprises Link (showcase), exhibition and expo, SME Infornet and resource centre. Interested firms to participate in all programmes and services provided by the SMIDEC are invited to register by filling forms and further information can be obtained from:

> Small and Medium Industries Development Corporation (SMIDEC),
> 9th. Floor, Block 10,
> Government Office Complex,
> Jalan Duta,
> 50662 Kuala Lumpur.

At the initial stage, the ILP will focus on the industry which has the biggest potential for linkages and critical to country's industrial development programme, among others include; electronic and electrical industry (which consists of consumer electronics semi conductor and electronic component, computer peripherals and communications, electrical/electronic appliances and apparatus); transportation equipment industrial group (which consists of automotive and motorcycle, marine transportation and aerospace); and machinery and equipment industrial group (which consists of machines and equipment, machine tools, mould and die, materials handling system and utilities); other industrial groups such as chemical and petro-chemical, the resource and agro-based are also be included under the programme.

In this relation, SMIDEC plays a co-ordinator or the project manager of ILP. Participants in the ILP among other can be; the linkages whereby SMEs as first or second tier suppliers; the lead whereby enterprises can be multi-national corporations (MNCs) or local large-sized enterprises; the financier which may consists of participating financial institution or bank or venture capitalists; and technology supplier which may be the lead enterprises. The ILP offers facilities to registered SMEs with paid up capital of not less than RM250, 000 and at least 70 percent of the equity must be Malaysians of which 60 percent must be directly held by the linkages/supplier enterprises. In order to encourage enterprises to participate in the Industrial Linkages Programme, the government will grant a number of other incentives, inter alia include:

i.   SMEs which produce intermediate goods in an approved scheme will be granted pioneer status with full tax exemption for 5 years.
ii. Expenses incurred by lead enterprises in developing the SMEs suppliers such as training, factory auditing and the technical assistance will be given tax deduction.
iii. Sales made by large enterprises located within Free Trade Zones (FTZ) and Licensed Manufacturing Warehouses (LMWs) who are participants in the programme will be treated as export for purpose of determining equity in these enterprises.
iv. Participating enterprises in the programme which has yet to comply with the equity condition in the licence, can use the ILP as trade off non-compliance in the equity condition.
v.   All other incentives under the Promotion of Investment Act 1986.

5 Human Resources Development, Technical and Vocational Programmes

Introduction

Rapid economic growth and sustainable industrial development will not easily and successfully attained without continuing contribution of efficient, capable and competent skills and knowledge of human resources and work force. In this regard, the availability of an adequate supply of well-trained skilled workers, engineers, technicians etc. is a paramount important for Malaysia especially in line to attain the status of a developed country by the year 2020. Concomitant to this, greater emphasis should be given to training, retraining and skills upgrading of the workforce. Indeed, all these are increasing essential not only to increase knowledge and skill intensity of the work force, but also to equip them with specialised and up to date skills as production techniques become increasingly automates and complex. Training, retraining and skills upgrading is also of paramount important to enhance the quality of the workforce so that it is versatile and adaptable to a changing technological and industrial environment.

In this connection, a human resources development policy that focuses on companies including small and medium enterprises and their workforce will also enable them to attain increases in workers' productivity, efficiency, value-added operations and their competitiveness both in the domestic and world markets. This chapter provides an overview of the current human resources development programmes particularly for the development of small and medium enterprises in Malaysia. The next part will elaborate on human resources development (HRD) in the country involving the approval of HRD Act 1992, Human Resources Development Council and Human Resources Development Fund (HRDF). The other following parts of the chapter will touch on specific government and/or private-related agencies and institutions which provide various programmes for human resources training, technical and vocational training such as Small and Medium Industries Development Corporation (SMIDEC), Centre for Instructor and Advanced Skills Training (CIAST), Industrial

Training Institute (ITI), Forest Research Institute of Malaysia (FRIM), Standard and Industrial Research of Malaysia (SIRIM), Malaysian Institute of Microelectronic System (MIMOS), Youth Training Centre (YTC), Secondary Vocational School, Polytechnic and Higher Education Institutions.

Human Resources Development Programme

The Human Resources Development Act 1992 was approved by the government that allow the establishment of the Human Resources Development Council under the Ministry of Human Resources. The council is responsible for determining objectives, plannings and direction of human resources development in the country. Its members comprise eight representatives of employers, four representatives of government agencies, responsible for human resources training and two independent members who in the opinion of the Minister of Human Resources, will be able to work with the Council. A year later, the council initiated the setting up of the Human Resources Development Fund (HRDF) to provide registered enterprises (with 50 employees and above) some rate of financial assistance and allowable cost. Nonetheless, effective from 1 January 1995, HRDF covered employers with a minimum of ten employees and above and a paid capital of RM2.5 million and above. For these employers they become mandatory to register with the HRD Council and pay the HRD levy at the rate of one per centum of the monthly wages of their employees. For employers having less than 50 to a minimum of ten employees and paid up capital of less than RM2.5 million, they will be given options to register with the HRD Council. Therefore, the council was set up to register, select, approve, monitor and control forms and types of human resources development training programmes pursued by employers. To complement this, HRDF is responsible in providing financial assistance, incentives and cost recovering allowance for employers who provide and send their workers for training approved by the HRD Council.

So far there are four training schemes introduced under the HRDF. They are as follow:

i.   The Funded Training Scheme (FTS). This scheme started in 1993 as the first scheme under the HRDF. Under the scheme, the HRD Council identifies several main trainings to upgrade skills of workers among most needed employers.

ii. The Approved Training Scheme (*Program Latihan yang diluluskan*). Under the scheme, training providers (agencies/institutions etc.) must register with the Council after which they may submit their training programmes which are relevant to employers' training needs for the award of the ATP (Approved Training Programmes) status. Employers can select any training programme with ATP status, sent their employees for training without the prior approval of the HRD Council Secretariat and claim for reimbursement, subject to terms and conditions imposed by the Council on completion of the training programme.

iii. The Annual Training Plan Scheme. Under this scheme, employers are encouraged to put annual training plans. The scheme provides further assistance to employers especially the SMEs' employers to engage consultants registered with the Council to assist them to identify training needs, systematically formulate training programmes and prepare annual training plans. The HRD Council had also engaged a local consultant two-days workshops for employers' representatives who would be invited to participate in these workshops.

iv. The Agreement Training with Training Providers Scheme. This scheme is basically a Training Agreement Scheme with selected training providers registered with the HRD Council. The objective of the scheme is to lessen the financial burden of employers. Under the scheme, employers sending their employees for training, retraining or upgrading skills (with these training providers) need not pay the full amount of fee charged. As an example, if the fee charged for a particular programme is RM1,000 and the rate of financial assistance under the HRDF is 80 percent, employers only need to pay RM200.00 upon registration. The balance of RM800.00 will be claimed by the training provider concerned from the HRD Council. With this small up front cost, the HRD Council hoped that more employees will be sent for retraining and skills upgrading.

Mode of Training

There are at least five modes of training conducted by the HRDF. These include the following:

i. Enterprise-based Training. The systematic development of enterprise-based training will not only produce a better trained, productive and efficient workforce, but also enhance productivity increases and ensure that the level of training can be fine-tuned to each enterprise's technological environment. This mode of training can combine both formal classroom study and factory training and can be designed to cause minimum disruption to production. Thus it can be provided either on-the-job and/or off-the-job. However, to qualify for training grants under the HRDF, training programmes must be structured with specific training objectives and training contents/lesson by plans.

ii. Institution-based Training. Under this mode of training, training providers (irrespective of whether they are public training institution, private sector training institutions, consultancy firms, trade or industry organisations) that can offers cost effective training needs of employers in the ever-changing technological and market environment will also be supported by HRDF.

iii. Industry-managed Training Centres. Under this particular training, the HRDF will support training conducted by employers. Industry-managed training centres are expected to better achieved relevancy of training viz. a viz. the knowledge and skill requirements of employers. In this relation, the HRDF will support the training by providing them financial assistance.

iv. Co-operative Training. Under this training, large enterprises having excess training capabilities are encouraged to offer training places to employees of scales of other enterprises, particularly SMEs which may not have the expertise and resources to formulate and run their own training programmes. This mode of training will be particularly effective in situations where SMEs do sub-contracting works for large enterprises. If employers send their employees for such training, there will be eligible for training grants under HRDF.

v.   Overseas Training. In cases where the training required is not available locally, and is absolutely necessary, request for overseas training can be considered on case by case basis by the HRD Council. Nonetheless, it has been the policy that training for upgrading skills should be ideally conducted locally as costs are much lower and large number of employees can participate in the training.

Procedures and Coverage

Once registered with the Human Resources Development Council, the employers will be liable to pay the monthly HRD levy at the rate of 0.5 per centum of the monthly wages of their employees. The Act will be amended to enable them to pay the levy at the reduced rate. Once the amendment is gazetted, these employers will be asked to exercise their options. To assist these employers, the government had decided to contribute RM2.00 for every RM1.00 contributed by them. In other words, if an employer under this category contributes RM5,000 per year, it will be eligible to apply for training grants up to the maximum of RM15,000 subject to the terms and conditions imposed by the Council from time to time. This subsidy scheme will be for a period of five years, after which it will be reviewed.

The payment of the HRD levy is the responsibility of employers. The wages of employees are not permitted to be deducted under any circumstances for the payment of the HRD levy. Employers who are entitle for this HRDF training programmes include those who registered and/or corporated in Malaysia. They have to register with HRD Council and contributed to the HRD levy for a period of six months and are eligible to apply for training grants (financial assistance) to defray a major position of the "allowance costs" of training their employees. Training must be in areas of direct benefit to their business operations. Financial assistance is, therefore, not given to individuals who enrol and finance their own training programmes and later request their employers for sponsorship. Neither is financial assistance given to employers earning the cost of training grants under the HRDF, trainers must be employees who are Malaysian citizens. Other than manufacturing sector, selected sub-industries in the services sector are also extended to the hotel, tour operations, telecommunications, computer, shipping, aviation and advertising industries as well as freight forwarded and the postal services including courier services.

Employers undertaking training and retraining and skills upgrading of their employees through any mode of training as discussed previously can

97

apply for training grants under any of the training schemes established and/or approved by the Council. It is pertinent to note that all training, retraining and skills upgrading programmes undertaken by employers should be seen as cost-sharing efforts. However, employers are eligible to claim up to the last sent of levy paid in any current year and it is hoped that the momentum of training and retraining of the workforce will be increased. Currently, the rates of financial assistance to the maximum allowance costs is presented in the Table 5.1 below.

Table 5.1 Rate of Financial Assistance by Skill Areas

Skill Area	Percentage of Maximum Financial Assistance
1. Technical skills	80
2. Craft skill	80
3. Computer-related skills	80
4. All other retraining & skill upgrading	75
5. Overseas training	50

Source: Human Resource Development Council 1995, Ministry of Human Resource, Kuala Lumpur.

Training grants in the form of financial assistance for approved allowable costs will be reimbursed on a claimed basis. Receipts and documents such as enterprises vouchers for payment of daily allowance and air ticket stubs must be attached to the appropriate claim forms submitted to the HRD Council Secretariat. Employers can be reimbursed up to the last sen to levy paid for any current year. Any unclaimed levy for any current year is allowed to be carried forward to the following year. In other words, employers have up to a maximum period of two years to claim back levies paid for any one year. Further information and all correspondence regarding the HRDF can be addressed to:

> Director-General,
> Human Resources Development Council,
> Lot 11.2, 11th Floor,
> Exchange Square, Off Jalan Semantan,
> Damansara Heights,
> 50490 Kuala Lumpur.

Small and Medium Industries Development Corporation (SMIDEC)

The Small and Medium Industries Development Corporation (SMIDEC) has also played an active role in providing technical assistance for SMEs, other than support programmes for entrepreneurial developing discussed in the earlier chapter. The most essential part of technical assistance provided by the Corporation are among others, the industrial technical assistance fund and skill development programme.

Industrial Technical Assistance Fund (ITAF)

This fund was set up in 1990 with an initial allocation of RM50 million. The introduction of this fund is expected to enhance the development of SMEs into cost efficient and competitive industrial sector. This fund is provided for the following SMEs: own production facilities or have access to facilities approved by the government (such as the Incubator Scheme and the Technical Park); involve in manufacturing or services or any related projects under the government franchise scheme; shareholders fund not exceeding RM2.5 million; at least 70 percent equity held by Malaysians; and at least 51 percent of their equity owned by SMEs or individuals. Priority will be given to SMEs which manufacture or intend to manufacture product(s). Assistance is given in the form of a matching grant where 50 percent of the project cost is borne by the applicant. Under the ITAF, there are four types of matching to SMEs to participate including:

i. Consultancy Service Scheme (ITAF 1). This scheme provides grants to SMEs to pay for consultancy and advisory services for eligible consultants for project expansion, and/or diversification, modernisation and upgrading of technical and management capacity; upgrading quality and increasing productivity; expenses for testing costs, purchasing computer and other related items related to the operation of the enterprises. Maximum grant provided is RM40,000 per project.

ii. Product Development and Design Scheme (ITAF 2). This scheme provides grants to SMEs for improving and upgrading local product development and design and indigenous technology through the development of new products/processes. Expenses eligible to be claimed under this scheme include: costs of technical manpower involved in development work, consultancy costs, cost acquiring technology and skills, service costs for related scheme, cost of acquiring equipment and designing, testing, security, costs of materials used and incidental costs. The maximum grant provided under this is up to RM250,000 per project.

iii. Quality and Productivity Improvement Scheme (ITAF 3). This Scheme provides grants to SMEs for upgrading of product quality and productivity and improving management and production systems. Expenses eligible to be claimed under the scheme include involvement cost during the implementation of the project, consultancy costs, costs of acquiring technology and skills through training, service costs for related schemes, costs of acquiring equipment for designing, costs of materials used and incidental costs. The maximum grant provided under this scheme is RM250,000 per project.

iv. Market Development Scheme (ITAF 4). This scheme is to introduced assist SMEs to enter the export market and develop export marketing expenses. Expenses which are eligible to be reimbursed under the scheme include costs of producing promotional materials for overseas publicity, costs of participating in overseas trade missions, costs of participating in overseas fairs (including cost of preparing samples and consultancy fees to assist SMEs to apply for overseas 'Certificate of Recognition'. Up to RM40,000 maximum grant per project is available under the scheme.

Skill Development Programmes

It is highly realised that skill development and/or upgrading programme are important to enhance SMEs' productivity and efficiency, to enable them to assume the role of reliable and efficient support and ancillary industries. Therefore, the main purpose of this programme is to upgrade knowledge and skill among technical and management groups of SMEs in critical areas, namely in electronics and information technology, industrial design and engineering skill. This programmes is offered to SMEs engaged in manufacturing activities, registered under Companies Act 1965 with the shareholders fund of below RM2.5 million and at least 70 percent of the shareholders are Malaysians.

These are a number of training areas provided under the Skill Development Programme. These include: electronics and information technology; industrial design and engineering skill; productivity and quality improvement skill; productivity and quality improvement scheme and; marketing skills and export development programme. This programme is conducted through workshops, businesses, clinics, seminars and attachment programmes in the manufacturing establishment. Normally, SMIDEC conducts this programme with the collaboration of existing training and technical institutions and agencies, industrial associations and larger companies. Further information regarding industrial technical assistance and skill development programme can be obtained from the SMIDEC, as the address is below:

Small and Medium Industries Development Corporation (SMIDEC),
9th. Floor, Block 10,
Government Officer Complex,
Jalan Duta,
50622 Kuala Lumpur.

Centre for Instructor and Advanced Skill Training (CIAST)

Centre for Instructor and Advanced Skill Training (CIAST) was established under the Ministry of Human Resources. The objective of its establishment is to provide courses for training instructor, supervisors and skilled workers sponsored by their employers. The CIAST provides a broad range of technical skills training in areas such as automotive, machinery operation, die making, forging heat treatment, welding and metal fabrication, press work techniques, foundry and casting, rubber moulding, plastic moulding, electrical and electronics training, instruments and automatic control equipment, instructors and supervisors training, quality control, production planning and control, and industrial safety. Most courses offered are for two to six week, provided at nominal charges and targeted at three main groups, viz. trade instructors, supervisors and skilled workers. Detailed information on fees can seen in Table 5.2 below.

Table 5.2 Category of Course by Fees Charged by the CIAST in 1997

Category of Course	Rate of Fee
Normal Course	
Tuition fee	RM150/week/participant
Hostel fee	RM50/week/participant
Workshop deposit	RM50/week/participant
Hostel deposit	RM50/week/participant
Evening Course	
Programmable controller application in foundry automation	RM350/participant (30 hours)
Plastic injection mould design fundamental	RM50/week/participant (75 hours)
NC turning	RM50/week/participant (30 hours)
NC machining centre	RM50/week/participant (30 hours)

Source: Centre for Instructors and Advanced Skill Training, *Annual Report 1997*, Ministry
of Human Resources, Kuala Lumpur.

Normally, interested employers or employees have to submit application to CIAST about six weeks prior to the commencement of the respective courses. Selection of participants for any course by CIAST is on the basis of first-come-first-served. All application, further information and correspondence should be sent to the address below:

Training Affairs Division,
The Centre for Instructor and Advanced Skill Training (CIAST),
Jalan Petani 19/1,
P.O Box 7012, Section 19,
40900 Shah Alam,
Selangor, Malaysia.

Industrial Training Institutes (ITIs)

Industrial Training Institutes (ITIs) established in 1982 under the Manpower Department, Ministry of Human Resources to provide formal technical training for workers in the industrial sector and school leavers to enable them to obtain technical skills in specific trades. Among the main objectives of the current ITIs are: i) to produce skilled workforce to fulfil the needs of industrial sector; ii) to upgrade skill of industrial workers to enable them to contribute effectively towards national development; and iii) to provide opportunity for school leavers to get jobs through systematic industrial skill training.

Responsibility for trades training is undertaken by five Industrial Training Institutes situated across the country such as Kuala Lumpur, Prai, Johor Bahru, Kuala Terengganu and Labuan. The trades training courses at these ITIs are grouped under five main categories: mechanical, electrical, construction, printing and metallic trades. The ITIs conduct four major training programmes as follows:

i.   The National Apprenticeship Scheme (NAS) in which new apprentices receive trades training over a three-year period including one and a half year in-plant training with the respective employers.

ii. Preparatory Trade Course (PTC) which is designed to provide school leavers with basic industrial trades skills to enhance their employment prospects. The courses cover a duration of 44 weeks of which 22 weeks involve training at the ITIs and another 22 weeks on-the-jobs training with employers. The annual output of this course is about 2,000 students.

iii. Skill Upgrading Course which covers six months duration is designed to upgrade the trades skills of persons who have been in employment for at least one year and who undertake semi-skilled work. The minimum qualification required for entry is standard six of primary schooling.

iv. The Industrial Training Course. The course is provided twice in a year to a small group of participants. The course is targeted to trade instructors and supervisors with the objective of upgrading their skills and more recent knowledge and producing competent level of trainers.

Forest Research Institute of Malaysia (FRIM)

The Forest Research Institute of Malaysia (FRIM) was established to provide effective research and development support for the forestry and forest products industries in Malaysia. Currently, the Institute has a number of facilities and expertise to offer technical services to the industries in addition to the long-standing research and development activities. Among the functions and services offered by the Institute include:

    i.   undertaking research project in wood, rattan and bamboo-based industry for the development of SMEs;

    ii.   disseminating information and advice in technical aspects whether in establishing new enterprises or modernising the existing production process;

    iii.   assisting entrepreneurs of SMEs to solve problems to related material selection, processing, preservation, utilisation, machines, operation etc;

    iv.   upgrading the skill of entrepreneurs and workers in specialised field by providing training courses such as saw doctoring, saw operation, cutter tool maintenance and wood moulding; and

    v.   developing suitable standards, techniques and guidelines in wood, rattan and bamboo utilisation.

In order to assist forest products industries and utilisation of wood and non wood-based producers, FRIM provides a range of testing, consultancy, advisory, training and technology diffusion services. All these can be seen from its three main services such as:

    i.   Training Services. The services offered various courses including: furniture making, glue-laminating techniques, machine maintenance, moulding operations, saw doctoring, wood drying, wood machining, wood preservation, rattan and bamboo processing, pulping and papermaking, paper testing, wood analysis, board making, wood preservatives analysis, charcoal making and briquetting and gasification.

    ii.   Technology Diffusion Services. The services provide assistance in a number of areas including machine demonstrations, production trial runs, publications, seminars and workshops.

    iii.   Publication. The services include a range of publishing materials such as Malayan Forest Record, research pamphlet, timber trade leaflet, FRIM report, Timber Digest, Bulletin Perhutanan Bandar, Research Report, FRIM Occasional Paper, FRIM Technical Information and Laporan Labuan. Further information and enquires can be made to:

Forest Research Institute of Malaysia (FRIM),
Kepong,
52109 Kuala Lumpur,
Malaysia.

Standards and Industrial Research Institute of Malaysia (SIRIM)

Standards and Industrial Research Institute of Malaysia (SIRIM) was established in 1975 to carry out a board range of functions relating to standards testing, registration for quality control, Research and Development (R&D), technical extension and consulting. It is the Institute which has a national multi-disciplinary research and development agency mainly to assist enterprises solve technical problems through the use of technology and help their business to grow. SIRIM has a quite large institute and its headquarters is situated in a 20-hectare campus in Shah Alam, Selangor, Malaysia. The site houses a number of main facilities such as technology centres, laboratories and officers. Presently SIRIM has seven branch offices throughout the country including Prai (Northern Region), Ipoh (Perak), Johor Bharu (Southern Region), Kuala Terengganu (East Coast Region), Kuching (Sarawak), Kota Kinabalu (Sabah) and Selangor (Central Region). The Institute now has a staff of 1,100 people, about one-third of whom are professional scientists and engineers, offering a wealth of skills and resources than can turn potential business opportunities into successful commercial ventures.

Practically, all aspects of the manufacturing sector encompass the main activities of SIRIM including from standards to calibration: from research and development of a product to prototype testing; production; certification and expert assistance; and from consultancy to training; technology dissemination and transfer. The organisational structure of SIRIM has been streamlined and its strategies realigned in order to be in a better position to assist the industrial sector to stay viable and competitive. Nowadays, SIRIM is made up of three technical divisions and one supporting division. The technical divisions are well-resourced in terms of both manpower and facilities cater for the diverse needs and expectations of industry. The technical arm of SIRIM endeavours to lead the industry towards greater innovativeness and growth. The Corporate Services Division provides the supporting services to the technical divisions including corporate planning and communications, marketing and business development, finance, human resource, engineering support services and general administration. The three technical divisions of SIRIM including Research and Development Programme (R&D), Standard and Quality Programme and Technical Services.

Research and Development Programme

SIRIM has strengthen its research activities and established mechanisms for contract research, which involves the provision of R&D services to enterprises on a free-for-service or contract basis. This will help translate the capabilities and technical capabilities of SIRIM into abilities for problem solving for the benefit of industrial enterprises that require them. A new dynamic partnership management has also been put in place between SIRIM and private sector to provide technological muscle and cost effectiveness. Under the Joint Research Venture Programme, SIRIM uses research funds to enable joint research project to turn innovative technology and promising ideas into marketable products, process and services. The Institute has a large pool of technical expertise. Eighteen specialist technology groups within four technology centres will work as a team operating in a matrix organisational mode to provide expedient solutions to industrial problems. The centres are the following below:

i. The Materials Technology Centre (MTC). The centre provides research services in the areas of ceramics, plastics and metal technology.

ii. The Advanced Manufacturing Technology (AMTC). The centre focuses on assembly technology, manufacturing systems, mechatronics, software development, and circuit and electronic systems.

iii. The Product and Machine Development Centre (PMDC). The centre offers expertise in product development, packaging development, machine development, production tooling, foundry and prototyping services.

iv. The Chemical and Biotechnology Centre (CBC). The centre undertakes projects relating to chemical technology, industrial biotechnology, environment technology, and energy conservation and auditing.

Quality Programmes

SIRIM is firm commitment to standardisation and quality is reflected in the many programmes aimed at upgrading the quality of Malaysian products. This high profile on standardisation and quality assurance activities has started to reap dividens as more and more Malaysian products are competing successfully in the foreign markets. Standardisation programmes under SIRIM over all the stages from the formulation of specifications for Malaysian Stand and to the provision of technical assistance to local exporters pertaining to improve regulations and requirements. Schemes on quality include product certification, product listing, laboratory accreditation based on ISO/IEC Guide 25 and registration of quality systems based on ISO 9000 series of standards:

i.   Product Certification. Third party product certification has been carried out for a long time. Licences have also been awarded to manufacturers whose products comply with either the Malaysian Standards or foreign standards issued by the relevant national standards organisation. Therefore, products certified by SIRIM will bear the Malaysian Quality Mark, the familiar "MS" or "Safety" mark to denote compliance with Safety Standards.

ii. Product Listing Scheme. This scheme was introduced in 1993 to fill a gap in our quality assurance activities. Under this scheme, product are evaluated in performances and/or safety compliance with specified standards. It is especially targeted to importers or products which are categorised as non-mandatory items by the government; local manufacturers of products that have no Malaysian or other national/international standards; suppliers to bulk purchase.

iii. Quality System Registration. This system was introduced in 1987 with the objective is to act as a catalyst to the adoption of cost-effective quality system that meets the requirements of MS/ISO 9000 series of quality management standards by Malaysian manufacturers.

iv. Laboratory Accreditation Scheme. The Malaysian ISO/IEC Laboratory Accreditation Scheme was established in 1990 in an effort to gain an international recognition for test and calibration reports produced by Malaysian laboratories. This will indirectly contribute towards the acceptance of Malaysian products in foreign markets. It is important to note that national laboratory accreditation scheme are becoming a global trend. Customers need assurance that the good they buy are of high quality, and accompanying test data will provide significant information concerning safety, conformity to certain specifications etc. In view of the GATT Code, industries should come forward to participate in the National Laboratory Accreditation Scheme based on ISO/IEC Guide 25.

   v. Measurement and Calibration. Accurate measurement underlies the quality of products and it is imperative that measurement instruments and equipment are calibrated periodically to maintain their accuvacies. Measurement Centre of SIRIM caters for precision measurement in the field of length, mass, flow, temperature, force, pressure and most of the electrical parameters. SIRIM also provides on-site calibration locally and even overseas.

Technical Services

Recognising the need for an efficient technical support services, SIRIM strives to build a responsive and consumer-oriented programme to meet the requirements of industries. SIRIM provides the following technical services:

   i. Testing. SIRIM laboratories are equipped with a comprehensive range of testing facilities to meet the industries' need in the mechanical and automotive, electrotechnical, civil and materials engineering, and chemical sectors. Tests are conducted according to company, national and international standards, professional organisation specifications and other prescribed specialisations and regulations. These laboratories are also supported by four Technology Centres, particularly for testing services in the fields of plastics, metals and ceramics.

   ii. Information Services. Industries can also draw upon a wealth of information contained in SIRIM's depository of six million patent document, 200,000 standards 19,000 technical books, 300 technical journal titles and technical regulations of various countries. Coupled with this, industries can also link on-line to source information on Malaysian Standards and Malaysian Patents. The SIRIM library also subscribes to the Dialogue Information Services, which is host system containing about 500 databases on a wide variety of subjects.

iii. Technology Consultancy and Dissemination. As a greater part of our national development role, SIRIM aims at creating a positive environment for the growth of small and medium enterprises (SMEs). Assistance is given by a way of advice and general consultancy. Two special programmes developed for SMEs are the Incubator and Quality Improvement Programme. In addition to this, SMEs who require financial assistance to develop a new product/process, or to improve their quality assurance system, can apply for aid under the Industrial Technical Assistance Fund. SIRIM helps the government to administer this scheme.

Besides, SIRIM also disseminates its technical know-how and expertise through training programmes for local industrialists and entrepreneurs. The latest technology and skills are passed on to the technical work force through seminars and workshop. Transfer of such technical capabilities are often affected through in-house technical training specially tailored to individual needs and they focus primarily on quality and manufacturing processes to enhance efficiency. Enquires, information and application forms for programmes introduced by SIRIM can be directed to:

> The Director-General,
> Standards and Industrial Research Institute of Malaysia
> (SIRIM),
> Persiaran Dato' Menteri, Section 2,
> P.O. Box 7035,
> 40911 Shah Alam, Selangor,
> Malaysia.

Malaysian Technology Development Corporation (MTDC)

Malaysian Technology Development Corporation was established by the government in 1992. This corporation is a joint-venture between the government and 17 major local corporations. The main objectives of its

109

establishment are to commercialise research results so as to realise the economic worth of such findings through developing indigenous technology and facilitate the absorption of technology developed by universities and institutions; and to encourage the growth of technology-based enterprises so as to broaden the industrial base of Malaysian economy through effecting technology transfer to local companies by gaining access to foreign technologies as well as being the catalyst to the development of venture activities in Malaysia. The focuses of this Corporation are on three main areas: i.e. commercialisation of local research results; introduction of strategic technologies to the country; and manufacture of product widely used as industrial inputs.

Commercialisation of Research Results

In commercialisation of research results, MTDC provides services for universities and other institutions to markets promising research results to private sectors. In addition to this, MTDC also provides capital to establish projects in joint venture with other companies to commercialise the research results. This will also cover the provision of seed capital to bring ideas to the stage where they would be attractive to the private sector enterprises. In the processes, technology is transferred to industry in return for agreed payment and royalties from the licensee. MTDC would identify technology-based profit opportunities, licence, sell or joint-venture the developed technologies for the profit. In the long run, it is the infection of MTDC to develop strengths in the areas such as evaluation of technology; management and leadership of research and development programmes, capital to invest in development of technologist, access to national and international sources of technology and markets for technology, international marketing of developed technology, and critical mass of expertise in technology transfer and development.

Introduction of Strategic Technologies to Malaysia

In the introduction of strategic technologies to Malaysia, MTDC undertakes tasks such as to develop enterprises to be involved in strategic sectors through the provision of venture capital, identified new technologies from abroad to be developed by targeted Malaysian enterprises, and develop linkages with institutions that can assist to identify and develop strategic industries.

MTDC also provides a range of services in line with functions to enhance the manufacturing capability of SMEs in Malaysia as financial services in the form of seed financing (at the idea stage of activity), start up financing (capital provided to initiate commercial, manufacturing and sales), and expansion financing (capital provided for extension financing of a enterprises). Meanwhile, a number of non-financial services is also offered, among others include: technical consultancy services (i.e. assistance provided to universities and research institutions to commercialise by "packaging" research findings with feasibility studies and business planning and assistance to companies to absorb new technologies through technology transfer); and technical support services (i.e. assistance provided to enterprises to evaluate equipment, assistance provided to enterprises to implement productivity improvement and other services such as registration of patients and industrial design). All information regarding programmes and facilities provided by the MTDC are obtainable from:

> Chief Executive Officer,
> Malaysia Technology Development Corporation (MTDC),
> 3rd. Floor RHB 1,
> 427 Jalan Tun Razak,
> 50400 Kuala Lumpur.

Malaysian Institute of Microelectronics System (MIMOS)

The objective of the establishment of the Malaysia Institute of Microelectronics System (MIMOS) is to play a pivotal role in the creation of a world-class electronics industry in Malaysia. It is the country's national centre-of-excellence in microelectronics and information technology. The Institute cultivates a variety of infrastructure needed to exploit Malaysia's multi-billion ringgit electronics industry. These ranges from specialised skills development to innovating highly sophisticated and intelligent industrial systems. The Institute was originally established in 1985 as a unit within the Prime Minister's Department, with a skeletal staff of 17 researchers. Currently, MIMOS has grown more than ten-fold to become a full fledged department of the Ministry of Science, Technology and the Environment.

111

MIMOS has numerous Research and Technology alliances with local and international organisations and is also a recognised reference site for international technology networks. MIMOS activities are driven by the nation's immense desire to score quantum leaps in technology excellence and superiority-preconditions needed to quickly push Malaysia into the league of developed economies. MIMOS has set out a number of directions since it was established especially to become a pro-active and high-technology research and development enterprises, among others include: to promote micro-electronics and information technology as strategic technologies for national development; to stimulate the co-ordinated development of an integrated electronics industry; to enhance industrial innovation and competitiveness; and to support the development of effective and efficient progress in production, manufacture, commerce and services. MIMOS is guided by the tenet that micro-electronics and information technology users in the country through technology excellence, strategic policy directions, applied research, industrial partnership and international collaboration. MIMOS is actively involved in the development of the following technologies:

i.   Semiconductor Technology. Malaysia is the world's largest exporter and the third world largest producer of semi-conductor devices. Semi-conductor technology is the foundation on which the world electronics industry thrives. In this relation, Malaysia has all the potentials to emerge among the world's best semi-conductor specialist and assume a leading role in the international electronics scene.

ii.   Design Methodology. Excellence in microelectronics entails the mastery of integrated circuit (IC) design and manufacture, the complexity of which compels the utilisation of highly sophisticated tools. MIMOS provides system designers, the expertise and facilities in IC design through its Design Methodology Division. Together with the Semiconductor Technology Division, it will offer the complete flow in IC development i.e. from design of working chip. MIMOS is committed to ensure a high rate of technology transfer. The Design Methodology Division seeks to bring the best international IC design techniques to local industries. Linkages with foreign research and IC foundries have been established to expedite technology transfer.

iii. Computer Technology. Computer technology continues to change all aspects of human life. Malaysia must strive to attain mastery over computer technology, both as a producer and a user. In this respect, the Computer System Division plays a significant role in supporting the growth of an indigenous computer industry. This is done by developing hardware and software for the domestic and international markets through joint and contract R&D with industry partners. The division is continuously exploring the latest technologies such as parallel processing, multi-media applications and object oriented techniques. The Computer System Division will continue to support the development of technical, educational and commercial applications. The division's future directions are towards hardware and software development in the real-time processing, computer and telecommunication sectors.

iv. Telecommunication Technology. Telecommunications need continuos improvement due to its entails a core infrastructure development which requires continuos development. More importantly, it regular doses of innovation to help the country maintain its competitive edge. Micro-electronics and information technology offer vast development opportunities when applied to telecommunications Technology Division's R&D activities are directed and creating the right infrastructure for information dissemination and utilisation for continued economic growth. The division emphasises the development of electronics sub-systems for use in the nation's telecommunication and information networks. The Telecommunication Technology Division is constantly exploring collaborative opportunities in the development of computers and communications.

v. Industrial Technology. Industrial growth is heavily influenced by technology and technological advancement. Malaysia as being a fast developing economy projects an increasing trend in industrial technology utilisation, acquisition and development. With increasing demand for industrial technologies, there is excellent potential for Malaysia to become a technology producer herself. The objective is to exploit this potential to the hit. In order to achieve this, the Industrial Technology Division has identified focused areas for industrial automation. These include the Supervisory Control and Data Acquisition (SCADA) System, Image Processing and Pattern Recognition Technologies, Speech Processing and Export System. Through this division, MIMOS is also willing to impart the benefits of applying high-technology processes in the country's industrial sectors.

vi. Product Development. It is highly realised that the electronics industry has normally a short product life-cycle. In this regard, an innovative product development programme forms part of an industrial imperative. This division is responsible to transform basic product ideas and functional specifications into cost-effective prototypes. The objective of this division is to encourage and develop a competitive industry through product innovation, focused studies on industrial needs and product improvisation and re-development. This division is also ready to take on sophisticated jobs that may arise from companies specialising in the manufacture of high value-added and innovative electronic products.

Besides actively involve in the development of technologies, MIMOS also provides some other services and facilities including:

i. Contract R&D i.e. offers the industry a variety of technology expertise through contract jobs and design services.

ii. Information services i.e. to nourish technology consumers and industries with a wide spectrum of information on microelectronic and information technology.

iii. Technology Licensing including develops products and technologies which can be licensed out to the private sector for commercialisation.

iv. Technical Services which include PLD Design, PCB Design and Fabrication, Reliability Analysis, ASIC Design and Computer Networking.

v. Technical Facilities which include a collection of sophisticated laboratories areas such as Open System, Semiconductor Technology, Image and Speech Technology, Software Development, Telecommunications, Computer Networking and Computer Technology. All activities, services and facilities provided and offered by MIMOS can be further obtained from:

114

The Public Relations Officer ,
MIMOS, 7th. Floor,
Exchange Square,
Off Jalan Semantan, Damansara Heights,
50490 Kuala Lumpur.

Malaysian Science and Technology Information Centre (MASTIC)

Malaysian Science and Technology Information Centre (MASTIC) was established in 1992 and now is under the Ministry of Science, Technology and the Environment. Its establishment is to play a more important role in the technological development through a number of mechanisms. First is to facilitate the efficient dissemination of management information on scientific activities, facilities, resources, research and development projects and their status, and other scientific information necessary to support and expand these efforts within Malaysia. Second, to assist other government ministries to research and analysis policy interactions between science and technology forecasting and impact assessment. Third, to assist research agencies to streamline, focus and evaluate research programmes and to provide an opportunity for end users of technology to be better informed about technology options both locally and abroad.

Therefore, the key goals of MASTIC, inter alia are: to establish an enhanced and permanent ability to service science and related policy development, analysis and measurement; to build strong relationship between the producers and users of S&T information in all sectors of the science and technology infrastructure in Malaysia; to facilitate the transfer of information to and between these sectors to improve the quality and efficiency which public scientific and technological activity is performed; and to acquire, enter relationships with, or to develop expertise and skills requirements for science and technology information, analysis by commerce and industry in their conduct of S&T activity in Malaysia, or by Malaysians.

In this respect, MASTIC provides four types of information services including:

i.   Science and technology (S&T) statistics and information analysis services. This service area will provide Malaysia's official statistics and indicators of S&T status, progress and trends. It will serve the public policy makers in the main. MASTIC is currently compiling the Malaysian research and development statistics, and the statistics on public S&T awareness in Malaysia.

ii. Educational, promotional and co-ordinating services. This service area will develop and recommend the adoption of consistent definitions and classification, standards of data and information care and access, and promote an appreciation of the uses of S&T management information, statistics and indicators among S&T information holders and users.

iii. S&T Management Information Reference Library and Directory Services. Directories of information on Malaysian scientist, their projects and facilities available as well as on the status of technologies and industries. Locally and overseas will be available for access to national and international databases will also be provided as well as connections to other data centres and libraries in these areas of speciality. Details of the library collection and coverage is available in a separate library brochure.

iv. S&T analytical services. These are services that will be provided for the public and private sectors that include the management and analysis of surveys, specialist information gathering, analysis and reporting, as well as technology management literature searching, research and reference work. The products and services are provided through a range of electronic on line services, as well as through other means.

MASTIC Network

MASTIC will acquire and store all its information and service its clients through a variety of electronic communications forms. At the centre of this scheme is a computer system controlled by MASTIC, which will be utilised for the capture, storage of data, information management and analysis, information "publishing" and dissemination. This system will be accessible both to suppliers of information and to potential users of information through various ways, such as:

i. Manual intervention of a MASTIC operator, in response to a request for information. Dissemination here may be by printed query, analysis and transmission of the response to the customer by facsimile, phone, e-mail, or other postal services.

ii. On line access to MASTIC is computer system using the Telekom telephone services and a modem. Essential to this type of access is a personal computer or similar equipment.
iii. On line access to MASTIC as computer system using dedicated TELEKOM lines.
iv. On line access using any one of a number of public network services including Malaysia's JARING network, through which international access to the Inter Net is also obtained.
v. Partial on line requestor services, using facsimile, E-mail and postal services.

Other network services, such as the establishment of special interest electronic mail groups, and of other research and academic groups are being encouraged, using the existing JARING network system and MASTIC's computer storage. This will include the automation of some key S&T grant and administrative systems. All enquires and information regarding MASTIC's activities should directed to:

Secretary General,
Ministry of Science, Technology and the Environment,
19th. Floor, Wisma Sime Darby,
Jalan Raja Laut,
50662 Kuala Lumpur
(Attn. MASTIC).

Malaysia External Trade Development Corporation (MATRADE)

Malaysia External Trade Development Corporation (MATRADE) was originally established in 1980 as a unit of the International Trade Division in the Ministry of International Trade and Industry known as Malaysian Export Trade Centre (MEXPO) before its was corporatised in 1993. Its establishment is to provide Malaysian exporters comprehensive marketing information, advisory services on exporting, and assistance with business appointments and participation in trade fairs and trade missions. It provides trade require and information services, has a company registry and an exhibition centre for export products. Currently, MATRADE is governed by a Board of Directors which comprises prominent leaders from Malaysia,s public and private sectors. These corporate captains are committed to assisting the Malaysian business community to venture into the international market place. MATRADE is the main export development organisation in Malaysia, therefore a range of trade promotion activities provides to achieve its objectives such as: to promote the export of Malaysia value-added products and services; to ensure their competitiveness in the dynamic international economic development; and to provide a comprehensive market information system and effective marketing strategies. Overall, MATRADE has five specialised bureau which co-ordinate their respective activities to provide a comprehensive range of services for Malaysia exporters and manufacturers, including Corporate Affairs, Trade Information, Trade Advisory and Training, Trade Promotion and Trade Research and Development:

i.   Corporate Affairs Bureau. Corporate Affairs Bureau is responsible for the overall planning and co-ordination of financial and administration activities and corporate matters of MATRADE.

ii.   Trade Information Bureau is responsible for the setting up of an external trade information database and the overall collection, documentation and dissemination of trade information. In this regard, MATRADE publishes several magazines and trade bulletin covering Malaysia's economy and trade for both the local and international business community. Among them include; Malaysia Trade Quarterly, Malaysia Trade Digest, Bulletin Dagang MATRADE, World Trade Fairs Calendar and Malaysia Export.

iii.   Trade Advisory and Training Bureau. This bureau is responsible for formulating, planning and implementing training programmes for the export community. They also handle trade enquiries from overseas and provide advisory services on trade technicalities. It organises workshops, seminars and clinics on the technicalities of international trade, the international market-place and trade opportunities. Offer areas covered include details on market access and strategies, general system of preferences, export documentation, electronic data information, product standards, export financing and insurance. Officers of Trade Advisory and Training Bureau to trade enquires directed at MATRADE and also provide advisory services in regards to market access, pricing, packaging and shipping. Equipped with the necessary knowledge and guidance, Malaysian Exporters are able to position their products or services attractively in competitive international markets, enabling them to further their interest abroad.

iv. Trade Promotion Bureau is responsible for planning, formulating and co-ordinating trade promotion activities within Malaysia and overseas. Therefore, MATRADE maintains a network offices and commissions in Malaysia and abroad for the expressed purpose of promoting trade. Information which is crucial commodity in international trade is organised by the network of trade commissions. This network deals with trade enquiries which arise from their respective markets. These enquires are channelled to Malaysia where MATRADE headquarters relay them to the appropriate parties. The Trade Commissions also promotes Malaysia exports in their respective overseas markets while leading the way into new market penetration. These commissions are also responsible for helping and encouraging the formation of joint ventures local and Malaysian businessmen, participating in international trade fairs and organising buying missions for overseas businessmen to Malaysia. Besides trade missions and exhibitions, international trade fairs are one of the most important marketing tools in the business of international trade. Participation in international trade fairs means being where the action is. Acknowledging the importance of such promotion activities, MATRADE manages Malaysia's participation in about 15-25 overseas trade fairs per year. Simultaneously, participation by Malaysian businesses continue to grow in the trade fairs, partly because of the incentives provided by the Malaysian government (such as double tax deduction on their expenses when participating in international trade fairs). To enable a wide-spread participation in trade fairs, MATRADE produces the World Trade Fairs Calendar, listing of all major trade fairs around the word.

v. Trade Research and Development Bureau which responsibles for the overall planning of MATRADE's trade development programme which includes conducting extensive studies in performances competitiveness and trade partners. This bureau plays vital role in linking both local manufacturers and foreign importers seeking trade-related information. Both its import register and export register help to meet the needs of interested parties. The Import Register offers a computerised list of overseas importers interested in linking up with Malaysian manufacturers, while the Export Register supplies information about Malaysia and international markets. Further information and enquires on activities and facilities provided by MATRADE can be obtained from:

Malaysia External Trade Development Corporation (MATRADE),
Ground and 2nd. Floor,
Wisma PKNS, Jalan Raja Laut,
50350 Kuala Lumpur.

Youth Training Centre (YTC)

Youth Training Centre was established in the late 1970s to provide youth in the age group between 18 and 25 years old with vocational training in a number of areas. The centres were established under the Ministry of Youth and Sports. Currently three YTCs are in operation i.e. in the states of Selangor, Perak and Terenganu. Areas of training provided by the centres include motor vehicle mechanics, agricultural plant mechanics, furniture making, carpentry and joinery, plumbing, bricklaying, general machinery, gas and arc welding, panel beating, radio and TV mechanics, air-conditioning, tailoring, plant operations, processing of agricultural products, electrical trades, printing, electronic engineering and other skilled traders. One of the most significant characteristics of the training provided is the emphasis on discipline and business attitudes. Most of the trainees are unemployed and lower secondary school leavers as well as after standard six of primary schooling level. The training takes between one and two years. During the first four months, trainees have to follow military types of training prior to undertaking skills training. This discipline and regimentation is maintained for the duration of the vocational training. It is noted that more than 1,000 youth per annum trained by YTCs.

Vocational Schools

Currently, there are 58 secondary vocational schools in Malaysia i.e. an increased of 12 schools from 1986. These schools are equipped with various amenities and equipment to cater for various skilled training programmes. The secondary vocational schools provided two years of full-time vocational education to students who have completed their lower secondary education. The school are also ready to offer various part-time courses for those interested in skilled training. In addition to this, the schools are also offering the use of their workshop facilities and equipments to members of the public who are keen to utilise these facilities.

The primary aim of full-time vocational training is to equip the students with skills that are in high demand in the labour market in the broad areas of engineering, trades, commerce and agricultural science. The courses offered include; woodworking and building construction, fitting and machining, sheet metal work and welding, air-conditioning and refrigeration, electrical installation and maintenance, radio, television and electrical servicing, motor mechanics (petrol and diesel), commerce, home science and agriculture. The vocational curriculum is designed to be flexible to adopt to the changing technology and needs. Basic scientific knowledge is included to provide students with some capacity to understand technology. About 75 percent of the curriculum is devoted to vocational education while the reminder is taken up by general education.

Polytechnics

The polytechnics play a significant role in providing the industrial sector with trained technicians and semi-skilled workers. They offer certificate as well as diploma levels to students. Besides, polytechnics provide various part-time courses for those interested in skilled training, and also offer the use of their workshop facilities and equipment to members of the public who are keen to utilise these facilities. The part-time courses are design to offer various skilled training courses such as construction, machinery and electrical programmes. Other areas of training offered include agriculture, commerce and economics. The objective of these courses, inter alia, include: to provide a variety of useful skills; to enroll in preferred courses which are useful to individuals; to increase future job prospects; to enhance current job skills; and to fruitfully utilise spare time. The first polytechnic was established by Ministry of Education in 1969, and there are now seven polytechnics altogether throughout the country producing an annual output of about 3,500 graduates per year. The courses cover a two to three year period. The emphasis is more on optical training and laboratory work. The number of students graduating from polytechnics has expanded rapidly during the 1980s and early 1990s.

Higher and Tertiary Education Institutes

In 1997, there were nine public universities and five institutes of higher learning which offered almost 400 courses and programmes at post graduate, degree, diploma and certificate levels in Malaysia. Currently, there are distance learning courses, off-campus programmes and twining university programmes have been established and introduced to enable a higher intake of students. This is apart from private higher institutions which are rapidly growing nowadays. Hence, the number of students graduating from tertiary institutions has been growing significantly over the last five years. During the period 1980-1995, enrolment in tertiary education increased from about 76,595 in 1980 to 136,277 in 1985. The number of enrolment expected to increased significantly over the last years especially for certificate, diploma and degree levels. This is mainly due to a rapid increase in enrolment in private institutions and twining programmes with universities and higher institutions abroad. Following recommendations of the Industrial Master Plan I (1986-1995) and Industrial Master Plan II (1996-2005) which identified short supply of high level technological manpower as one of the main constraints to industrial development in Malaysia.

6 Location and Infrastructure Facilities

Introduction

It is highly realised that one of the major constraints impeding the development of small and medium enterprises is the high cost of industrial land and factory space. This result in many of SMEs do not have adequate land, building or space for expansion or in some cases even for their present scale of operation. The shortage of appropriate land and building has forced some of SMEs to locate illegally in residential areas or backyard factories. A backyard factories, layout is not functional and the workspace is cluttered with raw materials, machinery and tools. Some of SMEs are often cramped on small spaces under cluttered conditions and with poor plant which in many cases affected their production. The constraint in locating operation in such a small space is the expansion since large machinery cannot be simply installed. In addition, labour's time and energy is also wasted in shifting raw materials to provide more space for work. Working condition in some SMEs which locate their operation in backyard location are often rather rudimentary with poor lighting and ventilation, and little regard safety as well as pollution control.

Meanwhile, a few other SMEs, particular those who operate in Klang Valley and in the east coast of Peninsular Malaysia face flood conditions. Operation and production is always interrupted during the monsoon season when premises are flooded. Meanwhile, some SMEs in the rural areas face the problem of low voltage of electric power, poor water supply and inadequate communications and transport facilities. Some SMEs are also occupying land on a temporary occupation licence, and the leases which are about to expire. Therefore, they face another form of insecurity of tenure when the factory is rented. If an enterprises is unable to secure the contract with the land lord, there will be a stoppage of work until the proprietor finds yet another premise. SMEs operating in a residential area also pose a number of other problems. Surrounding residents often complain about environmental pollution such as unbearable noise and polluted air. Some of the SMEs also impose an unbearable burden on the supply of electricity resulting in frequent breakdown of electricity supply, fluctuating voltage and fire hazards from overheated cables; and a severe strain of water supply, telephone and waste disposal services. In addition, some SMEs also cause traffic problems to residents since their operations frequently spill onto five-foot ways, side streets, traffic flow always interrupted when commercial vehicles deliver and obtain goods and materials from these firms. Because of all these, SMEs in residential areas are often a target of complaints from their neighbours and this creates a dilemma for the local authorities. If they strictly enforce the zoning codes, many SMEs would be forced to close, reducing further manufacturing outputs.

Relocation of SMEs from backyards to fully serviced industrial estates has a number of advantages including they can plan their activities without any constant threat of eviction from local authority; they can invest in new machinery and organise their lay-out in an efficient and effective way with more space for raw materials storage, manpower position etc.; they are better placed to attract skilled workers and to improve the quality of their products; and other related support services are more accessible in the industrial sites.

Presently, it is increasingly realised that the main problems for SMEs are costs and affordability rather than the supply of serviced industrial lands. In Malaysia, responsibility for land matters rests with the government especially the State Economic Development Corporation (SEDCs). Action has been taken by the state authorities to develop suitable land especially land close to urban centres in properly planned industrial estates. The Industrial Master Plan I (1986-1995) suggested that standardised, low-cost building be made available for sale or lease to SMEs especially those in the manufacturing sector. This specialised estates is established in view of achieving scale economies in the provision of support services to a cluster of firms engaged in the production of similar products. For example, specialised industrial estates are developed exclusively for engineering industries so that these locations become engineering centres. This chapter provides review of locational and infrastructure supports provided by several agencies both public and private agencies including Malaysia Industrial Estate Limited (MIEL), Urban Development Corporation (UDA), MARA, Technology Park Malaysia as well as other privisions and facilities in industrial locations in the country, MARA, Technology Park Malaysia as well as other privisions and facilities in industrial locations in the country.

124

Malaysian Industrial Estate Limited (MIEL)

Malaysian Industrial Estate Limited (MIEL) was established in 1964 and owned by Malaysian Industrial Development Finance (MIDF). Nonetheless, MIEL operates under the auspices of Ministry of International Trades and Industry and its has a close co-operation with other government agencies including with the respective State Economic Development Corporations (SEDCs). Presently, MIEL is the premier industrial estates development company in Malaysia and has played a significant role in providing factory units for enterprises in general and SMEs in particular. This is related to the MIEL primary role which is to assist the development of factory buildings in prime industrial estates to cater for manufacturing activities of small and medium enterprises (SMEs).

In the early stage, MIEL constructed factories to standardised design to cater for general manufacturing. Subsequently, this role has been diversified to include the demand for specially design units to cater the individual client requirements. Moreover, other than modern factory buildings for sale or lease for SMEs, large export-oriented industries are also provided by MIEL. Generally among services and facilities provided by MIEL include the following:

i.   Factory for sale. Factory buildings are available for sale on cash-basis. Finance can be obtained from financial institutions. Delivery of factory buildings will be upon full payments of all amounts due to MIEL.

ii.   Factory for rental. Standard factory spaces or specially constructed factory buildings are offered on three years tenancy with an option for subsequent renewals at very competitive rates. However, a shorter tenancy period can also be considered.

iii. Lease and purchase scheme. Factory buildings are initially let out on a three year tenancy which is renewable. Tenants will be given an option to purchase within five years and 20 percent of the rental paid will be recognised as part of payment of the purchase price. This scheme is applicable for 100 percent Malaysian owned companies only.

iv.   Factory Construction Scheme. MIEL constructs specially design building on land belonging to industrialists with approved projects. Factory construction on MIEL land may be considered for viable projects.

v. Special incentives for Bumiputera. MIEL offers special incentives to Bumiputera in the form of preferential purchase terms and lower price of factory buildings.

vi. Project management scheme. The professional services provided under the scheme comprises three main areas i.e. feasibility studies, project planning and construction management and supervision. These are provided to ensure the successful implementation and eventual completion of the project industrial estates. Further information and enquiry can be obtained from:

Malaysian Industrial Estates Limited (MIEL),
Tingkat 9, Bangunan MIDF,
195A, Jalan Tun Razak,
50400 Kuala Lumpur.

Map 6.1 Industrial Areas Built by MIEL in Malaysia

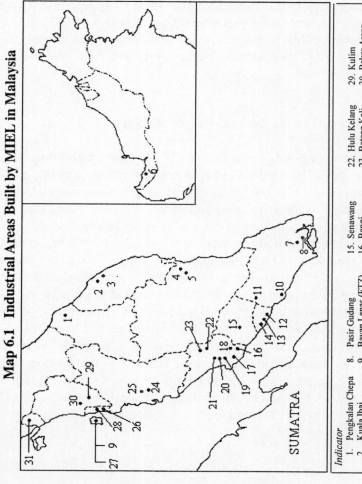

Indicator

1. Pengkalan Chepa
2. Kuala Ibai
3. Gong Badak
4. Padang Lalang
5. Semambu
6. Bintawa
7. Larkin

8. Pasir Gudang
9. Bayan Lepas (FTZ)
10. Tanjong Agas
11. Segamat
12. Alor Gajah
13. Batu Berendam
14. Ayer Keroh

15. Senawang
16. Bangi
17. Balakong
18. Petaling Jaya
19. Shah Alam
20. Pandamaran
21. Sungai Way

22. Hulu Kelang
23. Batang Kali
24. Silibin
25. Jelapang
26. Perai
27. Bayan Lepas
28. Mak Mandin

29. Kulim
30. Bakar Arang
31. Jejawi

Source: Moha Asri 1997, Industri Kecil dan Sederhana di Malaysia, Fajar Bakti, Petaling Jaya, Malaysia.

127

Urban Development Corporation (UDC)

Urban Development Corporation (UDC) previously known as Urban Development Authority plays a crucial role in the provision of business premises (offices and shop) in urban areas especially to Bumiputera. The UDC has a large organisation with over 700 staff including 60 economists as well as architects, planners, engineers and lawyers. UDC undertakes various forms of projects including new town development, urban redevelopment, builds up industrial and commercial spaces and buildings retail premises, as well as assists Bumiputera to establish new businesses in urban areas. In addition, UDC offers consultancy and project management services to Bumiputera landowners and assists them to go into business as land developers. Business properties that are developed by UDC are also sold to Bumiputera. This is done to assist Bumiputera enterprises gain access to good quality, well located business premises in urban areas at affordable prices or rents.

The Council of Trust for Indigenous People (TCTIP)

The Council of Trust for Indigenous People (TCTIP) plays a prominent role in encouraging SMEs' Bumiputera entrepreneurs to involve in business and commercial activities. The role is also vital in providing infrastructure facilities especially commercial and industrial spaces. Under TCTIP's Business Premises programme, a number of projects has been undertaken particularly in the construction of shopping and office complexes, arcades, shop houses, shop lots, bazaars and stalls. In terms of location, TCTIP concentrates both, the rural as well as urban areas. Before the premises are constructed, feasibility studies are usually conducted especially on the types of premises suitable for a particular area, the capability of the prospective entrepreneurs to be housed in the premises and their business requirement for space. Priority to rent premises is normally given to entrepreneurs who have already started their business in the area but who not situated are in suitable sites. The buildings are rented out at subsidised rentals. Provision of business premises is part of an integrated approach that MARA has adopted for entrepreneurial development of SMEs.

Technology Park Malaysia (TPM)

Technology Park of Malaysia (TPM) was established in 1987 under the Ministry of Science, Technology and Environment as part of the effort to stimulate indigenous technology development to spur Malaysia's drive towards industrialisation. Technology Park of Malaysia is basically a technology-based, value-added property and land development established to promote, stimulate, support and commercialise innovative concepts drawn for R&D activities in order to enable Malaysia industries to compete effectively in the international market. Among the objectives of TPM include; to promote private sector participation in R&D; to provide facilities and support to enable the commercialisation of research findings and innovations generated by the private sectors, government research institutions and the universities; to promote the growth and development of hi-tech industries; to facilitate collaboration between industry, government agencies research institutions and universities; to provide the necessary physical infrastructure, facilities and services to support local industries which are involved in manufacturing and R&D; to provide state-of-the-art information in marketing, management, financial and technical support to facilitate indigenous innovation and new product development.

TPM which has the area of about 150 acres is located in Bandar Tun Razak, Kuala Lumpur. Among the main focus of technology development include the following:

i.   Information Technology which concentrates on software development, database system development and telecommunication systems.
ii. Biotechnology includes molecular biology and genetic engineering in the fields of agriculture, health, food, energy and pollution control.
iii. Environmental Technology comprises R&D of environmental sustainability and quality of life with commercial and export potential, solar power system, biodegradable products, water and sewerage treatment systems as well as recycling.
iv. Resource-based Technology consists of development of new value-added products, labour saving devices and management systems to increase productivity using Malaysia's agriculture products and natural resources such as petroleum, rubber, palm oil, timber and jungle products.

v. Advanced Material focuses on the development of novel materials to improve and extend performance characteristic of devices, machines and products.

vi. Emergent Technology emphasises on the discover of new commercialisable principles and techniques to improve and perform new functions.

TPM encourages Malaysian enterprises to participate in R&D activities by providing support services and facilities for this purpose and to assist the start-up of small, high-technology especially in manufacturing enterprises. In order to attain its objectives, TPM has been strengthen a number of centres and units. These include, the following:

i. The Resource Centre. This centre is equipped with a number of facilities containing the management units, information division, conference and seminar facilities, computing services and other business services.

ii. An Incubator Centre. The centre designed to facilitate the establishment of small firms by providing them with subsidised shop floor working space of at least 1,000 sq. feet and central business service facilities, and the enterprises in the incubator centre are expected to relocate to the enterprises unit after two to four years operation.

iii. An Innovation Centre. This centre provides services to assist the start-up of high technology enterprises by making available support services and small modular units of 100 sq. meters for use as offices or laboratories.

iv. The Enterprises Units. The units comprise large flexible building modules catering for the needs of companies which have outgrown the incubation phase in the Innovation or Incubator Centre.

v. Industries Units for enterprises which have graduated from the above units and require factory spaces of up to an acre for their manufacturing and R&D activities.

vi. An institution Area reserved for new and relocated government R&D institutions such as MIMOS which is scheduled for relocation in the park and the proposed Institution of Biotechnology.

A tentative structure and progressive flow chart for enterprises which come to join the Technology Park in order to get facilities is presented in Figure 6.1. An enterprises or firms do not necessarily join the TPM from the early stage because they can do so at any one point of the chart if they fit into the criteria for selection. The TPM was established to attract many high-tech and innovative enterprises or firms especially SMEs in several industrial sub-sectors including; rubber-based industry, palm oil, food processing, wood-based industry, metal-based products, chemical, ceramics, micro-electronic and biotechnology-based industries. Nonetheless, other industrial sub-sectors are also eligible to obtain such facilities. All enquires should be directed to:

> Technology Park Malaysia,
> Ministry of Science, Technology and the Environment,
> Lot 10, Jalan Jaya 5,
> Bandar Tun Razak, Cheras,
> 56000 Kuala Lumpur.

There are now more than 215 developed industrial estates throughout Malaysia. These estates provide basic infrastructural amenities including roads, water, power and telecommunications facilities. There are also areas known as Free Trade Zones (FTZs) which specially designed for manufacturing enterprises producing or assembling products essentially for export. The objective of providing FTZ facilities to export-oriented industries is to enable them to enjoy minimum custom control and formalities in their import of raw materials, parts, machinery and equipment. Presently, more than 10 FTZs have been established including in Bayan Lepas, Prai, Mukim Pringgit, Bukit Baru, Tanjong Kling, Sungei Way, Ulu Klang, Telok Panglima Garang and Pasir Gudang. These FTZs are in the states of Penang, Melaka, Selangor and Johor.

Figure 6.1 Progressive Chart for SMEs in the Technology Park of Malaysia

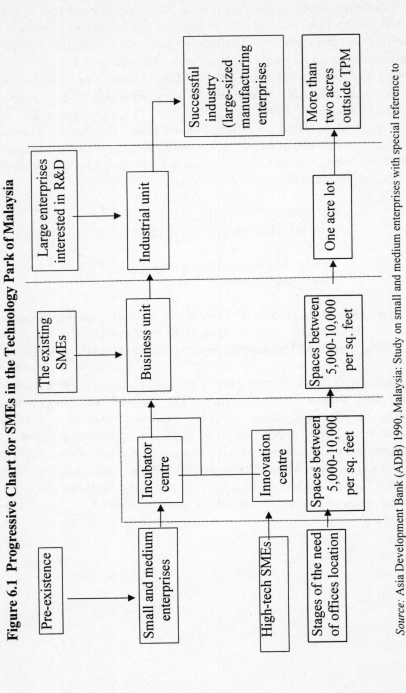

Source: Asia Development Bank (ADB) 1990, Malaysia: Study on small and medium enterprises with special reference to technology development (April).

Others

Enterprises or firms which can be considered for location in Free Trade Zones are those whose entire products are meant for export in exceptional circumstances firms or enterprises exporting not less than 80 percent of their products can also be considered for location in the Free Trade Zones; and those raw materials/component have to be imported. The government encourages FTZ enterprises to use raw local materials/components wherever possible. The enterprises are however, given the flexibility to choose their best sources of supply of raw materials/components.

Moreover, goods exported abroad from the Free Trade Zone are not liable to customs duty. If there are allowed to be imported from the Principle Customs Area (PCA) for domestic consumption they are subject to the prevailing customs duty as is applicable to foreign imports. Nonetheless, enterprises in FTZs may apply to the treasure for exemption on import duty for products which they wish to sell in the domestic market. Of the goods imported into the PCA are to be used as direct raw materials or compounds by manufacturers in the PCA, the importing company may apply for duty exemption in respect of imports from the FTZ in the same manner as if the goods are imported from abroad. Since the FTZ lies outside the Principles Customs Areas, goods exported therefore are eligible for duty drawback.

Another infrastructure facility provided by the Malaysian government is the establishment of Licensed Manufacturing Warehouses (LMW). This warehouse was established to encourage the dispersal of industries to less developed regions and states in Malaysia. Its establishment is also made in order to enable enterprises set up factories for the manufacture of products mainly for the export market. Nonetheless, LMW would be set up in areas where the establishment of a Free Trade Zone is neither practical nor desirable. These establishment are accorded similar facilities to those of factories operating in the Free Trade Zone. Enterprises usually approved for Licensed Manufacturing Warehouse are those whose entire products are meant for export. Enterprises exporting not less than 80 percent of their product also considered for approval; and whose raw materials/components are mainly imported as such gods are not available locally.

133

7 Fiscal Policy and Incentives for SMEs

Introduction

SMEs have been identified as an integral part of industrial development to spearhead economic growth in Malaysia. In recognition of the role of SMEs in the overall national economic development, the government has introduced a number of measures in relation to fiscal policy and incentives. It was highly hopes that will spur the individuals, entrepreneurs and private sector, to take advantages of the investment opportunities present in Malaysia, with that positive response from the private sector to take advantage of the investment opportunities intiated by the government which eventually will further contribute to the rapid growth of the Malaysian economy.

The principal incentives for the manufacturing, agricultural and tourism sectors are contained in the Promotion of Investment Act 1986 and the Income Tax Act 1967. These two incentives are designed to grant relief from taxes in various forms. The taxes applied to enterprises in Malaysia are in the form of income tax of 40 percent and development tax of five percent. Enterprises given pioneer status incentives are exempted from the payment of these taxes. In the case of the other incentives, the benefits are in the form of allowance given.

General Incentives

There are a number of general incentives initiated by the Malaysian government including pioneer status, investment tax allowance and reinvestment allowance.

Pioneer Status

The period of tax relief under this incentives is five years commencing from the production date as determined by the Minister of International

Trade and Industry. To encourage expansion and reinvestment, pioneer enterprises are eligible for a further five years tax relief period on meeting certain additional requirements. These include: the enterprise's fixed assets (excluding land) at the end of the initial five years period reaching at least RM25 million; or employment level reaching 500 full-time Malaysian workers; or other requirements, which in the opinion of the Ministry of International Trade and Industry, would contribute towards promoting and enhancing the economic or technological development of the country.

For small and medium enterprises, they are eligible to apply for pioneer status if one of the following criteria is fulfilled such as the enterprises produce components or input for supply to the manufacturing industry; 50 percent or more of the enterprise's products are exported. Exports include sales to companies located in Free Trade Zones (FTZs) or Licensed Manufacturing Warehouses (LMWs); produces import substitutes where local content of the materials used is more than 50 percent in terms of value; the project contributes towards the socio-economic development of the rural population; for a medium-sized enterprise, they applying for pioneer status must comply to the following criteria i.e.; any product being produced in Malaysia must be on a commercial scale and suitable to the Malaysian economic requirement or development; or favourable prospects for further development of the activity or product; sufficient facilities in Malaysia to enable the activity to be carried out; the national and strategic requirements of Malaysia.

Pioneer Status incentives are given in the form of total exemption from income tax ranging from two to eight years, depending on the level of fixed capital investment. The tax exemption period is set according to the total capital investment as follow:

i.   2 years for capital investment of less than RM250,000;
ii. 3 years for capital investment of less than RM250,000;
iii. 4 years for capital investment of less than RM500,000; and
iv. 5 years for capital investment of less than RM1 million.

Investment Tax Allowance (ITA)

An enterprise granted the investment allowance may be given an allowance of up to 100 percent in respect of qualifying capital expenditure incurred within five years from the date of approval of the project. The grant of either Pioneer Status or Investment Tax Allowance will be determined according to priorities termed as promoted activities or promoted products as determined by the Ministry of International Trade and Industry. The current list of promoted activities and promoted products is to be found in the Appendix. Meanwhile criteria for awarding Investment Tax Allowance (ITA) in manufacturing, agricultural and tourism sectors is presented respectively as shown in Table 7.1, 7.2 and 7.3 respectively as shown below.

Table 7.1 Investment Tax Allowance (ITA) for Manufacturing Sector

Criteria	Basis	Percent ITA	Maximum Percent ITA
Export Value	50%-less than 80%	15%	30%
	80%-100%	30%	30%
Value-Added*	Minimum 25%	20%	20%
Local Content*	Minimum 50%	20%	20%
Employment	Employ at least 100 full-timed paid Malaysian Workers	15%	15%
Location	Location in promoted areas as gazetted under section 32(4) of the Promotion of Investment Act 1986	15%	15%

Source: Malaysian Industrial Development Corporation (MIDA) 1993, Ministry of International Trade and Industry, Kuala Lumpur.

Note: Value added — Defined as gross sales less raw material costs
Local content — Defined as costs of Malaysian raw materials and/or parts and components manufactured in Malaysia, excluding wages, salaries, water, electricity and other domestic inputs, as a percentage of total cost of raw materials and/or parts and component.

Reinvestment Allowance (RA)

Reinvestment allowance is granted to enterprises engaged in manufacturing services and tourism sectors which incur qualifying capital expenditure for the purpose of approved expansion before 31st December 1990. The RA is in the form of an allowance of 40 percent of capital expenditure on plant, machinery and factory buildings incurred on or after 1st January 1988. An enterprise which incurred qualifying capital expenditure for the purpose of approved expansion before 1st January 1988, the previous RA rate of 25 percent will apply.

Table 7.2 Investment Tax Allowance (ITA) for Agricultural Projects

Criteria	Basis	Maximum of ITA Given
Primary Activities	Activities/products which are promoted under the National Agricultural Policy and which are gazetted under the Promotion of Investment Act 1986	50%
Export	Export 50 percent or more by value of its promoted agricultural products	50%
Import Substitution	Products currently imported in large quantities	50%
Integration	Integrated agricultural projects, involving both cultivation and manufacturing	100%

Source: Malaysian Industrial Development Corporation (MIDA) 1993, Ministry of International Trade and Industry, Kuala Lumpur.

Table 7.3 Investment Tax Allowance (ITA) for Tourism Sector

Criteria	Hotel Area and Percent ITA				Tourism Projects Area and Percent ITA			
	A	B	C	D	A	B	C	D
Location								
Fixed Assets of at least RM50 million (excluding land)	25	35	55	65	35	45	65	75
	10	10	10	10	10	10	10	10
Employment of at least 300 full-time Malaysian workers	10	10	10	10	10	10	10	10
Projects having international linkages	5	5	5	5	5	5	5	5

Source: Malaysian Industrial Development Corporation (MIDA) 1993, Ministry of International Trade and Industry, Kuala Lumpur.

Note: Area A - Covering the following areas such as Kuala Lumpur and State of Penang (except Area D).
Area B - Covering the following areas such as the States of Selangor, Perak, Negeri Sembilan, Melaka and Johor (except Area D).
Area C - Covering the following areas such as the States of Pahang, Terengganu, Kedah, Kelantan, Perlis, Sabah, Sarawak and Labuan (except Area D).
Area D - Covering island, hill resorts and such other areas as may be determined from time to time.

Incentives for Exports

Besides the above incentives, there are other incentives for enterprises which produce goods for export-market. Among them include export credit insurance premium, double tax deduction for promotion of exports and industrial building allowance.

Export Credit Refinancing Scheme

In line with the government's objective to promote the growth of exports of manufactured goods, Malaysia's Central Bank (Bank Negara) has implemented an Export Credit Refinancing Scheme (ECRS) which provides Malaysia exporters with short-term credit at preferential rates of interest to enable them to compete more effectively in international markets. The main features of the facility are as follows:

i. Credit is extended by commercial banks to exporters of goods manufactured in Malaysia. The maximum period of refinancing, for all eligible products for preshipment is four months and for postshipment is six months.

ii. Eligibility of goods for refinancing under the ECRS scheme is determined through a negative list concept, whereby products not listed in the negative list will be eligible for refinancing under the preshipment and postshipment refinancing schemes provided they satisfy the 20 percent value-added and 30 percent local content criteria. However, these criteria are being implemented flexibly taking into account special circumstances. Currently, crude rubber, vegetable oil products, cocoa products, agricultural food products and textile products are exempted from these requirements. For other products that do not fulfil the local content and value-added criteria, exemption is given by Bank Negara on a case by case basis.

iii. The current maximum interest rate for exporters under this facility is four percent per annum.

iv. The maximum amount of refinancing for each firm is RM5 million on an outstanding basis (for both post and preshipment), but higher limits may be given on a case based upon application to the Central Bank.

v. The minimum amount for refinancing, that is the minimum value of each substitution bill is RM20,000 expressed to the nearest thousand ringgit. Exporters can "bunch" several smaller bills to make RM20,000.

An Abatement of Adjusted Income for Exports

This incentives is granted to resident manufacturing enterprises exporting directly or through agents. Products should be manufactured in Malaysia. The amount of the adjusted income to be abated shall be an amount equal to the following items:

i.   a rate which is equivalent to 50 percent of exports sales as bears to total sales; and
ii. five percent of the value of indigenous Malaysian materials which are incorporated in the manufacture of the products exported. (indigenous Malaysian materials mean plants, animals, fisheries, minerals and any other materials grown, cultured, reared, captured, extracted or the extractions thereof in their raw or semi-processed forms in Malaysia).

Double Deduction of Export Credit Insurance Premiums

To encourage exporters to penetrate into non traditional markets, double deduction is allowed for premium payments in respects of export credit insurance insured with an enterprise approved by the Ministry of Finance.

Double Deduction for Promotion of Exports

Certain expenses incurred by resident enterprises for the purpose of seeking opportunities for export of products manufactured in Malaysia are eligible for double deductions. The expenses that qualify are expenses incurred on overseas advertising, supply of free samples abroad, export market research, preparation of tenders for supply of technical information abroad, exhibits and/or participation required in trade or industrial exhibitions approved by the Ministry of International Trade and Industry, services rendered for public relations work connected with export, fares in respect of travel overseas by employees of enterprises for business, accommodation and sustenance expenses incurred by Malaysian businessmen going overseas for business subject to RM200 per day, and cost of maintaining sales offices overseas for the promotion of exports.

Industrial Building Allowance (IBA)

An enterprise is eligible for International Building Allowance (IBA) in respect of buildings used as warehouses and as bulk storage installations for storing goods for export. The IBA consists of an initial allowance for 10 percent and an annual allowance of two percent.

Incentives for Research and Development

The following incentives are available to enterprises to encourage research and development in industry:

i. Expenses of a revenue nature incurred by a person on scientific research related to his business and directly undertaken by him or on his behalf, is eligible for deduction. Revenue expenditure incurred for research approved by the Minister of Finance is eligible for double deduction.

ii. Industrial Building Allowance in the form of an initial allowance of ten percent and an annual allowance of two percent is available for buildings used for purposes of approval research.

iii. Plant and machinery used for purpose of approved research are eligible for capital allowance.

Incentives for Training

In order to upgrade skills and impose productivity the following incentives have been provided:

i. Industrial Building Allowance (IBA) is granted to a company which has incurred expenditure on buildings used for approved industrial training. The incentives consists of an initial allowance of 10 percent and an annual allowance of two percent.

ii. Double Deduction of Operational Expenses is granted to an enterprise that has incurred expenditure for approved training.

Tariff Protection

It is the policy of the government to provide tariff protection to deserving industries or enterprises which are in a position to supply a major portion of the domestic market provided that the product is of acceptable quality and the price to customers is reasonable. In the granting of tariff protection, consideration will be given to the degree of utilisation of domestic raw materials and the level of local value added to be achieved and the level of technology of the industry. The long term need for tariff protection of industries already granted tariff protection however, will be reviewed from time to time, in order that protection is granted at an optimum level consistent with the needs of the industry and the welfare of consumers. Applications for tariff protection should be submitted to MIDA in the prescribed forms.

Customs Duty Exemption

The level of exemption from customs duty granted on raw materials/components depends on whether the finished products are sold in the domestic market or are exported. In the case of enterprises finished products for the export market, exemptions from customs duty or imported direct raw materials are normally granted on the following basis:

i.   full exemption from import duty provided such direct raw materials/components are not manufactured locally, or where they are produced and price; and

ii. full exemption from surtax, where applicable.

Meanwhile, an application from an enterprise is eligible for consideration if it complies with the equity condition as stipulated in the licence or unless an extension of time has been granted for compliance with the equity condition. In addition where it is established that the raw materials/components are not manufactured locally, treatment of exemptions from customs duties are as follows:

i.   Full exemption from import duties is normally given when the finished product made from dutiable raw materials/components is not subject to any import duty or surtax; and enterprise has complied with the New Economic Policy in terms of equity

142

participation, management and employment structure in all categories.

ii. In all other cases, partial exemption can be considered in which producers are normally required to pay two percent or three percent surtax or import duty.

iii. For raw materials which are subject to import duty of three percent or less, exemption will not be considered and enterprises are expected to pay the duty. All applications should be submitted to MIDA in the prescribed forms.

Double Taxation Agreements

Malaysia has comprehensive bilateral Double Taxation Agreements with a number of countries. These include Singapore, Japan, Sweden, Denmark, Finland, Norway, Sri Lanka, United Kingdom, Belgium, Italy, Switzerland, France, Canada, New Zealand, India, China, Germany, Poland, Australia, Thailand, South Africa, South Korea, Slovenia, Croatia, Romania, Philippines, Pakistan, Bangladesh, Russia, Netherlands, Indonesia, Hungary, Brazil, Chilie, Argentina, Peru, Malta, Turkey, Kuwait and Egypt. Moreover, Malaysia has intiated the similar agreement with some other countries. Some of the more important provisions of Double Taxation Agreement which are of relevance to foreign investors include:

i. The profit of an enterprise of a contracting country are taxed only in that country unless the enterprise has a permanent establishment situated in the other contracting country. If the enterprise carried on business through the permanent establishment can be taxed in the other country. Where tax is levied by other country, relief from the double taxation is given by the country of residence in respect of that tax.

ii. Dividends derived from Malaysia by residents of other countries having agreements with Malaysia are exempted from any tax in Malaysia which is chargeable in respect of the income of the company paying the dividend.

iii. Under the most of the agreements, interest on approved loans, approved industrial loyalties derived from Malaysia by residents of other countries having agreements with Malaysia are exemption from tax in Malaysia.

143

Tax Spring Provision

There is a provision for credit to be given by the country of residence in respect of tax spared by Malaysia under the repealed *Investment Incentive Act 1968*. Countries having agreement with Malaysia will continue to give credit for tax exemption under the *Promotion of Investments Act 1986* where the incentives are substantially similar to those under the repealed law.

Others

Besides the above incentives, there are numberous other incentives provided by the government to encourage investments and development of industrial sectors in Malaysia especially small and medium enterprises (SMEs). One of them is Labour Utilisation Relief. This incentive is quite similar to Pioneer Status incentives except that the basis for exemption is the number of full-time paid employees engaged as shown in Table 7.4 below. It is pertinent to note that for each of the incentive in the table, an extension of a further year tax relief is granted for each of the following conditions fulfilled, i.e. if the enterprise is sited in a development area; if the product or industry is a priority product or industry; and if the specified percentage of Malaysian content is attained in the final product.

Table 7.4 Incentive in the Form of Labour Utilisation Relief

Number of full-time paid employees	Tax Exemption Period
51 - 100	2 years
101 - 200	3 years
201 - 350	4 years
351 and above	5 years

Source: Malaysian Industrial Development Corporation 1990, Malaysia: Investment in the manufacturers sector, MIDA Kuala Lumpur.

Under the *Excise Duties (Drawback) Order 1977*, a drawback of excise duty in respect of raw materials can be claimed if such raw materials on which excise duty has been paid are used in the manufacture of goods and then exported. Movement of excisable goods from licensed premises for use in the manufacture of goods by a factory in a Free Trade Zone is considered as export of goods from Malaysia. There is also a provision of exemption from customs duty on machinery and equipments. Nearly all machineries and equipments which are not produced locally and which are directly used in the manufacturing process are not subject to import duty, surtax and sales tax. Quantitative controls on imports of these machineries have been removed. Machineries and equipments still subjected to import duty can be considered for tax exemption provided certain conditions and criteria are fulfilled.

Another form of incentives is drawback of customs duties. In this regards, all duty-paid goods used as parts or ingredients in the manufacture of other goods, which are subsequently exported, are eligible for drawback of duty in full. Packaging materials are not eligible for drawback. The detailed conditions for duty drawback as stipulated under Section 99 of the *Customs Act 1967* include: the goods exported have been manufactured on premises approved by the Director-General of Customs; provision to the satisfaction of the Director-General has been made for the control and supervision on such premises of the deposit and issue for use of the Director-General may require for the purpose of ascertaining the quantity of the prescribed goods used in such manufacture; such prescribed goods have been imported by the manufacturers; such prescribed goods are re-exported within 12 months of the date upon which import duty was paid; such claim in respect thereof is made in the prescribed form; duty payment receipts, invoices and other confirmation of importation shown in the statement by the claimant confirming exportation of goods.

If the documents are in order and all their particulars correct, payment is expected to be made within one month of the claims being lodged. Procedure and application for drawback facility should be made by the manufacturer on a special format. Claim for drawback of customs duty (import duty and surtax) under Section 99 of the *Customs Act 1967* must be made on Form Customs Number 15. The form should contain particulars of the claims including the method or formula for the calculating the drawback claim. The claim on Form Customs Number 15 should be supported by the three essential documents. These are: Import Form (Customs Number One) showing the importation of raw materials on which duty has been paid; Export Form (Customs Number Two) showing the

145

exportation of finished goods; and statement of claims signed by an authorised official of the enterprise confirming the exportation of goods on which drawback is claimed.

Movement of goods from the Principal Customs Area to a Free Trade Zone which is also liable for drawback of duty is regarded as export. Therefore, such goods if manufactured in the customs area will be eligible for drawback of duty. Similarly, goods moves to the Islands of Labuan and Langkawi from the custom Area is regarded as an export in so far as drawback of duty is concerned. In order not to delay the processing and payment of claims, all verification of factory stock records will be done after payment has been made. Under the provision of Section 99 of the *Customs Act 1967*, the manufacturer is required to maintain such books of the account as required by Customs for the purpose of ascertaining the quantity of raw materials used in the manufacture. Failure to maintain such records may jeopardise the processing of current and future claims and many result in the withdrawals of the drawback facility originally granted.

8 The Accessibility of Support Programmes for SMEs

Introduction

The recognition of the significant contribution of SMEs to national economic development has led to the prominent position of these enterprises in the Malaysia policy agenda. Various types of policy supports and the numerous agencies involved in promoting SMEs have already been discussed in five chapters, i.e. from Chapter Three to Chapter Seven. Corresponding to that background, this chapter examines four paramount issues based upon the empirical evidence supplied by the sampled enterprises. The first is to examine the nature and characteristics of the government assistance that has reached the SMEs. Reasons given by the sampled enterprises which do not use the government policy supports have impacts on the success of the SMEs, especially in comparison to SMEs that do not obtain any government assistance. Lastly, the implications of these policy supports for the different theoritical views in the study of SMEs in developing countries is discussed.

The chapter is divided into three main sections. The following section presents the first case study by revealing the evidence from a survey which was carried out in early 1996 on 51 SMEs in textile and clothing industry in Kuala Lumpur and Petaling Jaya. The detailed information on the research technique, sampling frame, organisations of the interviews, stages of data collection, criteria used in measuring the success of SMEs in the sampled enterprises and data entry and analysis are discussed in the subsequent subsections respectively. Meanwhile, the general existing policy supports used by the enterprises in the sample and the enterprises which have not used those supports are also discussed. The overall success of the enterprises which have used the policy supports as compared to the non-recipient enterprises in the sampled study is also revealed while the use of specific types of existing assistance and its relationship with the degree of success of the sampled enterprises will be analysed. The second case study will be presented on the basis of a survey which was carried out on 185 small and medium enterprises in the manufacturing sector in Penang,

Malaysia. The detailed information on research methodology and overall research and findings will be discussed in sub-sections Case Study Two's Research Methodology and Result and Findings. The chapter will end with a discussion on the main weakness of existing policy supports.

Case Study One

The Research Technique

Generally, three research techniques are adopted in the study. The first is the structured-interview based on a questionnaire. The structured-interviews are the most significant source of information in the study. The questionnaire used was designed to gather specific information on basic features of enterprises, their characteristic, types and sources of government policy support used and specific indicators to measure the success of firms.

The second is the unstructured interview. Several personal interviews conducted with selected personalities in SMEs and government as well as non-government officials in Kuala Lumpur and Petaling Jaya. General development, the nature of the operation, ownership status and characteristics of small and medium textile and clothing enterprises and the manufacturing sector in the country were given attention in these interviews. General issues about the government policy supports in relation to the development of SMEs were also discussed. Information gathered through this research technique was used to clarify and confirm information gathered from the written sources. Lastly, the study draws on written sources or secondary data. Selected published and unpublished reports, articles, technical papers and brochures produced by the numerous government departments and agencies as well as private organisation collected to provide information on the development of the manufacturing sector, SMEs and the textile and clothing industry, and on their roles, function and programme activities initiated for promoting SMEs in the country.

Sampling Frame

Due to lack of comprehensive information on the number of small and medium textile and clothing enterprises in the study area, a few preliminary steps were undertaken before the actual sampling survey could be determined. At the very beginning a general observation and scanning of various governmental and non-governmental agencies were made for any records, documents and information relating to the manufacturing sector, textile and clothing industry as well as small-medium textile and clothing enterprises in the country and the study area. This helped to avoid the inclusion of only registered textile and clothing enterprises in the sample. In so doing, the existing small-medium textile and clothing enterprises were given paramount attention. In particular, the identification of the existing textile and clothing in the area of the study was drawn mainly from three sources. The first was contact with the several government officers from different agencies through which government records were collected. This was very important to get to know which enterprises have received government support. Throughout this contact, lists of textile and clothing enterprises that do not receive policy assistance were also identified. Among these agencies were:

i.   Department of Statistics (Manufacturing Sector's Surveys and Census of Industries);
ii.   Malaysian Industrial Development Authority (MIDA);
iii.   Socio-Economic Research Unit (SERU);
iv.   Kuala Lumpur Municipality and Petaling Jaya Municipal Council;
v.   Small-scale Enterprises Division (SSED at MITI);
vi.   Registrar of Business (ROB) and Registrar of Companies (ROC);
vii.   Institute of Strategic and International Studies (ISIS); and
viii. National Productivity Centre (NPC).

Secondly, information on the textile and clothing industry was drawn from non-governmental organisations. Several main bodies were approached and these were:

i.   Federation of Malaysian Manufacturers (FMM);
ii.   Malaysian Textile Manufacturers' Association (MTMA);
iii.   Malaysian Knitting Manufacturers' Association (MKMA);
iv.   Malaysian Garment Manufacturers' Association (MGMA);
v.   Malaysian Institute of Management (MIM); and
vi.   Malaysian Trades Union Workers (MTUW).

Several textile and clothing enterprises were also identified through visits to areas in which businesses are most concentrated. Through extensive tours of the cities and with the assistance of experienced residents, several areas of concentration were identified. Among them are: Jalan Kuchai Lama, Jalan Sentul, Jalan Gombak and Jinjang in Kuala Lumpur and areas such sections 8, 9, 11 and 17 in Petaling Jaya. Some local newspapers in which SMEs usually advertise job vacancies were also quite helpful, especially daily local newspapers such as *Malays Mail* and *Metropolitan*. All above initiatives were used in order to estimate the total number of establishments in the area. The experience of compiling the list of textile and clothing firms in the study area was not a simple one. There was hardly any comprehensive source where the list of all textile and clothing enterprises could be obtained. There was certainly no published list or any compilation lists of small-medium textile and clothing industry.

The lists from these various sources were collected and processed to ensure that enterprises appear only once in the final list. A total of 219 textile and clothing enterprises identified in Kuala Lumpur. From 219 enterprises in our compiled list, 76 of them could not be traced when initial visits to their respective addresses were made. Two likely reasons for explaining these untraceable enterprises are: firstly that they may have gone out of business (bankruptcies), and secondly they may have moved out from the Kuala Lumpur and Petaling Jaya areas. Informal inquiry with their neighbours (for those who had operated close to other enterprises or residential areas) seemed to support these two reasons. Moreover, another 17 firms were well known as large companies and multi-national enterprises (according to our definition of SMEs). They were identified from the lists of approved enterprises from MIDA, (1991) and from the ASEAN Textile Directory 1990 (1991). In addition, 29 textile and clothing enterprises in the study area refused to cooperate or to give interviews. The reason given was that they did not have time and were too busy[1] to give an interview, although several (persuasive) measures were undertaken (see the following section).

Therefore, only 97 textile and clothing enterprises were interviewed in the preliminary survey. During this survey too, the willingness of the

---

[1] Phrases such as "time is money", "they did not want to waste time", etc. were always given. The researcher's impression was that they may be worried about "trade" secret being leaked and they may also be worried that the researcher may have been from or related to a government office, in addition to the fact that the individuals in business may genuinely be busy.

150

enterprises to give further co-operation was established. Another 37 enterprises did not want to give further co-operation and another nine enterprises were found to be still too large according to the definition adopted in the research study discussed earlier in the Chapter One. Eventually, from an initial 97 enterprises in Kuala Lumpur, 51 enterprises (or 56.2 percent of the total surveyed in the preliminary interviews) were available for an in-depth investigation of various issues relating to the objectives of the research. A pilot survey was undertaken interviewing five enterprises in order to test the appropriateness and timing of the designed questionnaire. Having done this, a revision of the existing questionnaire was accomplished before the actual in-depth investigation was undertaken.

Organisation of the Interviews

Because most the owners/managers of the establishments were Chinese, two Chinese economic (business studies) undergraduates from the University of Malaya who originated from Kuala Lumpur, were employed to assist in conducting interviews. These two interviewers were briefed to ensure that they were sufficiently well versed in the methodology and purposes of the survey. They were also selected for this particular job based on the criteria of self-confidence, clarity of expression and inter-personal presentation. On average, each interview lasted approximately one and half-hours in cases where the interview could be done all at once. Nonetheless, since many respondents did not wish to give that amount of time in one session, several visits had to be organised to the same enterprise.

Interviewees were designated to be the owner/manager. However, if the owner/manager was not available either the accountant or supervisor of the enterprises, as the representative for the owner/manager, was interviewed. In order to "build up" close co-operation with respondents, every effort was made to explain to the respondents that the survey was conducted independently of government agencies and was solely for academic purposes. In addition, the respondents were informed that all information would be kept strictly confidential and this was also written in a precise way in every questionnaire. Every assurance was given that no individual entrepreneurial establishment would be revealed/identified in the final research. Every completed questionnaire was carefully checked for consistency and completeness before the researcher left the site.

Corresponding to the sampling frame described in the previous sections, the fieldwork undertaken can be summarised in three main stages of data collection. The first is the collection of secondary resources from various government agencies and a number of independent bodies for general information on the manufacturing sector and textile and clothing industry in particular, including small-medium textile and clothing enterprises in the country and in the study area. The second stage was the interviews based on a short close-ended questionnaire directed at 97 firms. This questionnaire comprised brief information mainly on the scale of operation (number of employees, value of fixed assets or fixed capital), legal status of the firm, the year of establishment and whether they receive government policy supports or not. This preliminary survey was important to obtain general information for the following stage of interviews. Their willingness to provide further information for an in-depth survey was also identified.

The final stage was an in-depth open-ended questionnaire for 51 enterprises, entailing two sub-sets: i) a questionnaire for those enterprises that receive the government policy support programmes (a total of 23 enterprises), and ii) a questionnaire for the enterprises that do not receive any government policy support (a total of 28 enterprises). This questionnaire was basically the same as the previous one, but with additional information on the reasons why they do not receive any assistance and their opinion on what assistance they would like from government to promote the development of SMEs. It is relevant to note at this point that although the research attempted to allocate an equal number of sampling units between SMEs which enjoyed government assistance and those who do not, there is a disproportionate number of SMEs which do not receive support programmes in the final sample.

Criteria Used in Measuring the Success of the SMEs in the Sample

The available literature does not reflect a single way in which the success of SMEs can be measured. Their success, growth, performance and development are commonly measured using a range of indicators, including an increase in production, sales, turnover, profit, capital, number of employees, etc. Ideally, increased production is only beneficial if the goods produced can be sold, from which turnover or profit is accumulated. Likewise, an increase in the number of employees must be matched by an increase in production and sales, otherwise the enterprises might not be able to finance the retention of new employees.

Having noted this, however, an increase in production and sales do not always create an increase in employment in the enterprises. Introduction of machinery and new technology will also increase production without generating jobs. Besides, the introduction of new technology can lead to the loss of jobs whilst maintaining or increasing outputs. Therefore, an increase in production of a SME does not necessarily create jobs (this issue will be clarified later). In this relation, success may be synonymous with combined increases in production, sale, turnover, profit, capital and to some extent number of employees. However, in most cases, the elements of profit, capital and employment are used as indicators of success, either individually (separately) or in combination. Other indicators such as sales, turnover, fixed assets etc. are also adopted, however, less often as compared to the former indicators. To illustrate the range of empirical definitions of success for SMEs in developing countries adopted by earlier researchers, the following are presented. For the SMEs in Yaounde, Cameroon, the annual operating profit was used as an indicator for measuring the successful SMEs (Andersson 1987). A similar measure was also adopted by Apibunyopas (1983) in his study of the performance of SMEs in Thailand. In measuring the growth of SMEs in Turkey, Evcimen, Kaytaz and Cinar (1992) used the net profit before tax and paid up capital as the indicators. In a study of small and medium enterprises in Columbia, the ratio of value outputs to the cost of value inputs and the ability of an enterprise to maximise output from a given set of inputs were used as the criteria to assess the economic performance of an enterprise (Cortes, Berry and Ishaq 1987:232-235). Meanwhile, the success of Nigerian SMEs was measured by Nafziger (1977) in terms of value of the monthly income of entrepreneurs as a criteria for the success of small-medium Salvadorean urban enterprises in Costa Rice. Dijk (1980) measured the success of SMEs in Upper Volta in terms of profit, consumption and number of employees. In addition, both Amin (1982) and Quader (1985) in their studies of small-scale activities in Dacca have adopted the number of employees and capital accumulation as the main criteria/indicators for the success.

Therefore, success may be measured in various ways, both financially and in terms of the number of employment generation. The research study has adopted three indicators to record the success of the small-medium textile and clothing enterprises in Kuala Lumpur and Petaling Jaya. These are profit, capital and number of full-time employees (see definitions adopted for profit and capital indicators in Appendix II). The indicators are expressed in terms of: i) the change in the annual index (cumulative index) of the net profit before tax, ii) the change in the annual rate of return on paid up capital, and iii) the change in the annual index of the number of full-time employees. These indexes were based upon a five-year period from 1991 to 1995.

The study decided to develop a more balanced measure of indicators using both financial (profit and capital) as well as employment indicators. This correlates to the research's definition of the SMEs formulated in the Chapter One which considered both financial as well as employment aspects. The use of the employment indicator as well as profit and capital is also related to two main reasons. Although the introduction of new technology can lead to the loss of jobs (or can take place without creating jobs) whilst maintaining or increasing output, the introduction of high and sophisticated technology is unlikely for SMEs in developing countries where labour-intensive mode of production is commonly practised. This is specially so for the small-medium textile and clothing industry in Malaysia. Moreover, several studies of SMEs conducted in developing countries tend to show a significant relationship between financial indicators and number of jobs created (Ganesan 1982, Chowdhury 1982, Ayata 1984, Quader 1985, Andersson 1987 etc.).

The second is that in view of the rapid industrial development in Malaysia, there has been a great realisation of the need for the development of SMEs as one strand of the policy to support the big companies as well as to reduce unemployment. Employment generation is perceived as a pivotal reason for the government to promote SMEs It is, therefore, clear that SMEs growth in employment would be regarded as a measure of success of government policies or at least by those involved in the agencies assisting SMEs. This is highly relevant to the research as the impact of government supports is a major part of its focuses.

There are two main reasons why a five-year period was used. Firstly, it is felt that there would be more consistency in the data in terms of progress or change of success than a single year. This is particularly desirable when there is evidence which tends to suggest that business failure rates are disproportionately high for the youngest[2] enterprises. Taking this into consideration, the probability of an enterprise's survival after five years in

---

[2] For example Ganguly (1985) found that 50 percent of failure occur in the first two and a half years, 33 percent in the next two and a half years and only 17 percent in the following five years. See in D. Storey, K. Keasey, R. Watson and P. Wynarczyk 1987, *The Performance of Small Firms*, Croom Helm: London (p.95).

operation is far greater and this will provide useful data for the purpose of any inference that we will make relating to the development of SMEs in the study. The second reason is related to the reliability and consistency of the available financial information of the sample enterprises during this period.

The initial analysis of the correlation matrix between the three indicators of the success of the sampled enterprises shows that they are highly correlated. It strongly suggests that the three indicators have a close association, implying that an increase in the profit and capital indexes are also likely to be associated with an increase in the number of employment (a full computation of the indicators for an ENTERPRISE I as an example of the method of calculation and the results of correlation matrix are shown in Tables 6 and 7 in Appendix II). Despite the fact that the selected-indicators are highly correlated and could be combined into one-single indicator, the use of such a combination of components to provide standardised measures of success may result in problems in finding independent variables which correlate significantly with the measures of success. Moreover, combining them together as one unit may be arbitrary. Equally, a combination of the indicators may also have the effect of reducing the significance at any correlation with independent variables which may 'act' upon each of the indicators individually. Based upon these reasons, it was decided to analyse these indicators individually despite the earlier indications of a close correlation among them.

The next step is, therefore, to consider the degree of success of the SMEs in the sample in terms of the three dependent indicators. The research recognises that the available literature on the method of categorising the degree of success of SMEs is inconclusive. The arbitrariness of dividing successful categories is inevitable (a review of some existing methods of categorising the degree of success of SMEs is presented in Appendix III). The study rounded off the mean figures to classify the sampled enterprises as falling into either a less successful or a more successful category of performance. For the profit and capital indicators, the cut off point is that any firm which had an index of less than 10 percent of each indicator (or negative index), is identified as being in the less successful category. Therefore, those who attain a more than 10 percent increment would be classified as being in the more successful category. Meanwhile, for the employment indicator, the borderline is that any firm which has an index below five percent in increment index, is identified as being in the less successful category and those which have a five percent increment or more would be classified as more successful. Detailed explanations as to why a cut off line of ten percent is applied to the profit and capital indicators and five percent for the employment indicator are advanced in Appendix III. As shown in the Tables 1, 2 and 3 in the Appendix III, about 37.3 percent and 45.1 percent of the total enterprises are found to be in the more successful category in terms of profit and capital indicators respectively, while for the employment index the proportion is 31.4 percent.

Accessibility of Policy Support Programmes for SMEs

This section will examine two essential issues. The first is the number of sampled enterprises who have made use of support programmes. For the sampled enterprises not received any assistance, a discussion of the reasons as to why they have not received any assistance from agencies or institutions will be presented.

Table 8.1 shows that a total of 45.1 percent of the enterprises in the sample have received assistance in one form or another and 54.9 percent of them do not receive any assistance at all. It was relatively difficult to find small-medium textile and clothing enterprises in Kuala Lumpur area that had received assistance as compared to those who had not obtained any assistance.

Table 8.1 The Distribution of Recipient and Non-recipient Enterprises Assistance

Type of Enterprise	Number	Percent
Recipient Enterprise	23	45.1
Non-Recipient Enterprise	28	54.9
TOTAL	51	100.0

Source: Moha Asri 1996, Small and Medium Enterprises in Textile and Clothing Industry in Kuala Lumpur and Petaling Jaya, Research Report, Universiti Sains Malaysia, Penang Malaysia.

Information on why part of the sampled enterprises have not made use of assistance is shown in Table 8.2 below. From the Table, it is observed that 12 out of 28 of the non-recipient enterprises indicated that the assistance was not useful. A number of enterprises also claimed that much of the assistance given was not within their reach due to certain requirements or criteria specified by the agencies concerned. Among these criteria they included: a good track record, a guarantor, academic qualification as well as experience. They also highlighted that certain institutions and/or agencies provided for assistance for only 'Bumiputera' owners. Because of these criteria, some respondents cited that their applications, especially for financial assistance, were simply rejected. The Table also shows that there are six out of the 28 non-recipient enterprises said that they were not aware of the existence of such assistance. The same proportion said that they did not need the assistance. In addition, some of them also acknowledged that they do not have the time to work it out with the agencies and/or officers.

Table 8.2 The Distribution of Enterprises by Given Reasons for Not Using the Assistance

Reason for not Using the Assistance	Number
Assistance provided is not useful	12
Assistance procedures too tedious and outside their reach	9
Is not aware of such assistance	6
No such need	6
No time to work out with the government officer	4
Worry of "trade" secret being leaked out and does not kno how to apply	2

Note: Total number of responses exceeded the number of sampled size (28) may well be due to the fact that each firm gave more than one reason.

Source: Moha Asri 1996, Small and Medium Enterprises in Textile and Clothing Industry in Kuala Lumpur and Petaling Jaya, Research Report, Universiti Sains Malaysia, Penang Malaysia.

Two implications suggest themselves regarding this difficulty in finding enterprises that have obtained assistance. One possibility is that the policy supports are yet to reach many enterprises in general. Nonetheless, considering the substantial supports as discussed in five chapters (i.e. from Chapter Three to Chapter Seven) it seems curious that supports are used by less than half the sampled enterprises. Having said this, it is equally essential to acknowledge that enterprises are very numerous and tend to be geographically dispersed and divided between a variety of different economic activities across the country. Therefore, in a great majority of cases, the distribution mechanisms for assistance may fail to function in accordance with its targets and objectives. Another possible factor is that the existing policy supports are yet to cover the small-medium textile and clothing industry in particular.

Comparison of the Success of Recipient and Non-recipient Enterprises of Government Support Programmes

In order to fulfil the objective in the chapter, the survey data are tabulated in Table 8.3. A similar data is also presented in Figures 8.1 and 8.2 for much clearer illustration. It is observed that sampled enterprises who receive government assistance generally represent less than 40 percent in the more successful category of all three indicators that is generally 60 percent of the enterprises who have assistance are in the less successful profit, capital and employment categories. Detailed observation reveals that the 17.4 percent of enterprises who are recipients of assistance are in the more successful profit indicator, much lower in comparison to 53.6 percent of the non-recipient enterprises. A similar tendency is also observed in capital and employment indicators. For example, 39.1 percent of the recipient enterprises observed to be in the more successful capital indicator, much lower as compared to 50 percent of the non-recipient enterprises. In addition, the enterprises without assistance also performed better in the more successful employment indicator at 46.4 percent, in comparison to only 13 percent of recipient enterprises.

The data in the figures, thus, suggest that the SMEs which received assistance do not show more success in any of the three indicators. Inversely, the sampled enterprises which have not received assistance indicate a much better success, comparatively. This unexpected finding is hard to explain. It simply implies that policy supports do not appear to have any impact on the success of SMEs hence, thereby rejecting the hypothesis that there is a significantly positive relationship between the policy support programmes used by the SMEs and the degree of success they attain. However, several issues may be inferred from the finding above. Firstly, the existing policy supports are unlikely to be adequate and effective in catering for the existing problems confronting SMEs in Kuala Lumpur. The literature of SMEs in the country (see Lim 1986, Fong 1989, Salleh 1990 and 1991, Ebert-Stiftung 1990 and Hoong 1990) and elsewhere in the developing countries (see World Bank 1978, Harper and Tan 1979, Farbman 1981, Bromley 1985, Tsai 1990, Conti 1990 etc.) frequently emphasises that there is a cluster of problems and barriers that have appeared to inhibit the development of SMEs. Problems such as lack of access to financial institutions and commercial banks for credit, lack of management and marketing skills, unsuitable premises and other infrastructure facilities may not be, therefore, comprehensively addressed under the present assistance. Indeed, the fact that 12 out of the 28 non-recipient enterprises stated that assistance was not useful (Table 8.2) may further support this contention. This analysis, hence, confirms the previous studies, especially of Chee (1979), Institute of Development Research Centre (IDRC-1988) and the Federation of Malaysian Manufacturers (FMM-1988) which pointed out that SMEs in the country in general, do not receive adequate assistance from the relevant agencies/institutions.

Table 8.3 The Distribution of the Sampled Enterprises by Their Degree of Success

Assistance	Percentage (Number) of Enterprises in the Less and More Successful Categories					
	Profit Indicator		Capital Indicator		Employment Indicator	
	LSC	MSC	LSC	MSC	LSC	MSC
Recipient Enterprises	82.6 (19)	17.4 (4)	60.9 (14)	39.1 (9)	87 (20)	13 (3)
Non-recipient Enterprises	46.4 (13)	53.6 (15)	50 (14)	50 (14)	53.6 (15)	46.3 (13)

Notes: LSC- Less Successful Category
          MSC- More Successful Category

Source: Moha Asri 1996, Small and Medium Enterprises in Textile and Clothing Industry in Kuala Lumpur and Petaling Jaya, Research Report, Universiti Sains Malaysia, Penang, Malaysia.

160

Figure 8.1 Recipient Enterprises of Government Assistance and Their Degree of Success

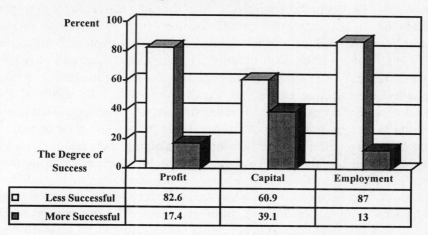

The Degree of Success	Profit	Capital	Employment
☐ Less Successful	82.6	60.9	87
▦ More Successful	17.4	39.1	13

Source: Moha Asri 1996, Small and Medium Enterprises in Textile and Clothing Industry in Kuala Lumpur and Petaling Jaya, Research Report, Universiti Sains Malaysia, Penang, Malaysia.

Figure 8.2 Non-recipient Enterprises of Government Assistance and Their Degree of Success

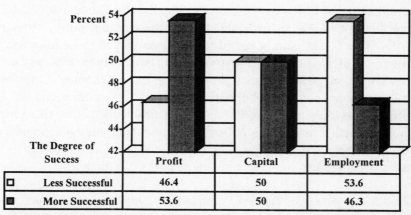

The Degree of Success	Profit	Capital	Employment
☐ Less Successful	46.4	50	53.6
▦ More Successful	53.6	50	46.3

Source: Moha Asri 1996, Small and Medium Enterprises in Textile and Clothing Industry in Kuala Lumpur and Petaling Jaya, Research Report, Universiti Sains Malaysia, Penang, Malaysia.

Secondly, the different performances shown in the findings between the recipient and non-recipient enterprises may also suggest another possibility. The sampled enterprises who do not receive assistance may already be in a relatively better off position (such as sufficient finance and/or internal working capital, competent management and marketing skills etc.) and are likely well-established enterprises which do not require any assistance. This assumption can be linked to some of the earlier reasons given by non-recipient enterprises. Apart from those who admitted that they do not need these supports, reasons such as: the assistance is not useful and that they were not aware of the assistance and had no time to work it out with the agencies, may be relevant in explaining their relatively better position in the businesses. Therefore, they might be expected to perform more successful than those who demanded such supports. This is different from those who have received the assistance, but are not "better-operational enterprises" and could in one form or another be having problems confronting their activity and hence required such supports. The ineffective assistance may not, however, fully solve their existing problems. Thus, the different "stages" of the sampled enterprises and their operational position coupled with incompetent policy supports may have synonymously determined our findings above.

Thirdly, it is interesting to note at this juncture that there may be other factors that are more influential than the policy supports in influencing the development of SMEs in the country. Finally, the above analysis has also contributed towards an understanding of the existing policy supports for SMEs. This is particularly useful for bureaucrats and those involved in the promotion of SMEs in the country. These findings may seriously question the existing supports, and they may have to be re-examined, reviewed and up-dated corresponding to the problems, barriers and needs of SMEs. Furthermore, they may be other numerous problems of overall shortage of resources and contradictory policy measures which may also contribute to the ineffective and inadequate assistance. A detailed discussion of these issues is undertaken in the concluding remarks (Chapter Nine).

The Use of Specific Types of Assistance and Its Associations with the Success of the Sampled Enterprises

The assistance received by enterprises in the sample as shown in Table 8.4 is quite diverse. It shows that while some enterprises have made use of only one type of assistance, others have used two or more categories of assistance. The largest group of the sampled enterprises has received two types of aid, i.e. financial assistance, and entrepreneurial and business management training comprising 34.8 percent of the total. This is followed by the sampled enterprises who receive entrepreneur and business management training only, comprising 26.1 percent. In addition, about 21.7 percent of them used the training and technical assistance only. A relatively smaller, i.e. 8.7 percent of the total sampled enterprises, used only financial assistance and factory premises. The remaining 8.7 percent of the total sample enterprises used all types of assistance with the exemption of factory premises. A number of points can be made about the finding above. The first is that no sampled enterprises receive all categories of assistance. Indeed, only small proportions received more than two types of categorise of assistance, and just under half receive only one type of policy support. This finding gives a useful indication of the nature of assistance which has reached SMEs in textile and clothing industry may imply and could further suggest that the focus and intensity of the existing assistance has yet to be fully implemented, particularly in the case of integrated packages. Since the 1980s the government has made efforts to promote integrated policy supports, covering all types of assistance (see MITI 1989).

Table 8.4 The Distribution of Enterprises by the Use of Specific Types of Assistance

Type of Assistance	Number	Percent
Single Recipient		
1. Entrepreneurial and Management Training	6	26.1
2. Human Resources Training and BusinessTechnical Assistance	5	21.7
Multiple-Recipient		
3. Financial Assistance and Entrepreneurial and Business Management Training	8	34.8
4. Financial and Industrial sites	2	8.7
5. Financial, training and technical and Entrepreneurial and Business Management Training	2	8.7
TOTAL	23	100

Source: Moha Asri 1996, Small and Medium Enterprises in Textile and Clothing Industry in Kuala Lumpur and Petaling Jaya, Research Report, Universiti Sains Malaysia, Penang, Malaysia.

While 12 out of 23 enterprises received financial assistance, this was always combined with other types of assistance (unlike the case of human resources training and technical assistance or entrepreneurial and business management training. It is also frequently observed that financial assistance will only be provided if the SME has already received other types of assistance, particularly the entrepreneurial and business management training and/or the human resources training and technical assistance. These other types of assistance are sometimes considered as the basic requirement for commercial banks and other financial institutions in approving the financial loans given by MARA and the NPC (in co-corporation with several commercial banks and DFIs such as Malayan Banking Berhad, Bank Bumiputera, Bank Pembangunan Malaysia Berhad and Malaysian Industrial Development Finance Berhad).

A further point of interest is the extremely limited numbers of sampled enterprises have made use of the provision of industrial site. This reflects the high cost of factory premises provided by the relevant agencies in the study area and the country elsewhere. Thus, claims in previous studies regarding the unsuitability of the factory premises provided in terms of the affordability to SMEs, may well be relevant to our finding (see Lim 1985:41-44 and ADB 1990:37). The findings also show that entrepreneurial and business management training were used most, with at least 16 enterprises in the sample of 23 having made used these services. This is correlated to the readiness of the government to provide full-scale advisory assistance to the small and medium-sized enterprises in the country. For example, NPC alone had 130 staff including 45 full-time professional trainers in the area in 1988. It also has four regional centres across the country besides its regional headquarters in Kuala Lumpur. The courses are conducted cover a wide-range of issues (see also the other agencies that are responsible for services discussed in Chapter Four). In addition, the requirements to use these services are not tedious in the sense that it does not require good track record and/or guarantor to attend the course. Anyone who is interested is qualified to be a participant. It is also regarded as the first type of assistance for a new entrepreneur who is interested in business and/or who intends to apply for other existing types of assistance, notably financial credit.

In order to provide a further detailed exploration on the possible effects of assistance, the information on specific types of assistance used by the sampled enterprises and their relative degree of success are drawn in Figures 6.3 and 6.4. It is observed that the sampled enterprises who received only human resources training and technical assistance are found

164

to be less successful. Only 20 percent are found in the more successful profit category and 40 percent in the capital category. In addition, they are not found at all in the more successful employment indicator. A similar tendency is also seen in the sampled enterprises who received only entrepreneurial and business management training with only 16.7 percent of their total represented in all three indicators of the more successful enterprises. This means that as much as 83.3 percent of them are found to be in the less successful category of profit, capital and employment indicators. The above data suggests that there is no direct relationship between the use of either human resources training assistance or entrepreneurial and business management only, and the relative success of the sampled enterprises. This may reflect that enterprises receiving only single assistance were unable to upgrade their existing operational activity due to a host of other constraints. It is also possible that the ineffectiveness of each of these kinds of assistance is due to the lack of application of the knowledge which, in turn, is likely due to a series of other barriers which together may relate to the poor performance of these enterprises. Furthermore, the different sources of training that were used by respective sampled enterprises may have resulted in the fluctuating data in the figures. These different sources of assistance will be examined in later sections of this chapter.

Unexpectedly, those who obtained two types of assistance, i.e. financial assistance and entrepreneurial and business management training, also have an unimpressive performance. They are not represented in the more successful profit and employment indicators respectively. Only about 37.5 percent of them are observed in the more successful capital category. Therefore, the finding suggests that there is no obvious impact of financial assistance and entrepreneurial and business management training on the success of SMEs. This finding is indeed hard to explain. However, it may be useful to point out two possibilities. Firstly, assistance may still be inadequate for SMEs in overcoming the overall problems in their business operations. Secondly, the amount of financial credit that was loaned to sampled enterprises may also be inadequate. In this connection, the lack of internal working capital emphasised in Lim (1986:39-41), which arises from either difficulty in obtaining loans or the loan provided being inadequate, may well be relevant. It is also possible that chronic shortage of working capital and insufficient finance may be symptomatic of poor production planning or other serious management and labour deficiencies that determine the whole operational performance.

**Figure 8.3 The Use of Specific Types of Assistance and
the Less Successful Sampled Enterprises**

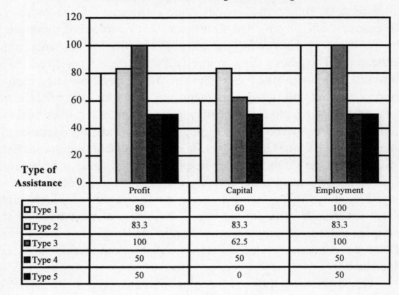

Type of Assistance	Profit	Capital	Employment
□ Type 1	80	60	100
□ Type 2	83.3	83.3	83.3
▨ Type 3	100	62.5	100
■ Type 4	50	50	50
■ Type 5	50	0	50

Source: Moha Asri 1996, Small and Medium Enterprises in Textile and Clothing Industry in Kuala Lumpur and Petaling Jaya, Research Report, Universiti Sains Malaysia, Penang, Malaysia.

Figure 8.4 The Use of Specific Types of Assistance and the More Successful Sampled Enterprises

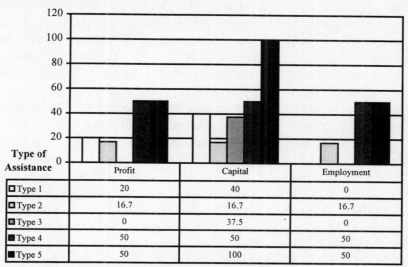

Type of Assistance	Profit	Capital	Employment
☐ Type 1	20	40	0
☐ Type 2	16.7	16.7	16.7
▣ Type 3	0	37.5	0
■ Type 4	50	50	50
■ Type 5	50	100	50

Source: Moha Asri 1996, Small and Medium Enterprises in Textile and Clothing Industry in Kuala Lumpur and Petaling Jaya, Research Report, Universiti Sains Malaysia, Penang, Malaysia.

Indicators:

Type 1 = Human Resource Training and Technical Assistance Only.

Type 2 = Entrepreneurial and Business Management Training.

Type 3 = Financial Assistance and Entrepreneurial and Business Management Training.

Type 4 = Financial Assistance and Factory Premises.

Type 5 = Financial Assistance and Entrepreneurial and Business Management Training.

A more modestly successful performance may be seen in the sampled enterprises who have obtained financial assistance and factory premises. About half of them are found in the more successful profit, capital and employment indicators. The finding suggests two implications. The first is that financial assistance and factory premises may relate to the most important needs of respective sampled enterprises. Moreover, it may also be pointed out that SMEs which obtained factory space are expected to have a relatively better position in terms of internal working capital and are well-established enterprises. This is because many of the premises provided by the authorities are not within an affordable price for SMEs (see for instance, in ADB 1990). Hence, only a few of them could afford to locate their operation in the proper premises provided. It may not be the financial

167

assistance and factory premises that have resulted in the more successful performance, but rather, a relatively better position in working capital and they are likely to be well-established enterprises which made access to financial assistance and factory premises easier. Finally, there are sampled enterprises who utilised three categories of assistance, namely financial assistance, human resources training and technical assistance, and entrepreneurial and business management training. It is found that about half of them are represented in the more successful profit. A similar percentage is also observed in terms of employment. In addition, 100 percent of them are found in the more successful capital indicator.

The data, therefore, suggests that the sampled enterprises who obtained the three stated types of assistance are relatively more successful. This implies that integrated assistance package could have more impact on the success of the sampled enterprises than just one type of assistance. This is simply based on the assumption that by having more types of assistance, there is an increased probability of addressing the problems that confront the sampled enterprises and hence, allows them to expand and grow. In terms of policy implications, therefore, our finding points out that assistance is more favourable and effective if the provision is not limited to just one or two types. Instead, a full range of support services such as financial assistance, training assistance, marketing and management and infrastructure supports in an integrated policy package is highly desirable if the accessibility to these services could be ensured. These inputs could be to up lift the full potential of SMEs development in the wake of the rapid industrialisation process of the country.

Case Study Two

There have been numerous support programmes provided by both government and non-government agencies and institutions aimed at fostering the development of SMEs as presented in the previous four chapters. Despite the fact that there are numerous types of assistance and as many as ten ministries and more than 30 governmental and non-governmental agencies and/or institutions that are involved in providing support programmes for SMEs, the accessibility of these supports to SMEs and how far SMEs make use of these is indeed difficult to ascertain. In this regard, another survey was carried out on 185 small and medium-sized enterprises in manufacturing sector in Penang, Malaysia from November

1996 to April 1997. Detailed information on the methodology and, results and findings of the study are presented below.

Research Methodology

Before the research determined the location of small and medium-sized enterprises in the state of Penang, (one of the most industrialised states in Malaysia) a number of agencies involves in the development of SMEs in the state had been approached. A list of SMEs in manufacturing sector was compiled from various sources such as Penang Development Corporation (PDC), Urban Development Authority (UDA), Federation of Malaysian Manufacturers (FMM), Penang Rural Development Authority (PERDA), National Productivity Centre (NPC), Department of Statistics, and several others. A total of about 369 small-medium manufacturing firms was identified from the list, however due to some problems like moving their sites outside Penang; firms no longer in business; could not be traced; and more importantly no co-operation from the managers, 185 firms have been investigated and interviewed using a set of questionnaires which comprise items relating to the government support programmes that small-medium enterprises have the access. The accessibility is considered for the SMEs who have gained benefits for the last six years period (from 1991 to 1996). These SMEs are widely spreaded across five districts of Penang. A total of 48.6 percent of them locate their operations in the North-East District, 25.9 percent in the Northern District and 12.4 percent in the South-West District. The rest are situated in the Southern District (7.6 percent) and Central District (5.4 percent).

Results and Findings

Of the 185 firms in the survey, 46.5 percent are sole proprietor status of ownership, while friend-partnership and family-partnership constitute 27.6 percent and 19.5 percent respectively (see Figure 8.5). Figure 8.6 shows that 34.1 percent of the SMEs in the survey locate their operation in the light industrial zones and another 33.5 percent situated in the shop-house type of location. Meanwhile, 16.8 percent of them operate in the backyard factories and the other 11.9 percent are in the trading and commercial areas.

Figure 8.5 Distribution of the Enterprises by Ownership Status

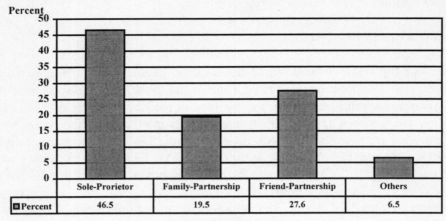

Percent

Percent	Sole-Prorietor	Family-Partnership	Friend-Partnership	Others
Percent	46.5	19.5	27.6	6.5

Ownership Status

Source: Moha Asri 1997, Small and Medium Enterprises in Manufacturing Sector in Penang, Malaysia, Research Report, Universiti Sains Malaysia, Penang, Malaysia.

Figure 8.6 Distribution of the Enterprises by Types of Location

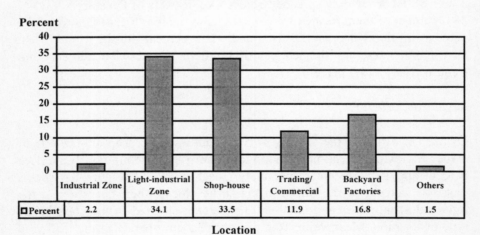

Percent

	Industrial Zone	Light-industrial Zone	Shop-house	Trading/ Commercial	Backyard Factories	Others
Percent	2.2	34.1	33.5	11.9	16.8	1.5

Location

Source: Moha Asri 1997, Small and Medium Enterprises in Manufacturing Sector in Penang, Malaysia, Research Report, Universiti Sains Malaysia, Penang, Malaysia.

The finding reflects the continuing problem of inadequate land or building for SMEs in the country to locate their operation. With the exception of 36.3 percent of SMEs in the survey operating in the proper site (industrial zone and light-industrial zone), the rests are forced to operate in residential and commercial areas or in backyard factories. This is also a serious problem faced by many SMEs in the country despite efforts have been made to provide them a suitable land or building by the various government-sponsored agencies and institutions over the last decades. Figure 8.7 shows that 39.1 percent of the SMEs in Penang began their operation less than five years ago, while another 41.4 percent started their operation between five and 14 years ago. This finding may correlate with economic growth of the country i.e. many SMEs in Penang were established after a brief recession period (1985-1986) that provides ample of opportunities for SMEs to grow in the wake of rapid economic growth in the country particularly from the late 1980s. In the view of the actual number of the full-time employees of SMEs in the survey, it is observed that almost 81 percent employ between 20 and 29 workers. Only 0.6 percent employ 100 workers and above. The survey also reveals that 35 percent of them have paid up capital of RM120,000 and above, while another 14.4 percent have between RMl00,000 and RM119,999.

Figure 8.7 Distribution of the Enterprises by Year in Operation

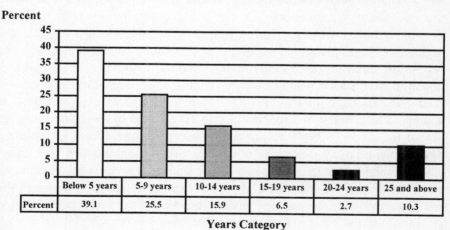

	Below 5 years	5-9 years	10-14 years	15-19 years	20-24 years	25 and above
Percent	39.1	25.5	15.9	6.5	2.7	10.3

Years Category

Source: Moha Asri 1997, Small and Medium Enterprises in Manufacturing Sector in Penang, Malaysia, Research Report, Universiti Sains Malaysia, Penang Malaysia.

It is also observed that from the 185 SMEs in the survey, a substantial proportion of them do not receive assistance from the government-sponsored agencies/institutions as compared to only 28.1 percent of SMEs received the assistance (see Table 8.5). Since the methodology of the survey is not a sampling technique, this finding clearly indicates the lower level of accessibility of government-sponsored support programmes to SMEs operating in Penang.

Table 8.5 The Distribution of Recipient and Non-recipient Enterprises of Government Assistance

Type of Firm	Number	Percent
Recipient firm	52	28.1
Non-Recipient Firm	133	71.9
Total	185	100

Source: Moha Asri 1997, Small and Medium Enterprises in Manufacturing Sector in Penang, Malaysia, Research Report, Universiti Sains Malaysia, Penang Malaysia.

Of the 52 enterprises who received the government assistance, 75.0 percent are Malays-ownership enterprises, 28.1 percent are Chinese while the rest is Indian-ownership enterprises (see Figure 8.8).

The substantial proportion of the Malay-ownership who has gained to the assistance may reflect the emphasis of the government efforts to produce Malay entrepreneurs for the last decades in line with the New Economic Policy (NEP). In Malaysia, it is widely documented that the Malays or Bumiputeras ("sons of the soil" which refer to the indigenous people of Malaysia and include mainly Malays, Kadazans, Ibans and few others) have been far behind in terms of their socio-economic fortunes and their participantion in the business, trade and commercial activities as compared to Chinese and Indians. The NEP adopted in 1971 and covering the period of 1971-1990 has served as a cornerstone of the government development policy. Its main objectives are to achieve national unity, eradicate and to reduce ethnic and regional imbalance in terms of income, employment and the ownership of productive assets. The main thrust of the societal restructuring policies under the NEP has been to uplift the economic status of the Bumiputera Malaysia by ensuring their greater access to education, employment and business opportunities. Although some adjustments and liberalisations have been introduced in the New Development Policy (NDP) which covers the period of 1991 to 2010, the original aim was to raise the Bumiputera participation and ownership of the corporate sectors at least 30 percent (supposedly by 1990, but it had not been achieved, and therefore this aim carried on during the NDP) as well as to promote greater participation in commercial and business activities. This aim, has been very much translated in the government policy support programmes for the development of SMEs in the country.

More essentially, there have been claimed that the Chinese-based ownership of SMEs generally ethnic groups in the country such as Malays and Indians because of their traditionally predominant involvement in the business and commercial sectors of the country (see for instance in Popenoe 1970, Charlesworth 1974, Lim, Cheok and Othman 1978 and Aziz 1980). In this relation, Malay-based ownership enterprises are less capable survive and grow as they tend to be inexperienced, late in joining business world with less business exposure, less innovativeness and creativeness generally as compared to the Chinese-based ownership enterprises (Popenoe 1970:344-346). The Malay-based ownership enterprises are also noted to be low on individualism, activism, trust and risk-taking and high on conservatism. Therefore the Malay-based enterprises are also seen to be less effective at delegating functions, affecting their overall performance as compared to the Chinese entrepreneurs, (Charlesworth 1974:17). On the basis of those evidence and other similar arguments that the government efforts to produce competent, capable and strong business leadership of enterprises and this apparently found in the study. This is indeed in line with the broader objectives of the national development strategy to uplift the economic status of the Bumiputera Malaysians by ensuring, among others, greater access to business opportunities. Meanwhile Figure 8.9 show that more that more than half of the recipient sole proprietor status of ownership as compared to family partnership (23.1 percent) and friend partnership (11.3 percent).

Figure 8.8 Distribution of the Recipient Enterprises by Ethnic-based Ownership

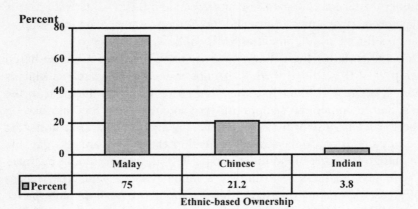

	Malay	Chinese	Indian
☐ Percent	75	21.2	3.8

Ethnic-based Ownership

Source: Moha Asri 1997, Small and Medium Enterprises in Manufacturing Sector in Penang, Malaysia, Research Report, Universiti Sains Malaysia, Penang, Malaysia.

Figure 8.9 Distribution of the Recipient Enterprises by Ownership Status

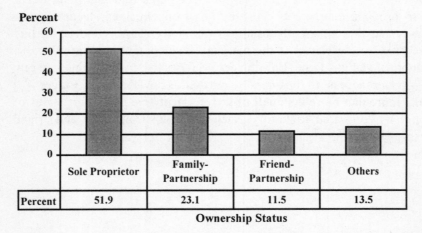

	Sole Proprietor	Family-Partnership	Friend-Partnership	Others
Percent	51.9	23.1	11.5	13.5

Ownership Status

Source: Moha Asri 1997, Small and Medium Enterprises in Manufacturing Sector in Penang, Malaysia, Research Report, Universiti Sains Malaysia, Penang, Malaysia.

Out of the 52 recipient enterprises, a large proportion of them (42.4 percent) have access to only one single type of assistance mainly marketing and market research, and infrastructure supports which form a large percentage. In addition to this, the finding also indicates that the number and percentage of the recipient enterprises decreases with the number of the types of assistance increases. It is observed that only two recipient enterprises (3.8 percent) have received all five types of support programmes. This finding indeed further validates the earlier finding that the accessibility of go support programmes to SMEs is still limited despite the fact that numerous efforts are undertaken to promote their development.

Conclusion

This chapter has presented two essential analyses relating to the accessibility of the government policy support programmes for SMEs in the country. The first was the characteristics of these programmes that have reached the sampled enterprises from the two specific case studies. We found that of the enterprises receiving several types of assistance, not all enjoyed an equal privilege. Only few sampled enterprises were provided more than two types of available assistance, while others had only one or two types of supports. We have found that not all institutions and agencies that were described in the previous four chapters have been involved in assisting the SMEs in the sample. In the entrepreneurial development and business management training, two agencies of National Productivity Centre (NPC) and Malaysian Entrepreneurial Development Centre (MEDEC) seemed to be most active. The National Productivity Centre was also prominent in providing technical and training assistance to the enterprises in the sample. An extremely limited number of the sampled enterprises have received factory premises. On examining the effects of existing support schemes on the sampled enterprises in Kuala Lumpur from the Case Study One, on the whole, at least several salient points emerge. Firstly, contrary to what was expected, those enterprises receiving government assistance were not predominantly found to have a more successful performance than those enterprises not receiving assistance. Secondly, the number of types of assistance received by sampled enterprises seems to be correlated to their degree of success, reflecting the need for a fuller range of assistance to ensure more successful growth. Lastly, there is a possibility that assistance is not the main contributor to the success of the SMEs in the sample.

There are theoretical implications on the basis of our evidence that the effects of the existing Malaysian policy supports on the development of small-medium textile and clothing enterprises in Kuala Lumpur appear to be unfavourable, if not fully ineffective. The assumption that policy supports would have straight-forward beneficial effects on the development of SMEs, as suggested by many scholars of the liberal neo-classical approach, may be less accurate. It is clear that policy supports have not always benefited SMEs or made them more success than non-recipient enterprise. There are many other factors affecting the success of SMEs that have to be investigated in their development process. In addition, the diversity of economic activity, various degrees of policy implementation in different places, all cautions raised by the petty commodity production and flexible specialisation analysts may be very important in the light of our finding. This raises a number of questions about the purpose of policy assistance, the target group of assistance, the implementation of multi-types of assistance, types of economic activity as well as the application of the knowledge and/or credit assistance by recipients. This reinforces the position of flexible specialisation analysts about the need to consider the specific context of SMEs within a particular economic and socio-cultural environment.

The study's assessment is that many SMEs in the country do not receive adequate assistance despite the existence of numerous policy-oriented supports and various agencies being involved. This inference has given some credence to those who were earlier unable to conclude on the policy supports' effectiveness on the SMEs performance (Lim 1986, Salleh 1990 and 1991, and F. Ebert-Stiftung 1990). Furthermore, this inference also supports the conclusion of Chee (1979), IDRC (1988 at the National Agricultural University) and FMM (1988). A general observation is that the majority of SMEs do not have access to government inputs, while some simply are not even aware of the existence of the government policy supports. While SMEs-oriented loan schemes have reached some targeted enterprises many of them still continue to experience difficulty in raising finance and working capital and in the modernisation of their plants because of lack of collateral, while new firms could obviously not produce the track record that is required. Therefore it can be stressed that although the government has stated its strong commitment to and interest in SMEs promotion, the intention has not been translated into effective action. In other words, the outreach and effectiveness of most of the public agencies involved at the level of individual SMEs are indeed limited and fragmented. Based upon our finding and indeed other reports in the country, the lack of effectiveness is likely to be due to several reasons.

The first is that the stated support and interest in the promotion of SMEs to represent sometimes little more than a "half-action" service. A relatively few SMEs have received the government supports and an extremely limited number of them that have received a fuller range of assistance have proven this phenomenon. In practice, preference and priority in terms of incentive and programmes is overwhelmingly given to large industry. For example, under the *Investment Incentives Act 1968* which incorporated Pioneer Status, Investment Tax Credit, Labour Utilisation Relief, Locational Incentives and Export Incentives was mainly based upon capital investment, employment and export features that favoured only big enterprises or companies. As a result SMEs were unable to benefit from those incentives. *The Promotion of Investment Act 1986 (PIA)* replaced the 1968 Act, in order to give more concessions to small and medium-sized firms: These include namely: specific incentive in the form of a five percent abatement on adjusted income, and the pioneer status which is no longer given on the basis of capital investment but on activities and products (the promoted list of products).

Nonetheless, the incentives provided under the PIA 1986 are still biased towards big export-oriented, capital intensive industries. They are still based on profit and performance and do not really benefit SMEs who produce mainly for the domestic market. It is also observed that these incentives are given to companies and hence do not benefit SMEs which mainly operate on a sole proprietorship or partnership basis. Similarly, most of the heavily subsidised space in industrial estates such in Cheras, Jinjang, and Kepong and elsewhere in the country have been allotted to large rather than SMEs. Perhaps what SMEs require is not so much incentives but rather measures that will address the problems and weaknesses of SMEs that is, management advice, easy access to capital, technical and marketing assistance as well as industrial sites.

The second reason for the apparent ineffectiveness of policy supports for SMEs is that the allocation of resources for them is indeed insufficient. This is compounded by inefficient ways in which the programmes are implemented. Besides the limited amount of credit given to the enterprises in the sample, it was also estimated in 1985 that SMEs needed at least RM10,000 million in bank loans, but it was recorded that less than RM300 million was available (see for instance, Lim 1988:122 and 1989). Even then, this amount was reported not to have been properly distributed. Some of the loans went either to undeserving SMEs or even to large enterprises (ADB 1990). Thirdly, it is also imperative to point out that the existing policy programme focuses predominantly on the development of new Bumiputera enterprises, most of which are domestic-orientated business and which are mostly "saturated" such as food, furniture and handicraft industries. While the choice of policy programmes lies in the wider political judgement in a specific economic and socio-cultural context of a given society, continuing supports for these enterprises may be among the reasons for inefficiency in terms of the general net benefit to society. This is because as new enterprises enter the market, other less efficient or less subsidised enterprises are forced out. Since competition is strong in the domestic market, the profit margin are expectedly low and mortality rates are high.

To conclude, although policy supports are ineffective, vast majorities of SMEs in Malaysia have demonstrated their ability to go into business and survive without supports. This is clearly linked to the earlier contention that the support programmes are not currently the major factor in determining their development. Nevertheless, it is possible to argue that survival is not sufficient, especially for a country which is now poised to enter the ranks of the New Industrialised Countries (NICs). This transitional period to NICs can be considerably distorted if inadequate attention is paid to the development of SMEs, widening and strengthening Malaysian domestic industrial-structure. There is indeed scope and ample evidence that many SMEs can increase substantially their productivity and rate of growth, and new enterprises can be established in a number of product lines and sub-industries in the wake of the rapid industrialisation development in the country. If government policies were more favourable and if adequate financing, technical assistance, entrepreneurial development and business training, as well as infrastructure supports were made readily and cheaply available, a more prosperous growth and development of individual SMEs could be anticipated.

9 Conclusions and Recommendations

Concluding Remarks

There has been ample evidence from this study and other reports that the Malaysian industrial sector has, under an induced export-led strategy, experienced high and sustained rates of growth over the past two decades. However, concerns have been expressed on the potential vulnerability of the pattern of industrialisation which concentrates on electronics and electrical goods and an almost total reliance on multi-national corporations (MNCs). The latter, which is dominated by foreign investor, engages in an "enclave-type" development with high capital intensive/import incentive activities and contributes little to extending and deepening domestic technological capacity for a more diverse domestic industrial-base. It is reported that the backward linkages of these corporations with indigenous economic activities have been very weak (ADB 1090:I). The study has stressed that, in recent years, the main preoccupation of policy- makers in Malaysia has been to extend the input-output linkages in the national economy and re-direct externally-determined growth towards an indigenously-induced industrial development. The promotion of SMEs, among other policies, has emerged as a complementary policy instrument envisaged to modify the existing structure of the industrial development in the country.

The policy reflects a recognition of the fact that SMEs posses several socio-economic attributes and potentialities, and that can be promoted to achieve a more balanced industrial development. The attributes listed are that: i) SMEs could strengthen the country's industrial-base and are seen as a major outlet for the absorption of the unskilled, a large segment of the population; ii) they are one of the major networks through which the benefits of economic growth spread to the poor, leading to income re-distribution; iii) they provide an excellent training ground for the development and upgrading of entrepreneurship skills, and serve as an important vehicle for promoting forward/backward linkages in geographically and economically diverse economic activities as well as play an important complementary role; iv) they use largely labour-intensive

179

technologies leading to employment generation and utilising mainly local resources; and v) they help to increase total saving in economy and help to have a favourable trade-balancing payment.

The Malaysian government has, therefore, embarked upon the promotion of SMEs in attempting to tap their potentialities within the overall national industrial strategy. This can be seen clearly in five-year national plans since the early 1970s, the Industrial Master Plan I (1986-1995), Industrial Master Plan II (1996-2005), and the efforts of publicly-funded agencies as well as annual budget plans. While there is no ambiguity about the requirement of such assistance, there are however, unresolved issue as to the extent, role and effects of these existing support programmes on the developments of SMEs at the individual level. These issues are indeed contentious at the conceptual level. Among the different theoretical approaches to the study of SMEs in developing countries, the study found that the petty commodity approach and the flexible specialisation approach are more appropriate in guiding a conceptual framework for a more critical analysis, than the dualist approach. These two approaches (i.e. petty commodity production and flexible specialisation) appear to have a strong conceptual and analytical power in explaining various aspects and characteristics of SMEs to identify those factors which play a crucial part in contributing to the development prospects of SMEs in developing countries. The cautious optimism of some petty commodity analysts about the possible positive affects of government support programmes for specific types of SMEs activities, while recognising the numerous constraints and obstacles, are highly relevant to this research. More importantly, so too are flexible specialisation analysts who recommend policy support for SMEs but, are aware that its effectiveness largely depends upon the particular conditions in the context of a specific economic sub-industry and in a given society.

Moreover, petty commodity production and flexible specialisation approaches are most relevant for their recognition and emphasis on inter-dependent relationships between small-medium and large enterprises in the total economic system. Whether the position of SMEs is subordinated to or exploited by large enterprises, whether their relations with large enterprises have favourable and complementary effects can only be ascertained by an empirical study located in a historically specific socio-economic context. To a large extent, flexible specialisation approach recognises the importance of organisational characteristics and the internal dynamism of SMEs which generate the possibility for natural growth and expansion.

These factors are widely shown in developed countries (Storey 1983, Foley 1987, Babber, Metcalfe and Porteous 1989 etc.).

Having stated the required conceptual clarifications in Chapter Two, the study focuses on the elaboration of the objective, i.e. the exploration of the characteristics, sources and the extend of the existing support programmes that have reached individual SMEs and their possible association with the success these enterprises attain; and an understanding of the major weaknesses of policy support programmes in the context of one country, Malaysia, and some possible considerations for strengthening efforts in promoting the development of SMEs.

Issues and Challenges

The policy issues and implications of the findings may be stated with reference to several aspects. These include: the research findings on the overall support programmes; the fundamental weaknesses of the existing supports, and ways to improve existing programmes. The study assessment was that many SMEs in the country did not receive adequate assistance despite the existence of numerous policy-oriented supports and the involvement of a wide variety of agencies. This inference has given some credence to those who were earlier unable to conclude on the effectiveness of policy supports with respect to the SMEs performance (Lim 1986, Salleh 1990 and 1991, and F. Ebert-Stiftung 1990). Furthermore, this inference lends its supports to other analysts in the country such as Chee (1979), IDRC (1988 at the National Agricultural University) and FMM (1988). The research indicated that the majority of the SMEs did not have access to support programmes with some enterprises simply not even aware of the existence of the policy supports. While small-medium enterprises oriented loan schemes reached some targeted enterprises, many of them were still continuing to experience difficulty in raising finance and working capital reflected in their views about the credit advantages of contractual arrangements with large enterprises, and in the modernisation of their plants because of lack of collateral, while new enterprises obviously not produce the qualifying track record that was required. The study, therefore, stressed that although the government has stated its strong commitment and interest in the promotion of SMEs, the intention has not been translated into effective action. In other words, the outreach and effectiveness of most of the agencies involved at the level of individual SMEs was indeed limited and fragmented. Based upon our findings, and indeed other reports, the research stated that lack of effectiveness is probably due to several fundamental reasons. The first is that stated support programmes for SMEs represented merely a "half-action" service. From the Case Study One, out of 23 sampled enterprises who received assistance, 11 of them have received one single category of support, while eight of out them have received only two categories of assistance. Interestingly, no sampled enterprises receive all categories of assistance. Meanwhile, out of 185 SMEs in the Case Study Two, 71.9 percent do not receive assistance and from 52 recipient enterprises, only two of them received all five types of support programmes. In practice, it is clear that preference and priority in the incentives and programmes is primarily given to large industry. The research cited two examples of the support programmes that had been biased towards large firms, these were: i) the *Investment Incentives Act 1968* which was originally introduced to promote large industry and its amendment the *Promotion of Investment Act 1986 (PIA)* which, although it was reported to have given more concessions to small and medium enterprises, was found. to be of Iittle benefit to SMEs (see for instance in MIDA 1988), and ii) the heavily subsidised industrial estates as in Cheras, Kepong , Bayan Lepas, Prai and elsewhere the country, which were found to have been allotted to large rather than SMEs.

The second reason for the ineffectiveness of the support programmes is the allocation of resources for SMEs which is indeed insufficient. This is compounded by inefficient ways in which the programmes are implemented. Besides a limited amount of credit given to the SMEs in the sample, it was also estimated in 1985 that SMEs needed at least RM10,000 million in bank loans, but it was recorded that less than RM300 million was available (see for instance, Lim 1988:122). Even then, this amount was reported not to have been properly distributed. Some of the loan went either to undeserving SMEs or even to large enterprises (ADB 1990). Lastly, the research noticed the existing policy programmes focused predominantly on the development of new Bumiputera enterprises, most of which were domestic-orientated businesses and which were mostly "saturated" such as food, furniture and handicraft industries. While, it is clear that the basic choice of policy programmes on SMEs rest on the wider interest of political judgement in a given specific socio-economic context of a country, continuing supports to these enterprises may be among the reasons for inefficiency in general terms of the net economic benefit to society. This is because as new enterprises enter the market, other less efficient or less subsidised enterprises are forced out. Since competition was strong in the domestic market, the profit margin was expectedly low and their mortality rates were high.

Policy Recommendations

In light of the above-mentioned weaknesses of the existing support programmes in the country, the research study stressed several elements which could potentially be given some consideration in the promotion of SMEs. Firstly, there is a need for more realistic objectives for the policy support programme over the medium and long term programmes among the various government and non-government agencies, with adequate financial resources. The boundaries of responsibility, priorities and targets should be clearly defined. Secondly, there is a need for the identification of potential areas of growth for destined for the domestic market and for exports. It was emphasised that in textile and clothing industry are among the sectors that should be given attention. Since the textile and clothing industry ranks second after electronic and electrical industry in terms of share of the total employment and manufacturing exports in the country, it is crucial to maintain and expand the potential market for its products. For more significant than its outstanding position was the predominance of the small and medium-scale nature of activities within this industry. The need for the government to establish a Research and Development Centre for the industry, as has been done for others such as Metal Industry Development Centre, Plastic Technology Centre and Foundry Technology Centre, was further emphasised.

Throughout this observation, it has been emphasised that policy supports for SMEs have to be selective in nature due to limited resources and the nature of SMEs which are numerous, geographically diverse, divided between a variety of different economic activities and heterogeneous in terms of their age, sex structure and social composition (see also in Bromley 1985). Indeed, it cannot be denied that this is a difficult issue when often in the wider interest of political influence, and those who are responsible for the development of SMEs, policy supplies are tied to biological characteristics such age, sex and ethnicity. To exclude people from public supports on these biological grounds poses a clear direction of discrimination. In this respect, the basic choice and objective of the government policy support for SMEs in the country should be explicitly directional, either to support and encourage successful enterprises or those which have the potential characteristics for success, or to support those enterprises that are not doing so well or have "potentially" disadvantageous characteristics.

Observing the trend of government support programmes since the 1970s when the significance of promoting the development of SMEs was re-stated under the New Economic Policy (1970-1990), the focus has been predominantly on the development of new Bumiputera enterprises most of which are small-scale operations and domestic-orientated businesses in industries such as food processing and handicrafts which are mostly saturated. Competition is strong in the domestic market for the sale of products which these enterprises seek to produce. Moreover, the profit margins of these SMEs is low and their mortality rates are high. Therefore, the objective and focus of government policy programmes in the past two decades has been to support SMEs which were not doing so well or have potentially disadvantageous characteristics. The implication of such supports may be that the net benefit to society of these new and small-medium enterprises is low because as new firms enter the market, other less efficient or less subsidised enterprises are forced out. Those who fail often lose their land or the few assets they posses in the process. The creation of further new businesses in such low technology, easy entry activities such as food processing and handicraft production generally does not lead to a net increase in employment because demand for their products is income inelastic and grows slowly. However, the implication of policy programmes on the development of SMEs may be different if a re-direction of support resources and services to new business venture concentrating on areas with growth potential in the manufacturing services and other sectors. At present, there are a few of the "on-going" support programmes which concentrate on nurturing and developing such relatively successful SMEs so that they may move up the ladder into the next firm-size category under the New Development Policy for the year 1990-2020 (see for instance MITI 1990 and ADB 1990).

Based upon our findings and in view of the need for policy supports for successful SMEs or those which have potential characteristics of success, the focus predominantly on the development of new Bumiputera enterprises has to be re-considered with respect to other entrepreneurs as well. In this respect, one may argue that the Chinese owner/managers who have shown relatively better success as compared to their Malay and Indian counterparts, are deserved to be given "a priori" attention by support programmes. This is due to the net benefit and scale of economies in terms of the broader utilisation of public resources that may form the basic progress in the overall development of SMEs in the country. However, there may be reasons as to why Chinese entrepreneurs are more successful than their Malay and Indian counterparts. Besides, business exposure and traditionally wider business-connections among Chinese business community in Malaysia as well as in the Southeast Asia, they are also able to raise their capital investments much higher to start off their businesses as compared to Malay and Indian entrepreneurs.

For example, further analysis on this issue shows that all 24 sampled enterprises (in the Case Study One) which have the value of fixed capital of RM60,000 and above, are found to be managed by Chinese entrepreneurs. In particular, low individualism, activism, trust and risk-taking, and high on conservatism among Malay entrepreneurs (as noted by Charlesworth, 1974:17) are also among the seasons why Malay entrepreneurs are less successful (see Moha Asri 1997b). Having noted the brief advantage and disadvantage positions of the owner/manager among the three main ethnic groups, consideration for policy supports may be more relevant if it is implemented within the wider context of the existing social composition (of the Malaysian society) and the country's need for the racial harmony in order to maintain and sustain its momentous economic development and progress. In this regard, the selection of support programmes for the entrepreneurs from one ethnic group should not necessarily deny access of others for the sake of the contribution of the existing "harmony-atmosphere" of the country in which the implementation of support programmes for SMEs may play its part in her rapid industrialisation process.

Specifically, based on our findings too, and if the choice of the government policy supports is to assist enterprises that have potential characteristics for success, aspects of sex and educational level of the entrepreneurs, should not be considered as priorities in assisting SMEs since our research has proven that they have no influence on the success of the individual SMEs (see Moha Asri 1993). Nevertheless, some consideration should be given to the age and experience of the owners/managers and the enterprises which practice a regularly written business plan. In particular, the relatively younger entrepreneurs, but with more experience either in general business or in the same industry as well as the use of a regularly written business plan in their operations may be accountable for such consideration. This is due to the fact that SMEs are likely to have the technical and managerial capacity to produce and market products that cannot be expected to come from the relatively inexperienced entrepreneurs but from those with "sound business experience" and technical skills as well as the requisite access to capital resources with a greater vision for international markets.

Fourthly, the study noted that the approach of private agencies and commercial banks appear to be rather passive. Commercial banks for instance, practised the policy of waiting for clients to approach them with investment loan proposals. Thus, there is scope for these banks to adopt a marketing-orientated approach in dealing with SMEs. This approach, for instance, would involve the banks undertaking market research on selected growth industries and then directly approaching some of their existing clients. This would be desirable particularly for existing clients who have good business records to discuss financial expansion programmes related to production for domestic and/or overseas market niches. By initiating this, the commercial banks would, hence, actively play an important role in the development of SMEs in the country. in this respect too, it is suggested that the cooperation of public and private agencies should also be further co-ordinated in terms of objectives, targets, types of SMEs involved, types of assistance etc.

Fifthly, the study appears to suggest that the ancillary role of SMEs to large enterprises in terms of inter-firm linkages could be further explored, not just within the same industry but across other industries and sectors of economic activity. The positive effects of inter-firm linkages on the development of the SMEs generally shown elsewhere have indeed provided very useful information for policy makers and those who are involved in the promotion of SMEs in the country (see Basok 1989, Evcimen, Melmet and Cinar 1991 and Moha Asri 1996). Further support programmes for more integrated linkages should be strengthened and enhanced, not merely in the textile and clothing industry but also in other industries and across sectors. Thus, potential backward and forward linkages should be fully realised especially when similar evidence has been proven elsewhere in developed countries such as Japan (Watanabe 1975) and NICs such as Hong Kong and Singapore (Ganesan 1982), Taiwan (Tsai 1991) and South Korea (Yoon 1991). In proposing support programmes for inter-firms linkages, several areas were suggested including: inputs and outputs, subcontracting works and putting-out systems.

Lastly, the study noted that consideration might also be given to subsidising space in industrial estates for SMEs. As the SMEs located in industrial sites were proven to be more successful (see Moha Asri 1993) many SMEs scattered outside industrial estates deserved to have a subsidise space in industrial estates. The prolonged preference of continuing support programme for large firms should at least partly be diverted to SMEs need.

Supports for SMEs in this respect could be intensified in view of the current evidence of high cost of developed industrial land in the country (see ADB 1990:36).

To conclude, although government policy supports were largely ineffective, a majority of SMEs in Malaysia demonstrated their ability to go into business and to survive without government support. This is clearly linked to the earlier findings that the support programmes were not currently a major factor determining the development of SMEs. Instead other aspects emerged as more critical. Nevertheless, it is possible to argue that survival is not sufficient especially for the country which is now poised to enter the ranks of the New Industrialised Country (NICs). This transitional period to NICs can be considerably distorted if inadequate attention is paid to the development of SMEs. What seems to be most important is growth and development of SMEs at the individual level which would form the base for widening and strengthening the domestic industrial-structure. There is indeed scope and ample evidence that many SMEs can increase their productivity and rate of growth substantially and new enterprises can be established in a number of product lines and sub-industries in the wake of the rapid industrialisation process in the country. If government policies were more favourable and if adequate financing, technical assistance, extension and advisory services as well as infrastructure supports were made readily and cheaply available, a more prosperous growth and development of individual SMEs could be achieved.

Appendix I

LIST OF PROMOTED ACTIVITIES AND PROMOTED PRODUCTS

Agricultural Production

(1)   Cultivation of cocoa, coffee or tea
(2)   Cultivation of fruits
(3)   Cultivation of vegetables, tubers or roots
(4)   Cultivation of cereals
(5)   Cultivation of herbs or spices
(6)   Cultivation of essential oil crops
(7)   Production of planting materials
(8)   Cultivation of medicinal plants
(9)   Cultivation of fodder crops or animal feed ingredients
(10)   Cultivation of tobacco
(11)   Floriculture
(12)   Sericulture
(13)   Apiculture
(14)   Livestock farming
(15)   Spawning, breeding or culturing of aquatic products
(16)   Off-shore fishing
(17)   Any other agricultural activity, except planting of rubber, oil palm and coconut

Integrated Agriculture

(1)   Cultivation and processing of cocoa, coffee or tea
(2)   Cultivation and processing of fruits
(3)   Cultivation and processing of vegetables, tubers or roots
(4)   Cultivation and processing of cereals
(5)   Cultivation and processing of herbs or spices
(6)   Cultivation and processing of essential oil crops
(7)   Cultivation and processing of medicinal plants
(8)   Cultivation and processing of fodder crops or animal feed ingredients
(9)   Cultivation of tobacco and curing of tobacco
(10)   Floriculture and packaging or processing of its produce
(11)   Sericulture and processing of its produce
(12)   Apiculture and processing of its produce
(13)   Breeding and rearing of livestock and processing of livestock and livestock products
(14)   Spawning, breeding or culturing and processing of aquatic products
(15)   Off-shore fishing and processing of its produce

The list of promoted activities and promoted products is gazetted under Gazatte Notification No. P.U. (A) 391 dated November, 1986.

Agricultural Processing

(1)   Cocoa and cocoa products
(2)   Coffee
(3)   Tea
(4)   High fructose syrup
(5)   Coconut products except copra and crude coconut oil
(6)   Fruits
(7)   Vegetables
(8)   Cereal products
(9)   Starch and proteins
(10)   Herbs or spices
(11)   Essential oils
(12)   Fodder or other animals feed ingredients
(13)   Tobacco
(14)   Flowers or ornamental foliages

(15) Honey
(16) Meat
(17) Livestock products
(18) Aquatic products, including seaweed
(19) Agricultural waste and by products
(20) Sugar
(21) Aquaculture feed

Forestry and Forestry Products

(1) Reafforestation
(2) Forestry products
(3) Rattan products
(4) Basketware and other rattan products
(5) Bamboo products

Manufacture of Rubber Products

(1) Tyres, all types
(2) Retreading of aircraft tyres
(3) Tubes
(4) Precured retreads
(5) Moulded rubber products
(6) Latex dipped products
(7) Extruded rubber products
(8) General rubber goods
(9) Foam rubber products
(10) Rubberised fabrics
(11) Inflatable rubber products
(12) Conveyor belts, transmission belts, V-type belts and other rubber belting
(13) Engineering components of rubber (e.g. building mounts, anti-vibration mounts)
(14) Reclaimed rubber
(15) Rubber compound
(16) Rubber-based (elastomeric) specialty coating

Manufacture of Palm and Palm Kernel Oil Products and Their Derivatives

(1) Fatty acids and their derivatives, fatty esters and their derivatives inclusive of metallic esters, fatty alchohols and their derivatives, fatty amines and their derivatives and glycerine (crude and refined)

(2) Cocoa butter replacers (such as cocoa butter substitutes, cocoa butter alternatives, cocoa butter modifiers cocoa butter equivalents); palm oil mid fraction, special olein II and special olein III

(3) Margarine, vanaspati, shortening and other manufacturing fat products

(4) Crude palm kernel olein and stearin, neutralised or refined and bleached palm kernel olein and stearin and neutralised or refined, bleached and deodorised palm kernel olein and stearin

(5) Hydrogenated and/or interesterified oils and oil blends, all types

(6) Crude palm kernel oil

(7) Refined palm oil

(8) Neutralised palm kernel oil

(9) Refined, bleached and deodorised palm kernel oil

(10) Palm kernel meal

Manufacture of Chemicals and Pharmaceuticals

(1) Chemical derivatives obtained from methyl and ethyl alcohol

(2) Plant and vegetable extracts for pharmaceutical, perfumery, cosmetics and food flavouring industries

(3) Antibiotics

(4) Basic manufacture of pharmaceutical

(5) Basic manufacture of fertilisers

(6) Basic manufacture of pesticides

(7) Chemical intermediates derived from petroleum, natural gas or coal

(8) Fine chemicals

(9) Animal vaccine and clinical diagnostic reagents

(10) 2, 4-DiCholoro Pheyln Acetic Acids, Methyl Chloro Phenyl Acetic Acids

(11) Synthesised raw materials for advanced ceramic

(12) Specialised paints and coatings

(13) Common salt

(14)   Soap, cleaning preparations, cosmetics and other toilet preparations
(15)   Chemical derivatives from inorganic sources
(16)   Recycling of chemicals and plastic wastes
(17)   Injections, sterile solutions and gelatin capsules
(18)   Carbon black master batch
(19)   Industrial gases, whether compressed, liquefied or in solid state
(20)   Chemical for fire extinguishers
(21)   Fertilisers

Manufacture of Leather and Leather Products

(1)   Tannery
(2)   Leather products

Manufacture of Wood and Wood Products

(1)   Integrated timber complex
(2)   Plywood, fancy plywood, prefinished and printed plywood
(3)   Building and insulating boards, such as blockboards, laminated board, batten board, medium density board, soft board, hard board, wafer board, lamin board, particle board and chipboard
(4)   Timber mouldings, all type
(5)   Prefabricated housing units and components
(6)   Wooden cabinets for electrical or electronic products
(7)   Builders carpentry and joinery, assembled parquet flooring panels
(8)   Wooden staircases
(9)   Wooden doors and windows
(10)   Products derived from utilisation of wood waste (e.g. activated charcoal, wooden briquettes, wood wool)
(11)   Wood pellets
(12)   Article of turned wood
(13)   Rubberwood veneer

Manufacture of Pulp, Paper and Paperboard

(1)   Pulp
(2)   Newsprint

(3)   Printing and writing paper
(4)   Security paper
(5)   Household and sanitary paper
(6)   Wrapping and packaging paper and board
(7)   Linerboard
(8)   Kraft liner
(9)   Fluting medium
(10)   Sack kraft
(11)   Folding boxboard
(12)   Other paper and paper board

Manufacture of Textiles and Textiles Products

(1)   Man-made fibre, all types excluding polyester staple fibre
(2)   Silk, silk yarn and fabrics of silk
(3)   Continuous yarn or filament yarn of man-made fibres
(4)   Woven fabrics of higher counts
(5)   Special fabrics for upholstery and furnishing fabrics '
(6)   Commission dyeing, bleaching, printing and finishing facilities of high standard for yarn and fibre
(7)   Cord fabrics including tyre-cord fabrics
(8)   High quality made-up garments and made-up textile articles
(9)   Made-up garments
(10)   Natural fibre
(11)   Batik printing
(12)   Knitted fabrics
(13)   Accessories for the textile industry

Manufacture of Clay and Sand-based Products and Other Non-metallic Mineral Products

(1)   High grade processed kaolin
(2)   High grade processed ball clay
(3)   High alumina and basic refractories
(4)   Kiln furniture refractories
(5)   Laboratory, chemical or industrial wares
(6)   Ceramic artware, ornaments and articles for adornment
(7)   Medium and high tension porcelain insulators

(8)   High grade silica sand and powder
(9)   Glass inners for vacuum flasks or for other vacuum vessels
(10)   Decorative glass and glassware
(11)   Glass ornaments and articles of adornment
(12)   High tension electrical glass insulators
(13)   Bricks, tiles, slabs, paving block, squares and other articles of pressed or moulded glass used in building
(14)   Mirrors
(15)   Glass envelopes (including bulbs and tubes) for electrical lamps, electric valves or the like
(16)   Glass fittings for lighting purpose
(17)   Sand lime bricks
(18)   Glass pellets
(19)   Glass fibres (staples and continuous) for reinforcement and textiles, produced from basic raw materials.
(20)   Polished slabs of locally sourced marbles and granite.
(21)   Panels, boards, tiles, blocks and similar articles of vegetable fibre, wood fibre, straw, wood shavings or wood wastes, agglomerated with cement plaster or with other mineral binding substances.
(22)   Cellular concrete blocks and panels
(23)   Rice-husk ash cement
(24)   High quality calcium carbonate powder
(25)   Advanced ceramics and its derivatives
(26)   Ceramic floor tiles
(27)   Abrasive products for grinding, polishing and sharpening
(28)   Bricks
(29)   Prestressed spun concrete piles
(30)   Ceramic wall tiles
(31)   Vitrified clay pipes

Manufacture of Iron and Steel and Their Products

(1)   Pig iron, sponge iron and hot briquetted iron
(2)   Ingot, billet, bloom and slabs of all grades of steel
(3)   Bars and wire rods (except those of mild steel), angles, shapes and sections of all grades of steel either hot-rolled cold-rolled of cold-finished
(4)   Plates, sheets, coils, hoops and strips of all grades of steel either hot-rolled, cold-rolled, cold-finished, coated, or plated

(5)   Welded pipe, seamless pipe and pipe fittings of iron and steel including hydro-electric conduits
(6)   Wire and wire products of iron and steel
(7)   Cans and drums of iron and steel
(8)   Steel fabricated products
(9)   Steel structures
(10)   Gas cookers

Manufacture of Non-ferrous Metals and Their Products

(1)   Dressing and smelting of non-ferrous metals
(2)   Ingots, billet and slabs of non-ferrous metals
(3)   Bards, rods, shapes and sections of non-ferrous metals
(4)   Plates, sheets, coils, hoops and strips of non-ferrous metals
(5)   Pipes and tubes of non-ferrous metals
(6)   Wire and wire products of non-ferrous metals
(7)   Cans and drums of non-ferrous metals
(8)   Fabricated products non-ferrous metals
(9)   Powder of non-ferrous metals

Manufacture of Machinery and Machinery Components

(1)   Industrial processing machinery
(2)   Agricultural machinery and equipment
(3)   Mining and mineral processing machinery including equipment for oil and gas exploration and extraction
(4)   Power generation machinery
(5)   Material handling equipment
(6)   Industry machinery and equipment including engines, motors, generators, compressors, welding equipment, fans and blowers
(7)   Machine tools
(8)   Machinery components including ball bearings, valves, pumps, gears and gear boxes, couplings and mechanical seals
(9)   Duplicating machines
(10)   Typewriters, all types
(11)   Construction machinery and parts thereof
(12)   Automatic gate systems, burglar alarm systems and parts thereof

Supporting Products/Services

(1) Iron and steel castings
(2) Iron and steel forgings
(3) Precision machining
(4) Precision stamping
(5) Precision electroplating
(6) Moulds, tools and dies
(7) Non-ferrous metal castings
(8) Non-ferrous metal forgings
(9) Galvanising shearing and slitting of metal sheets and other related engineering services

Manufacture of Handtools

(1) Handtools, all types (such as axes, pliers, spanners, screwdrivers, wrenches, hammers, pincers, riveting tools and other handtools)

Manufacture of Motor Vehicles, Components and Accessories

(1) Manufacture of motorised vehicles
(2) Engines of all types and their parts
(3) Transmissions, final drives and wheels of all types, including their parts
(4) Chassis bodies including fuel tanks and their parts
(5) Suspension systems, stablising system and their parts
(6) Electrical or electronics systems, instrumentation and their parts
(7) Fuel systems, braking systems, ignition systems, steering systems, cooling system, ignition systems, steering systems, cooling systems, air-inlet systems, exhaust systems, and engine-starting systems and their parts
(8) Any other automotive component and accessories

Manufacture of Other Transport Equipment

(1) Non-motorised vehicles such as bicycles, tricyles and gliders
(2) Locomotives, coaches, wagons and their parts

(3)   Pleasure crafts, hydrofoils, hovercrafts and their parts
(4)   Aeroplanes, helicopters and their parts
(5)   Any other type of transport equipment

Manufacture of Electrical and Electronic Products and Components and Parts Thereof

(1)   Colour television receivers and parts thereof
(2)   Audio or video cassette recorders or players and part thereof
(3)   Tuners
(4)   Computers, computer peripherals and parts thereof
(5)   CAD, CAM or CAE equipment and parts thereof
(6)   Controllers, all types
(7)   Modems
(8)   Telephones including cellular radios, walkie-talkies
(9)   Telecommunications equipment and parts thereof
(10)   Intercoms
(11)   Optical fibre products and parts thereof
(12)   Counters
(13)   Piezoelectric frequency units
(14)   Voice and data synthesis equipment
(15)   Earphones
(16)   Hearing aids
(17)   Microphones
(18)   Smoke detectors, fire alarms, electronic counters
(19)   Automatic fare collection machines
(20)   Automatic traffic control equipment
(21)   Automatic vending machines
(22)   Automatic parking meters
(23)   Automatic teller machines
(24)   Computing scales
(25)   Cash registers
(26)   Telemetering requipment
(27)   Telex machines
(28)   Photocopying machines and parts thereof
(29)   Robots and robotics
(30)   Electrical lawn mowers
(31)   Ovens
(32)   Washing machines and parts thereof

(33)	Vacuum cleaners and parts thereof
(34)	Floor polishers
(35)	Shavers
(36)	Hair dryers
(37)	Decorative lights
(38)	Industrial furnace and parts thereof
(39)	Button cells
(40)	Rechargeable cells or batteries
(41)	Dischargeable tubes
(42)	Antennae
(43)	Speakers
(44)	Microswitches
(45)	Power supplies
(46)	Quartz crystals
(47)	Sensors and transducers
(48)	Solar cells
(49)	Motors, all types
(50)	Relays
(51)	Resistors
(52)	Capacitors
(53)	Printed circuit boards
(54)	Printed circuit board connectors and parts thereof
(55)	Charge-couple devices
(56)	Displays - electroluminescent plasma, liquid crystal
(57)	Ceramic substrates or packages
(58)	High density memory storage media
(59)	Gold and aluminium bonding wires
(60)	Headers and cans
(61)	Lead-frames
(62)	Magnets or ferrite cores
(63)	Semiconductor, water fabrication integrated circuit design
(64)	Semiconductor, all types
(65)	Semiconductor testings, all types
(66)	Electronic modules
(67)	Magnetic heads
(68)	Magnetic webs and pancakes
(69)	Static convertors
(70)	Compressors for refrigerators
(71)	Wire harnesses
(72)	Timer switches

(73)   Thermostat
(74)   Power tools
(75)   Electric door bell
(76)   Protective switchgear and parts thereof
(77)   Electric cookers
(78)   Electric rice cookers
(79)   Video cassette tapes and cassette casings
(80)   Quart blanks
(81)   Silicon wafers
(82)   Computer diskettes
(83)   Electric fans
(84)   Air conditioners, components, parts and accessories
(85)   Transistor radio
(86)   Compressors for air conditioners
(87)   Wireless coded door bell
(88)   Solar powered outdoor lights
(89)   Digital encoder
(90)   Digital decoder
(91)   Audio cassette tapes
(92)   Jigs and fixtures
(93)   Compact disc players and parts thereof
(94)   Silicon elastomer switches (key pads) for electrical and electronic instruments/appliances
(95)   Steam iron
(96)   Flat type PVC elevator cables
(97)   Fire resistant cables

Manufacture of Professional, Medical, Scientific, Measuring Equipment and Components and Parts Thereof

(1)   Medical, surgical, dental, veterinary, instruments and equipment and parts thereof, all types
(2)   Scientific gauges and measuring apparatus, all types
(3)   Surveying, hydrograhic, navigational, meteorological, hydrological, geophysical instruments and parts thereof, all types
(4)   Testing equipment and parts thereof, all types
(5)   Meters - gas, liquid or electric measuring

Manufacture of Photographic, Cinematographic, Video and Optical Goods and Components

(1)   Cameras and accessories, all types
(2)   Projectors, all types
(3)   Sound recorders and reproducers
(4)   Lenses
(5)   Films-unexposed
(6)   Binoculars
(7)   Telescopes, magnifying glasses and microscopes
(8)   Cinematographic and video equipment
(9)   Any other photography apparatus and accessories
(10)   Semiconductor photolithographic equipment

Film Industry

(1)   Film and video production
(2)   Expansion/modernisation of film and video production
(3)   Post production for film and video
(4)   Expansion/Modernisation of post-production for film and video

Manufacture of Clocks, Watches and Components

(1)   Clocks and watches, all types
(2)   Parts for clocks and watches

Manufacture of Musical Instruments and Components

(1)   Musical instruments and parts, all types

Manufacture of Kitchenware

(1)   Kitchenware, all types
(2)   Cutlery
(3)   Tableware

Manufacture of Furniture

(1)　　Furniture, all types

Manufacture of Souvenirs and Handicrafts

(1)　　Souvenirs, handicrafts and giftware, all types

Manufacture of Educational Objects

(1)　　Educational objects, all types

Manufacture of Toys

(1)　　Toys, all types

Manufacture of Footwear

(1)　　Footwear, all types

Manufacture of Sports Goods and Equipment

(1)　　Sport goods and equipment, all types

Manufacture of Jewellery and Related Products

(1)　　Jewellery
(2)　　Processed gems

Hotel Business and Tourist Industry

(1)　　Establishment of hotel
(2)　　Expansion/Modernisation/Renovation of hotel

(3)   Establishment of tourist project
(4)   Expansion/Modernisation of tourist project

Miscellaneous

(1)   Photo album
(2)   Stationery
(3)   Wax products
(4)   Barbecue charcoal set
(5)   Arms and ammunition and part thereof
(6)   Name plate and sign plate, all types
(7)   Art and design apparatus, all types

Manufacture of Fire Fighting and Detection Systems and Parts Thereof

(1)   Fire fighting and detection systems and parts thereof

Manufacture of Plastic Products

(1)   Expanded polystyrene sheets
(2)   Plastic products for building and construction
(3)   Plastic product for electric, electronics and telecommunications industry
(4)   Plastic products for medical and veterinary use
(5)   Plastic products for engineering use
(6)   Magnetic and non-magnetic cards
(7)   Plastic pellets
(8)   PU foam mattresses and cushions
(9)   Plastic tarpaulin
(10) Plastic packing products

Appendix II

Measuring the Indicators of Success, Resultant Computation and the Correlation Matrix Between the Three Indicators of Success

An Example of Measuring the Indicators of the Success for Enterprise I

a) The change in the annual index[1] of the net profit before tax for the Firm I is:

Year	Deflated Value of Net Profit	Index	Cumulative Change
1991	4,777.13	100.0	-
1992	17,734.56	371.2	271.2
1993	25,938.31	146.3	46.3
1994	30,832.64	118.9	18.9
1995	48,268.98	156.6	56.6
			393.0

Therefore the average change in the annual index of the net profit before tax is 78.6 percent (393.0 divided by 5).

---

[1] The construction of an index number can be seen in most statistical texts. Among those to mention are: i) G. Bancroft and G. O'Sullivan 1988, *Maths and Statistics for Accounting and Business Studies*, McGraw-Hill Book Company: London, pp. 155-167; ii) T. Wonnacott and R. Wonnacott 1990, *Introductory Statistics for Business and Economics*, (Fourth Edition), J. Wiley and Sons: New York, pp. 664-677; iii) R. Hammond and P. S. McCullagh 1982, *Quantitative Techniques in Geography*, Clarendon Press: Oxford, pp. 86-110; iv) L. Kazmier and G. Pohl 1987, *Basic Statistics for Business and Economics*, McGraw-Hill Book Company, New York.

Procedure Used to Calculate Net Profit before Tax

Net profit before tax is calculated using the annual operating profit, i.e. the year's total sales (income/revenue) minus the year's total costs (the year's cost of raw materials and services used, wages, depreciation and interest foregone). Services included electricity, water, transportation rent for hired equipments, premises etc. (if any), cost of necessary repair, advertisement etc. Wages include the year's total salary paid to the owner /manager and all employees involved in the establishment. Depreciation is computed on the basis of a remaining economic life expectancy (Malaysian Standard) of five years for machinery, equipment, vehicles, furniture, fixture etc. and 20 years for building and plants. Interest rate is measured on the basis of individual enterprise's borrowing from particular bank/financial institutions that charges differently, according to the amount of lending as detailed in Chapter Three. The reasons for using the annual operating profit as a basis for the operational definition in the present research are due to several factors as follows: i) it may monitor more precisely the progress of individual enterprises annually, ii) it is a much more practical way to measure profit when this calculation is made at a single point in time, and iii) it is made with the sole objective of comparability with the balance-sheets of some sampled enterprises that had been using private consultants for their financial reports (especially in auditing). It is essential to note that all the values (of fixed assets, paid up capital and net profit before tax) are at 1980 prices, used as the based year. This is done by applying the official consumer price index and deflating current prices so as to make them comparable to the based-year-price. (Annual growth rate of the country's consumer prices and/or consumer price index from 1991 to 1995 as well as deflator value are shown in this Appendix below.)

b) The change in the rate of return on paid up capital for ENTERPRISE I

Year	Deflated Value of Net Profit	Index	Cumulative Change
1991	59,194.95	7.5	-
1992	58,049.54	30.0	22.5
1993	70,046.44	37.0	29.5
1994	67,942.94	45.4	37.9
1995	66,058.395	52.7	45.2
			135.1

Therefore, the average change in the rate of return on paid up capital is 27.0 percent.

Procedure Used to Calculate the Annual Rate of Return

The annual rate of return on paid up capital is calculated using a common accounting procedure, i.e.:

$$Rt = \frac{P}{K} \times 100$$

where, Rt = Rate of Return
P = The Value of Net of Profit Before Tax
K = The Value of Total Paid up Capital.

Paid up Capital in the study is considered on a yearly continuing basis in the enterprise's activities. These include: i) intangible assets - development and management costs, concessions, licences, and any payment on account for intangible assets, ii) tangible assets - land and buildings, plant and machinery, fixtures, fittings, tools and equipments, assets in course of construction and any payment on account for tangible assets, and iii) investments - shares in and loans to other banks or finance institutions or companies.

c) The change in the annual index of the number of full-time employees for ENTERPRISE I

Year	Number of Employee	Index	Cumulative Index
1991	9	100.0	-
1992	11	122.2	22.2
1993	11	122.2	22.2
1994	13	144.4	44.4
1995	16	177.8	<u>77.8</u>
			<u>166.6</u>

The average change in annual index of the number of full-time employee is 33.3 percent.

The Resultant Computation of Individual Enterprises for the Three Indicators

Table 1   The Distribution of Enterprises by the Average Change in the Annual Cumulative Index of Net Profit Before Tax Between 1991 and 1995

The Average Change of Index	Percent
-5.0 to less than 0.0 percent	2.0
0.0 to less than 5.0 percent	25.5
5.0 to less than 10.0 percent	35.3
10.0 to less than 15.0 percent	9.8
15.0 to less than 20.0 percent	9.8
20.0 to less than 25.0 percent	7.8
25.0 percent and above	9.8
TOTAL	100(51)

Table 2   The Distribution of Enterprises by the Average Change in the Annual Cumulative Rate of Return on Paid up Capital Between 1991 and 1995

The Average Change of Index	Percent
-5.0 to less than 0.0 percent	2.0
0.0 to less than 5.0 percent	35.3
5.0 to less than 10.0 percent	13.7
10.0 to less than 15.0 percent	3.9
15.0 to less than 20.0 percent	11.8
20.0 to less than 25.0 percent	9.8
25.0 percent and above	23.5
TOTAL	100(51)

207

Table 3   The Distribution of enterprises by the Average Change in the
           Annual Cumulative Index of the Number of Employees Paid up
           Capital Between 1991 and 1995

The Average Change of Index	Percent
-0.5 to less than 0.0 percent	7.8
0.0 to less than 5.0 percent	60.8
5.0 to less than 10.0 percent	19.6
10.0 to less than 15.0 percent	3.9
15.0 to less than 20.0 percent	5.9
20.0 to less than 25.0 percent	2.0
25.0 percent and above	-
TOTAL	100(51)

Correlation Matrix Between the Three Indicators of Success

Based on a full computation of the indicators for ENTERPRISE I as an example of the method of calculation above, together with the resultant computation the three indicators for individual enterprises, these three indicators were initially analysed using a correlation matrix (part of statistical option in SPSS) to examine whether there is any positive relationship among them. The findings are shown in Table 4.

Table 4   Correlation Matrix Between the Three Indicators of Success

Correlation Matrix of the Indicators	Net Profit	Paid up Capital	Employment
Net profit	1.00000		
Paid up capital	.68719	1.00000	
Employment	.61525	.57615	1.00000

Notes: *Profit = The average change in the annual index of the net profit before tax.*
       Capital = The average change in the annual rate of return on paid up capital.
       Employment = The average change in the annual index of number of employees.

It is observed that the pairwise coefficient correlation matrix between them are indeed very high, comprising more than 0.5000, particularly between the profit and capital indicators which accounted for 0.68719. It strongly suggests that the three indicators have a close association implying that an increase in the profit and capital indexes are also likely to be associated with an increase in the employment index. In addition, Table 5 shows a final statistical matrix of approximately 75.1 percent of the total variance of the three indicators, illustrating further validification of a strong relationship among them.

Table 5   Final Statistics of the Factor Analysis for the Total Percentage Variance in the Matrix Solution

Variable	Communality	Factor	Eigenvalue	Percentage of Variance
Profit	.79092	1	2.25354	75.1
Capital	.87247			
Employment	.83750			

Notes: *Profit = The average change in the annual index of the net profit before tax.*
Capital = The average change in the annual rate of return on paid up capital.
Employment = The average change in the annual index of number of employees.

Appendix III

The Degree of Success of the Sampled Enterprises

The main problem in categorising the degree of success of SMEs is that there has been no standard procedure to quantify the concept of business success. There has been no consensus on what the dividing line is by which SMEs should be categorised as less successful and more successful (Foley 1987, Blackburn 1987, Andersson 1987, etc). It is a subjective issue that is often open to criticism. In view of this difficulty, it is not surprising that many of the research methodological texts tends to indicate that a conceptual and/or operational definition of variable, though it is very essential part, it does not necessarily accurate/true[1]. This is clearly illustrated by Judd, Smith and Kidden as:

> Operational definition are never completely adequate. They are necessary but rarely seem sufficient to capture the rich and complex ideas contained in a theoretical construction. The beauty of an operational definition is that it specifies precisely how to measure a variable on such a concrete and specific manner... (1991:43)

This may be among the reasons why many researchers measure a variable in different ways such as rating scales etc. for quantifying judgments, especially in psychology, sociology and economics (Howard and Sharp 1983:99-120). However, it is important to be aware that the above views are reliant upon the use of precise and concrete measurement, appropriately conceptualised and based on evidence elsewhere (if any). As

---

[1] Nachmias and Nachmias 1981, *Research Methods in the Social Sciences*, Edward Arnold: London, state that there is no point in criticising a conceptual definition for not being accurate and/or less accurate if it is used consistently throughout a research study. A similar view is shared by Babbie (1992) who points out that it does not have to be agreed or even pretend to agree that a particular specification may be worth using in conceptualising the variable. See also in E. Babbie 1991, *The Practice of Social Research*, Wadsworth Publishing Company: California, (p.118).

there has been no concensus on the degree of success that should be applied, it may be useful to observe some evidence with respect to studies on SMEs.

In describing the profitability rate averaged over a four-year period (from 1975/76 to 1978/79), Storey, Keasey, Watson and Wynarczyk (1987: 28-30) note that the 590 firms under the Industrial and Commercial Finance Corporation (ICFC) have a relatively better performance with an overall profitability mean of 15.9 percent as compared to 8.5 percent for 373 Northern independent manufacturers over the same period. However, they did not categorically mention the border line of what is defined as a more or less successful category for the individual performance of enterprises.

From an extensive search of the literature of SMEs, it is found that there are some studies previously conducted in Malaysia. In a study of small and medium-sized businesses in the Malaysian manufacturing sector, Lam (1989:45-49), for example, used a composite index to measure growth based on the performance of business over a five year period (1981-1985) in terms of increase in net profit, paid up capital and fixed assets. Any firm which had performed below than 10 percent performance index was categorised as a poor performance firm while 10 percent and/or above the performance index was classified as good performance. This is seen to have been similar to a measurement adopted by Aziz (1981) previously. Both studies, unfortunately, did not give any reason why a 10 percent performance index was used as a cut off point. The Survey Research Malaysia Ltd. (SRM - 1991)[2] conducted a study of 13,992 small enterprises across Malaysia. This survey noted that enterprises which had increased their value added from 0 to 25 percent were classified as lower profit margin enterprises while those which managed to achieve more than 25 percent of value added as higher profit margin enterprises.

Perhaps the most useful information in considering the merit and demerit of the growth-performance of the enterprises in the sample is by observing official statistics (from the National Productivity Centre) relating to the overall performance of the same industry, i.e. textile and clothing industry in Malaysia over a decade or so[3]. It is recorded that between 1980 and 1985, the textile and clothing industry achieved an

---

[2] This study was commissioned by the Small-scale Enterprise Division at Ministry of International Trade and Industry which was conducted in 1989.

[3] See the National Productivity Centre (NPC) 1991, Seminar on Productivity Measurement and Improvement in the Textile and Wearing Apparel, Petaling Jaya: Selangor, (1st October 1991). All figures were calculated on the basis of 1991 prices.

annual average growth rate of real added value of about 10.5 percent. The figure increased to 20.9 during the period 1985-1988.[4] This is found to be exceedingly higher than the overall figures for the manufacturing sector which is 4.7 percent during the same period (1985-1988). In addition, the real value of gross output is also reported to be high. During the period 1980-1985, this industry experienced an annual rate of 8.9 percent which increased to 19.6 percent for the period of 1985-1988. Meanwhile, it is also recorded that the annual growth rate of the number of employees in this industry was 5.3 percent between 1985 and 1988.

Bearing this in mind and looking at Tables 3, 4 and 5 in section C of the Appendix II, it is calculated the mean for the profit and capital indicator is 10.7 percent and 12.9 percent per enterprise respectively. Meanwhile the mean of the increase in the index of the size employment is 4.8 percent enterprise. Observing evidence in the previous studies and the annual growth rate recorded in official statistics of the same industry in the country as well as considering the mean for each indicator, the study classified the sampled enterprises into two categories of success, i.e. the less successful and the more successful categories of the sampled enterprises.

Table 1 The Distribution of the Enterprises by the Degree of Success in Terms of the Increase in the Annual Index of Net Profit Before Tax (1991-1995)

The Average Increase in Annual Index of the Net Profit Before Tax	Percent	The Degree of Success
-5.0 to less than 10.0	62.7	Less Successful
10.0 percent and above	37.3	More Successful
Total	100(51)	Two Categories

---

4 See NPC 1991 in Appendix II - 'Productivity indicators for textile and wearing apparel (clothing) industry for the period of 1975 - 1988' (pp.1-3).

Table 2 The Distribution of the Enterprises by the Degree of Success in Terms of the Annual Increase in the Rate of Return on Paid up Capital (1991-1995)

The Average Increase in Annual Rate of Return on Paid up Capital	Percent	The Degree of Success
-5.0 to less than 10.0	54.9	Less Successful
10.0 percent and above	45.1	More Successful
Total	100(51)	Two Categories

Table 3 The distribution of the Enterprises by the Degree of Success in Terms of the Increase In the Annual Index of the Number of Employees (1991-1995)

The Average Increase in the Number of Employees	Percent	The Degree of Success
-5.0 to less than 5.0	68.6	Less Successful
10.0 percent and above	31.4	More Successful
Total	100(51)	Two Categories

Corresponding to the inconclusive discussion on the merit of categorising the degree of success of SMEs, the research advances some explanations as to why a cut off line of 10 percent is applied for profit and capital indicators and 5 percent for employment indicator. Firstly, the level of 10 percent is adopted for the profit and capital indicators recognising that the textile and clothing industry in Malaysia has generally shown a high average annual growth rate over the last decade or so, as compared to other industries in the manufacturing sector in the country (see Malaysia 1991 and 1996). This coincides with the average annual increment index in our sample. These two indicators are also found to be very closely integrated (see Table 6 of section D in Appendix II) as compared to the employment indicator. Meanwhile, the level of 5 percent is applied for the employment indicator because of average growth rate of 5.3 percent of growth workers in the same sector in the country.

Secondly, it could be expected that the enterprises which have reached a 10 percent annual increase (of index) in profit and capital and 5 percent in employment, are likely to survive much longer in the future. In addition, evidence revealed by Storey, Keasey, Watson and Wynarczyk (1987:125-127)[5], it is essentially based upon the assumption that even during the difficult years (recession of the country from 1985 to 1986)[6] this industry had gained a steady and outstanding annual growth rates of gross (real) value outputs, added (real) value, number of workers etc, unlike other industries in manufacturing sector. Thirdly, it is also decided that the enterprises with 10 percent or more annual increase in profit and capital and 5 percent or more annual increase for employment are the more successful enterprises because these percentages are the closest to the mean per enterprise of each indicator which gives a more practical and balanced pattern of the distribution among the enterprises in our sample in the analysis.

Fourthly, it should be noted that a less successful enterprise is deemed such only in the context of comparison with the more successful enterprise in the sample. Lastly, this research study recognises that the percentage index above can be transformed into a more complex mathematical calculation for categorising a less and more successful enterprises. This is, however, less desirable in the study's context which attempts to reduce 'arbitrary figures'.

---

[5] They found that enterprises making positive levels of profit in the base year tended to be more persistent in terms of their profitability (p.125).

[6] It is recorded that Gross Domestic Products in 1985 was -1.0 percent, which the growth rate of manufacturing outputs was -3.8 percent before it was slightly recovered in 1987 (1.2 percent and 7.5 percent respectively, see i) Ministry of Finance 1986, *Economic Reports 1986/87*, Government printer: Kuala Lumpur, ii) Ministry of Finance 1987, *Economic Reports 1987/88*, Government Printer: Kuala Lumpur.

Bibliography

Abell D. and Hammond J. (1979), *Strategic Market Planning*, Prentice-Hall International Inc.: Englewood Cliffs, New Jersey.

Akerredolu-Ale O. (1975), *The underdevelopment of indigenous entrepreneurship in Nigeria*, Ibadan University: Nigeria.

Al-Quader A.S. (1985), *Making it on the Margins: An Analysis of the Performance, Growth and Potential of the Informal Sector in Dhaka*, Ann Arbor Film, University of Syracuse.

Amin A.T.N. (1982), *An Analysis of Labour Force and Industrial Organisation of the Informal Sector in Dacca*, Ann Arbor Film, University of Manitoba, Canada.

Allen L. (1973), 'Factor affecting the profitability of small firms' in *The Vital Majority*, Carson D. (ed.) U.S Small Business Administration, Washington D.C.

Anderson D. (1982),'Small industry in developing countries: a discussion of issues', *World Development*, Vol 10, No. 11 (November).

Andersson T. (1987), *Profit in Small Firms*, Avebury: Aldershot, England.

Anuwar Ali (1995), *Globalisasi pembangunan industri dan peranan pemerintah di Malaysia*, Penerbit UKM, Bangi.

Apibunyopas P. (1983), *An Analysis of the Small Rural Non-Farms in Thailand*, University Microfilms International, Ann Arbor

Aryee G. (1977), *Small-scale Manufacturing Activities: A study of the Interrelationships between the Formal and Informal Sectors in Kumasi, Ghana*, Geneva: ILO.

ASEAN Federation of Textile Industries (1991), *ASEAN Textile Directory '90*, Kelvin Printing Company: Singapore.

Asian Development Bank (1990), *Malaysia: Study on small and medium enterprises with special reference to technology development*, ADB. Kuala Lumpur.

Asian Development Bank (1990), *Malaysia: Study on small and medium enterprises with special reference to technology development*, Staff Working Paper, (April).

Asian Development Bank (1989), *Regional cooperation in technology ventures in small and medium industry*, ADB Seminar, (Sept 6-9): Seoul.

Ayata S. 1984, 'Capitalist subordination of household production. Carpet industry: Turkey' in Moser 1984b (op.cit).

Aziz A. (1981), *Malay Entrepreneurship: Problems in Development, A Comperative Empirical Analysis*, Heng Lee Press: Kuala Lumpur.

Babbie E. (1991), *The Practice of Social Research*, Wadsworth Publishing Company: California.

Bancroft G. and O'Sullivan G. (1988), *Maths and statistics for accounting and business studies*, McGraw-Hill Book Company: London.

Banerjee N. (1981), 'The Weaknest Link, *IDS Bulletin*, 12 (July).

Basok T. (1989), 'How useful is the "Petty Commodity Production" approach? Explaining the survival and success of small salvadorean urban enterprises in Costa Rica' *Labour, Capital and Society*, Vol 22 (1), April (pp. 42-64).

Berlinct M.T., Boyo J.M. and Cintra L.C. (1981), 'The urban informal sector and industrial development in a small city: The case of Campinas' in *The Urban informal sector of developing countries*, (ed.) Sethuraman S.V. ILO: Geneva.

Bernstien F. (1988), 'Capitalism and Petty-Bourgenous Production: Class Relations and Divisions of Labour' *Journal of Peasant Studies*, 15(2), January (pp.271-322).

Beza L. (1989), 'SME development financing services in Malawi: retrospect and prospective', *The Courier*, No. 115 (May-June) (pp. 80-84).

Bienefeld M.A. (1975), 'Informal Sector and Peripheral Capital: The Case of Tanzania', *Institute of Development Studies*, Bulletin 6.

Blincow M. (1986), 'Scavengers and recycling: A neglected domain of production', *Labour, Capital and Society*, 19 (1) April (pp.94-115).

Bose A.N. (1978), *Calcutta and Rural Bengal: Small Sector Symbiosis*, Calcutta: Minerva Associates.

Bromley R. (1978), 'Organisation, regulation and exploitation in the so-called "Urban Informal Sector", The street traders of Cali, Colombia', *World Development*, Vol. 6 (9/10).

_____ (1985), *Planning for small enterprises in Third World World cities*, Pergamon Press: Oxford.

Broom H. (1971), *Small Business Management*, South-Western Publishing Company: New York..

Byrman A. and Cramer D. (1990), *Quantitative Data Analysis for Social Scientists*, Routledge: London.

Chapham R. (1982), *Small and Medium Enterprises in South East Asia*, Institute of Southeast Asian Studies: Singapore.

Charlesworth H.K. (1974), *Increasing number of Bumiputra entrepreneurs*, MARA Institute of Technology: Kuala Lumpur.

Charlesworth H. (1974), *Increasing the Supply of Bumiputra entrepreneurs*, Research Report, MARA Institute of Technology, Selangor.

Chee L.P. (1987), *Industrial development: An introduction to the Malaysian Industrial Master Plan*, Pelanduk Publications: Petaling Jaya.

_____ (1979), *A Study of Small Entrepreneurs and Entrepreneurial Development Programmes in Malaysia*, University of Malaya: Kuala Lumpur.

Chowdhury N. (1982), *A Study of Cotton Weaving in Bangladesh: The relative advantages and disadvantages of Handloom weaving and factory production*, Dphil Thesis, University Cambridge.

Conti R. (1991), *The role of business association in the promotion of SMIs: The Philihines Experience*, ISIS Regional Workshop (Nov. 12-13): Kuala Lumpur.

Cooper A. (1982), 'The entrepreneurship –Small business Interface' in *Encyclopedia of Entrepreneur* Kane C., Sexton D. and Vesper K. (eds), Prentice-Hall Inc.: New Jersey.

Cortes M., Berry A. and Ishaq A. (1987), *Success in Small and Medium-Scale Enterprises – The Evidence from Columbia*, A World Bank Research Publication: Oxford University Press.

De Connick J. (1980), *Artisans and Petty Prodcers in Uganda*, D.Phill thesis, University of Sussex.

Drakakis-Smith D. (1987), *The Third World City*, Methuen: London and New York.

Drucker P. (1974), *Management*, Allied Publisher Private Ltd. New Delhi.

Estanislao A. and Antiono G. (1980,) *Comperativee Advantage of Textile and Cement Industries in the Philihines*, CAM Series, No. 4 Institute of Developing Economies: Tokyo.

Evcimen G., Mehnet K. and Cinar E.M. (1991), 'Subcontracting, Growth and CapitalAccumulation in Small-Scale Firms in the Textile Industry in Turkey', in *The Journal of Development Studies*, Vol 28., No. 1 (Oct.)(pp. 130-149).

Fapohunda O.J. (1981), 'Human Resources and the Lagos informal sector' in Sethuraman ed.) *The Urban Informal Sector in Developing Countries*, Geneva: ILO.

Federation of Malaysian Manufacturers (1995), *Small and Medium Size Industries: FMM Business Guide*, FMM, Kuala Lumpur.

Foley P. (1987), *Marketing Management Policies and Small Businesses: An Investigation of the Factors Contributing to Small Business Success*, Ph.D., Leed Polytechnic.

Fong C.O. (1987), *New Economic Dynamo: Structure and investment opportunities in Malaysian economy*, Allen and Unwin: Sydney.

Fong C.O. (1987), *Technological leap: Malaysian industry in transition*, Oxford University Press: Singapure.

Fong C.O. and Mahani A. (1985), *Electronic sector: Final Draft Report for Malaysian Industry Master Plan Study*, Universiti Malaya: Kuala Lumpur.

Fong F. Lim C. and Mahani A. (1985), *Electronic sector: Draft report for Malaysian Industrial Master Plan Study*, Faculty of Economics and Administration, University of Malaya: Kuala Lumpur (January).

Freeman H. (1952), 'Effective management in small business' *Harvard Business Review*, Mar-April.

Friedman H. (1986), 'Postcript: Petty Commodity Production' in *Labour, Capital and Society*, 19 (1).

Friedmann J. and Sullivan F. (1974), 'The Absorption of Labour in the urban economy: a case of developing countries', *Economic Development and Cultural Changes*, 22 (3), 358-413.

French D. (1985), *Dictionary of Accounting Term*, Corner Publication: London.

Ganesan S. (1982), *Management of Small Construction Firms*, Asian Productivity Organisation: Tokyo.

Gerry C. (1974), *Petty Producers and the Urban Economy: A case Study of Dakar*, ILO Geneva.

_____ (1978), 'Petty production and capitalist production in Dakar: the crisis of the self-employed', *World Development*, Vol 6, (9/10).

Gibb A.A. (1981), *A working approach for stimulating new enterprise development*, Working paper series, Business School, University of Durham.

Golde R. (1964), 'Practical planning for small business' *Harvard Business Review*, Sept-October.

Hamid A. A. (1994), 'Pembangunan Rakyat Termiskin (PPRT): Pengalaman Daerah Hulu Terengganu', in *National Seminar of Malaysian Geography 1994*, 17-19 August 1994, Universiti Sains Malaysia, Penang, Malaysia.

Harper M. (1984), *Small business in the Third World*, John Wiley and sons: Chinchester, U.K.

Harriss J. (1982), 'Character of an urban-economy – small-scale production and labour-markets in Coimbatore', *Economic and Political Weekly*, Vol 17, No. 23.

Hansohm D. (1992), 'Small Enterprise Flexibility in Sudan' in *Flexibility Specialisation: A New View on Small Industry*, J. Ramussen, H. Schmitz and M. Dijk (eds.) (op.cit).

Harper M. and T.T Soon (1979), *Small Enterprises in Developing Countries: Case Studies and Conclusions*, Intermediate Technology Publications Ltd: London.

Harper M. (1984), *Small Business in the Third World*, John Wiley and Sons: Chichester.

Harrison B. and Kelley M.R. (1993), 'Outsourcing and the Search for "Flexibility" in *Work, Employment and Society*, Vol 5, No. 3 (pp.397-415).

Hart K. (1973), ' Informal Income Opportunities and Urban Employment in Ghana', in *Journal of Modern African Studies*, 11 (1) 61-89.

Hill H. (1985), 'Sub-contracting, Technological Diffusion and the Development of Small Enterprise in Philipine Manufacturing', *The Journal of Developing Areas*, Vol. 19 (Jan.) (pp. 245-262).

Hing A.Y. (1986), *Malaysia Textile workers: A case study*, Institut Pengajian Tinggi, University of Malaya, Kuala Lumpur.

Hoong S.S. (1990), 'The role of business associations in the promotion of small and medium-sized industries: Malaysia's experience', *ISIS Regional Workshop*, 12-13hb. November, Kuala Lumpur.

ILO (1982), Small enterprise development programe. Working Paper, Management Development Brach, Geneva.

Institute of Developing Economies (1987), *Changes in the industrial structure and the role of small and medium industries in Asian countries: The case of Malaysia*, (February): Tokyo.

Institute of Strategic and International Studies (ISIS) (1991), *Promotion of SME's: Policy Environment and Institutional Framework*, ISIS Regional Workshop (Novem. 12-13, 1990), Percetakan Tenaga: Kuala Lumpur.

International Development Research Centre (IDRC) (1988), *Technology adoption by small and medium enterprises in Malaysia*, (August), University of London.

International Labour Organisation (ILO) (1986), *The promotion of small and medium-sized enterprises*, Persidangan ke 72, Pejabat ILO, Geneva.

Ishak Shaari and Halim A. (1995), 'Globalised economy: Implications for equity in Malaysia', in *International Conference on Globalisation: Local Challenges and Responses*, 19-21hb. Januari 1995, Universiti Sains Malaysia, Pulau Pinang.

Ismail M. Salleh (1990), Small and medium scale industrialisation: Problems and prospects, ISIS, Kuala Lumpur

Ismail M. Salleh (1991), *The role of small and medium-scale industries in Malaysia's industrial development: Problems and issues*, Third Southeast Asia Roundtable on Economic Development, (23-24 September), ISIS, Kuala Lumpur.

Ismail M. Salleh and Fichtner G. (1991), *Promotion of SMEs: Policy environment and institutional framework*, Friedrich-Ebert Stiftung, Kuala Lumpur.

Jabatan Perangkaan (1975), *Industrial Surveys*, Kuala Lumpur.

_____(1981), *Manufacturing Sector Surveys*; Kuala Lumpur.

_____(1985), *Industrial Surveys*; Kuala Lumpur.

_____(1992), *Industrial Surveys*, Kuala Lumpur.

_____(1993), *Industrial Surveys*, Kuala Lumpur.

Jomo K.S. (1989), *Beyond 1990: considerations for new National Development Strategy*, Universiti Malaya, Kuala Lumpur.

_____1990, *Growth and structural change in the Malaysian economy*, Macmillan: London.

Jomo K.S. and Shari I. (1986), *Development Policies and Income Inequality in Peninsular Malaysia*, Institute of Advanced Studies, University of Malaya: Kuala Lumpur.

Kaplinsky R. (1981), *From Mass Production to Flexible Specialisation: A case Study from a Semi-Industrialised Economy*, IDS Discussion Paper (No.295), University of Sussex.

Khanthachai N. (1991), *Creating the conducive environment for small and medium-sized enterprises promotion: Thailand experience*, ISIS Regional Workshop, (Nov. 12-13): Kuala Lumpur.

Lan K. (1989), *The Performance of Small and Medium-sized Business in the Malaysian manufacturing sector*, MBA Dissertation, University of Malaya.

Larson M. and Chute C. (1979), 'The failure syndrome', *American Journal of Small Business*, Vol. 4.

Lassort J. and Clavier L.J. (1989), 'SMEs in the ACPs' in *The Courier*, No. 115 (May-June).

Levy B. (1991), *Obstacles to Developing Small and Medium-Sized Enterprises: An Empirical Assessment*, Working Papers (WPS 588), the World: Washington.

Lim C. , Cheok C. A. Othman (1978), *A study of small Bumiputra enterprises in Kuala Lumpur and Johor Bharu*, University of Malaya: Kuala Lumpur.

Little I.M.D. (1987), 'Small manufacturing enterprises in developing countries'. *World Bank Economic Review*, Vol. 1 (2).

_____ (1988), 'Small manufacturing enterprises and employment in developing countries', *Asian Development Review*, Vol. 6 (6).

Lyberaki A. (1989), *Small Firms and Flexible Specialisaton in Greek Industry*, Dphil Thesis, University of Sussex.

Majlis Amanah Rakyat (MARA) (1988), *The rle of technology towards entrepreneurial development –MARA's Approach*, MARA: Kuala Lumpur.

Malay Mail June 24th, 1981.

MALAYSIA (1966), *The First Malaysian Plan 1966-1970*, Government Printer: Kuala Lumpur.

_____ (1971), *The Second Malaysian Plan 1971-1975*, Government Printer: Kuala Lumpur.

_____ (1976), *The Third Malaysian Plan 1976-1980*, Government Printer: Kuala Lumpur.

_____ (1981), *The Fourth Malaysian Plan 1981-1985*, Government Printer: Kuala Lumpur.

_____ (1986), *The Fifth Malaysian Plan 1986-1990*, Government Printer: Kuala Lumpur.

_____ (1991), *The Sixth Malaysian Plan 1991-1995*, Government Printer: Kuala Lumpur.

_____ (1996), *The Seventh Malaysian Plan 1996-2000*, Government Printer: Kuala Lumpur.

Malaysian Industrial Development Authority (MIDA) (1985), *Industrial Master Plan 1985-1995*, Government Printer: Kuala Lumpur.

_____ (1988), *Investment in the manufacturing sector: Policies, incentives and procedures*, (March), Government Printer: Kuala Lumpur.

_____ (1990), *Investment in the manufacturing sector: Policies, incentives and procedures*, Percetakan Mega: Kuala Lumpur.

_____ (1991), *Textile and Clothing Industry: A List of Registered Firms*, Government Printer: Kuala Lumpur.

Manuh G. and R. Brown (1987), *Resources of the development of entrepreneur: A guided reading list and annotated bibliography*, Commonwealth Secretariat: London

MARDI (1985), *Proposed Research programmes-MARDI 1985-1990*, Unpublished, MARDI: Kuala Lumpur.

_____ (1990), *Circular letter-The new structural organisaton of MARDI*, (March) MARDI: Kuala Lumpur.

Ministry of Education (1991), *Public Development Expenditure for Education and Training in Malaysia*, Government Printer: Kuala Lumpur.

Ministry of Finance (1980), *Economic Reports 1980/81*, Government Printer: Kuala Lumpur.

_____ (1981), *Economic Reports 1981/82*, Government Printer: Kuala Lumpur.

_____(1982), *Economic Reports 1982/83*, Government Printer: Kuala Lumpur.

_____ (1983), *Economic Reports 1983/84*, Government Printer: Kuala Lumpur.

_____(1984), *Economic Reports 1984/85*, Government Printer: Kuala Lumpur.

_____ (1985), *Economic Reports 1985/86*, Government Printer: Kuala Lumpur.

_____ (1986), *Economic Reports 1986/87*, Government Printer: Kuala Lumpur.

_____(1987), *Economic Reports 1987/88*, Government Printer: Kuala Lumpur.

_____(1988), *Economic Reports 1988/89*, Government Printer: Kuala Lumpur.

_____(1989), *Economic Reports 1989/90*, Government Printer: Kuala Lumpur.

_____ (1990), *Economic Reports 1990/91*, Government Printer: Kuala Lumpur.

_____ (1991), *Economic Reports 1991/92*, Government Printer: Kuala Lumpur.

_____ (1992), *Economic Reports 1992/93*, Government Printer: Kuala Lumpur.

Ministry of Labour (1985), *Occupational Profile of the Textile and Clothing Industry in Malaysia,* Government Printer: Kuala Lumpur.

Ministry of International Trade and Industry (1987), *Annual Report 1987/88*, Government Printer: Kuala Lumpur.

_____(1988), *Annual Report 1988/89*, Government Printer: Kuala Lumpur.

_____(1990), *Annual Report 1990/91*, Government Printer: Kuala Lumpur.

Moha Asri A. (1994), 'Aspek sosio-ekonomi pekerja-pekerja industri kecil tekstil dan pakaian' *PERANTARA*, April, Buletin Universiti Sains Malaysia, Pulau Pinang.

Moha Asri A. (1994), 'Hubungan dengan firma-firma besar dan kesannya ke atas kejayaan dan pembangunan industri kecil di bandar', *Seminar Kebangsaan Geografi Malaysia 1994*, 17-19hb. Ogos, Universiti Sains Malaysia, Pulau Pinang.

Moha Asri A. (1994), 'Forms and characteristics of inter-firm linkages in urban economic activities: A case study of small textile and clothing firms in Kuala Lumpur, *The Third International Conference on Geography of the ASEAN Region*, 25-29hb. Oktober, Universiti Malaya, Kuala Lumpur.

Moha Asri A. (1995), 'Globalised economy and Malaysian policy support programmes for small-medium industries: Some critical issues and needs' *International Conference on Globalisation: Local Challenges and Responses*, 19-21hb Januari, Universiti Sains Malaysia, Pulau Pinang.

Moha Asri A. (1995), 'Policy support programmes for SMIs: Towards more participation of wider social groups in Malaysia', *ASEAN Inter-University Seminar on Social Development*, 23-25hb. November, University of San Carlos, Cebu, Filipina.

Moha Asri A. (1997), *Industri kecil di Malaysia : Perkembangan dan masa depan*, DBP, Kuala Lumpur.

Moha Asri A. (1997), *Industri Kecil dan Sederhana di Malaysia : Tinjauan terhadap pembangunan program bantuan*, Fajar Bakti, Kuala Lumpur.

Moha Asri A. (1997), *Pembangunan Perindustrian di Malaysia : Perkembangan dan Permasalahan*, Fajar Bakti, Kuala Lumpur.

Moha Asri A. (1998), 'Altitudes of entrepreneurs in SMEs towards training in Malaysia', *Industry And Higher Education*, Vol. 12, No.2, (April).

Mohd Yusuf I. (1991), 'The establishment of small and medium scale enterprise development corporation-Towards creating a better environment for the promotion of small and medium-scale industries', *Promotion of SMIs: Policy Environment and Institutional Framework*, ISIS Regional Workshop (November 12-13) Kuala Lumpur.

Morris A.S. and Lowder S. (1992), 'Flexible Specialisation: The Application of Theory in a Poor-Country Context: Leon, Mexico', *International Journal of Urban and Regional Research*, Vol 16, No. 2 (June) (pp. 190-201).

Moser C.O.N. (1978), 'Informal Sector of Petty Commodity Production: Dualism or Dependent in Urban Development' in *World Development*, Vol. 6 No. 9/10, 1041-1064.

_____ (1984), *A Survey of Empirical Studies in Industrial and Manufacturing Activities in the Informal Sector in the Developing Countries*, Development Planning Unit, University College London.

National Productivity Centre (NPC) (1988), Annual Report, NPC: Kuala Lumpur.

_____ (1991), *Seminar on Productivity Measurement and Improvement in the Textile and Wearing Apparel*, (1st. Oct. 1991), Petaling Jaya.

Naumes W. (1978), *The entrepreneurial manager in the small business*, Addison-Wesley Publishing Company: Sydney.

Naumes W. (1978), *The entrepreneurial manager in the small business*, Addison-Wesley: Sydney.

Neck P. (ed) (1977), *Small Enterprise Development: Policies and Programme*, Management Development Series No. 14, ILO: Geneva.

Nooriah, Morshidi and Abibullah (1994), 'Regional industrialisation, labour supply problems and manufacturing plants' responses- the Penang Case', *The Third International Conference on Geography of the ASEAN Region*, 25-29hb. Oktober 1994, Universiti Malaya, Kuala Lumpur.

Perbadanan Produktiviti Negara (1988), *Laporan Tahunan*, Kuala Lumpur.

_____ (1991), *Seminar on productivity measurement and improvement in the textile and wearing apparel*, 1hb. Ogos, Petaling Jaya.

_____ (1995), *Program peningkatan produktiviti dan kualiti 1995*, NPC, Kuala Lumpur.

Perbadanan Pembangunan Bandar (UDA) (1987), *Annual Report 1987*, Kuala Lumpur.

Persatuan Pengilang Malaysia (FMM) (1988), *Memorendum on small and medium-sized industries*, Julai, Kuala Lumpur.

Piore M. and Sabel C. (1984), *The Second Industrial Divide: Possibilities for Prosperity*, Basic Books: New York.

Popenoe O. (1970), *An analysis of the social background careers and attitudes of the leading Malays businessman in Western Malaysia*, Ph.D. Thesis, LSE, University of London

Portes A. (1985), 'The Informal Sector and the World Economy: Notes on the Structure of Subsidzed Labor' in Timberlake M. (ed.) *Urbanisation in the World-Economy*, Orlando: Academic Press

Rahmah Ismail (1995), *Industri Kecil di Malaysia : Isu Pembiayaan, teknologi dan Pemasaran*, Penerbit UKM, Bangi.

Rainnie A. (1991), 'Just-In-Time, Sub-Contracting and the Small Firm' *Work, Employment and Society*, Vol. 5, No. 3 (pp. 353-375).

Rasmussen J. (1992),'The Small Enterprise Environment in Zimbabwe: Growing in the Shadow of Large Enterprises', *Flexible Specialisation: A New View on Small Firms ?*, J. Rasmussen, H. Schatz and M. Dijk (eds.): (op.cit).

Rasmussen J., Schmitz H. and Dijk M. (eds.) (1992), *Flexible Specialisation - A New View on Small Industry ?*, IDS Bulletin, Vol.23 (July).

Robinson R. and Pearce J. (1983), 'The impact of formalised strategic planning on financial performance in small organisation', *Strategic Management Journal.*, (Vol.4) (pp. 197-206).

Sanyal B. (1988), 'The Urban Informal Sector Revised', in *Third World Planning Review*,10 (1) 65-83.

Salleh A. (1985), *Management of the Small Firm*, MBA Thesis, University of Sheffield.

Salleh M.I. (1990), *Small and Medium Scale Industrialisation: Problems and Prospects*, Institute of Strategic and International Studies (ISIS), Kuala Lumpur.

_____(1991), *The Role of Small and Medium-Scale Industries in Malaysia's Industrial Development: Problems and Prospects*, Paper presented at the Third Southeast Asia Roundtable on Economic Development, (23-24 Sept. 1991), Kuala Lumpur.

Salleh M. Fichtner G. (1991), *Promotion of SMEs: Policy environment and institutional framework*, Percetakan Negara: Kuala Lumpur.

Sayer A. (1986), 'New Development in Manufacturing: the "Just-In-Time" System', in *Capital and Class,* No. 30.

Schmitz H. (1989), *Flexible specialisation- a new paradigm of small-scale industrialisation ?*, Institute of Development Studies, University of Sussex, U.K.

Schmitz (1990), 'Small Firms and flexible specialisation in developing countries' *Labour and Society*, Vol. 15 No. 3.

Schumacher E.F. (1974), *Small is beautiful - A Study of Economics as if People mattered*, Abacus ed. Sphere Books: London.

Scott A.M. (1986a), "Introduction: Why rethink Petty Commodity-Production ?" in Scott A. (ed.) Rethinking Petty Commodity-Production, *Social Analysis*. Special Issue Series, Vol. 20, December (pp.3-10).

Scott A.M. (1986b), 'Towards a rethinking of petty commodity Production' in Scott A (ed.) 'Rethinking Petty Commodity Production' *Social Analysis*, Special Issue Series, Vol. 20, December (pp.93-105).

Sethuraman S. V. (1981), *The Urban Informal Sector in Developing Countries,* ILO: Geneva.

Sien Lee Mei Ling (1990). *Malaysia's Industrial and Entrepreneurship Profile*. Malays Management Review, v25:3-10.

Soon T.T. (1983), 'Southeast Asia' in *The Small firm: An International survey*, (ed.) by Storey D.J. Croom Helm: Kent.

Stanworth K. and Curran J. (1973), *Management Motivation in the Smaller Businesses*, Gower: Epping.

Steel W.F. (1977), *Small-Scale Employment and Production in Developing Countries*, New York: Praeger Publ.

Storey D.J. (1983), *The Small Firm: An International Survey*, Croom Helm: Kent.

Storey D.J., Keasey K., Watson R. and Wynarczyk P. (1987*), The Performance of Small Firms*, Croom Helm: London.

Storey D.J. and Johnson S. (1987), *Job Generation and Labour Market Change*, MacMillan: London.

Syarikat Jaminan Kredit (CGC), (1981), *Garis Panduan Skim Pinjaman CGC*, Kuala Lumpur.

_____ (1993), *Garis Panduan Skim Jaminan Utama Baru, Skim Jaminan Tabung Usahawan Baru dan Skim Jaminan Penjaja dan Peniaga Kecil*, Kuala Lumpur.

UNIDO 1985, *Medium and Long Term Industrial Master Plan, Malaysia 1986-1995 (IMP),* (August); Kuala Lumpur.

_____ (1986), *Policies and strategies for small-medium industry development in Asia and the Pacific Region*, (Mac) ; Kuala Lumpur.

_____ (1991), *Promoting of supporting industries in Malaysia* (Januari) ; Kuala Lumpur.

_____ (1993), *Techno-Economic Environment in the Textile and Clothing Industry: Implications for the Role of Women in Asian Developing Countries,* Final Draft of a Study by HRD Unit, REG (29 January 1993): Vienna.

Urban Development Authority (1987), *Annual Report*, Government Printer: Kuala Lumpur.

Watanabe K. (1975), 'Subcontracting, industrialisation and employment creation', *International Labour Review.* 104 (1).

Watanabe S. (1978), *Technological Linkages between Formal and Informal Sectors of Manufacturing,* Working Paper No. 34, Technology and Employment Programme, Geneva: ILO.

World Bank 1978, Employment and Development of Small Enterprises: Sector Policy Paper, World Bank, Washington D.C.

_____ (1982), *Malaysia: Development issues and prospects of small enterprises*, Report No. 3851-MA (June).

_____ (1984), *Malaysia: Development Issues and Prospects of Small Enterprises,* Vol.1

_____ (1990), *Poverty: World Development Report 1990.* World Development Indicators, Oxford University Press: Washington D.C.

Yonzon M. (1990), *The role of government in the Promotion of small and medium industries: The Philippines Experience*, ISIS Regional Workshop, (Nov. 12-13): Kuala Lumpur.

Yoon D.H. 1990, *The Promotional policv of SMIs: Korean experience*, Paper. Presented at ISIS Regional Workshop, (November 12-13): Kuala Lumpur.

Index